ROCK ISLAND, CROOKHAVEN

A COASTAL TOWNLAND'S HISTORY SINCE 1800

AIDAN POWER

Published by Aidan Power (aidan@crookhaven.ie)

Printed by Inspire Printing, Skibbereen

This publication has received support from the Heritage Council under the 2006 Publications Grant Scheme.

Cover Picture: Patrick Roach www.patrickroach.com

ISBN 10: 0 9552684 0 0
ISBN 13: 978 0 9552684 0 3

© *Aidan Power 2006*

All rights reserved. No part of this publication may be reproduced, stored in a retrieval system, or transmitted in any form or by any means, electronic, mechanical, photocopying, recording or otherwise, without the prior permission in writing of the publisher.

CONTENTS

Acknowledgements		ii
I	Introduction	1
II	Crookhaven Lighthouse	10
III	Crookhaven Coast Guard	123
IV	Notter's & Other Resident Families	160
V	Rock Island School	189
VI	Rock Island Post Office	195
VII	Lobster Ponds	198
Appendix I	Miscellaneous Events: Rock Island, Fastnet & Mizen Lighthouses	207
Appendix II	Lightkeepers based at Station	212
Appendix III	Crookhaven Coast Guard Personnel	217
Bibliography		222
Index		228

ACKNOWLEDGEMENTS

This book is primarily a review of the archival records of the Commissioners of Irish Lights, National Achives, Dublin, National Archives, London, Land Commission, Dublin and the National Maritime Museum, London. I acknowledge that it has many gaps in the story of Rock Island and focuses principally on the institutions which functioned here.

Thanks must firstly go to all those who helped me with information on this little townland: Richard Craig-White, Tony Doyle, Dermot Griffin, Ronan Hamilton, Gerard Harrington, Mary Lannin, Tony Lonton, Pete Notter, Denis (Sonny) O'Driscoll, Denny O'Meara, Jim O'Meara, Angela O'Sullivan, David Roberts, Peter Shortt and Craig Treeby. I am particularly grateful to Mel Boyd, former Chief Executive, and Captain Kieran O'Higgins of Irish Lights for allowing access to their archives. Also thanks to the Commissioners of Irish Lights for permission to use the photographs on pages 33, 86, 87 and 89.

Thanks must also go to all the helpful librarians at the various libraries and archives in Ireland and Britain.

I am most grateful to Kevin Lynch and Therese Laycock for their time given proof-reading. All errors, however, are solely my responsibility.

Finally I must thank my wife Angelique for her patient encouragement.

INTRODUCTION

Rock Island (Oilean na Carriage) is a townland in the parish of Kilmoe located in the barony of West Carbery. It is two km south of the village of Goleen and at its nearest point, by sea, 0.5 km north-east of Crookhaven village. Its significance is due to its location at the north entrance to Crookhaven harbour. Crookhaven harbour is now primarily used by pleasure craft in the summer months but historically it was heavily used by coastal craft, fishing fleets and transatlantic sailing craft. It is an excellent harbour providing shelter from most winds. With this shelter came its economic significance as a provisioning port.

Richard Pococke on an Irish tour in 1758 visited Crookhaven. He described the harbour as follows:

> It is a very fine haven opening to North east, & is made by a head of land extending to that point which ends in a rock head called the Alderman, through which there is a passage for a boat, a point of land comes from the north-west [Rock Island] and defends it against the easterly winds: It is a very fine bason (*sic*) about a league in Length & half a mile broad, with the ruins of a fort & of a Barack (*sic*) & there is a church built in it…The West India fleet often puts in here, by contrary winds going or coming. When an East India fleet or indeed any other puts in here, it raises provisions to an exorbitant price[1].

From Rock Island, Ballydevlin Bay, parts of Roaring Water Bay, the open sea out to Fasnet and Crookhaven harbour are all visible. At Rock Island's north-easterly extreme, Fastnet Rock is 12km to the south-east and can be seen through the gap between the Alderman Rocks and Streak Head. These properties made it an ideal location during the 19th century for a Coast Guard station, a Lighthouse and as the base for the Fastnet Lighthouse.

---

[1] McVeagh, J., ed., Richard Pococke's Irish Tours, Dublin, 1995.

The townland is made up of slate and grits. The land is marginal; most is rough pasture with afforested areas around Rock Island House and Lannin's house and farm. It measures 24.8 hectares (61 acres and 34 perches). From one end to the other it is about 1.2 km long. Its width varies from around 100m to 300m. Its highest point, at the easterly tower is 26m high. There is over 3km of coastline with the townland almost separated from the mainland where it meets Shanavally, the only other townland it touches. The proximity to the sea results in a very moderate climate. Frost is rare, possibly once a year on average. As a result there is a profusion of plants flowering almost 11 months of the year. Due to the undulating nature of the landscape there are many sheltered areas even allowing plants averse to salt to survive.

Crookhaven harbour entrance with Rock Island lighthouse on right

In the early 1800s the whole of Rock Island was owned by Lord Riversdale[2]. Lord Riversdale may have been the ancestor of Arthur Annesley, first Earl of Anglesea, who was granted large areas of West Cork after the uprising of 1641[3]. The title of Lord Riversdale was created in October 1783 when "Richard Tonson, controller of Rathcormac Borough, traded his [parliamentary] seats for the Riversdale title". He had been born as William Hull (1724 – 1787), the illegitimate son of Richard Tonson (1689-1773). Hull "employed as a menial in his father's kitchen before a short army career, inherited the estate worth upwards of £10,000 p.a." as a result of Tonson's only legitimate son predeceasing him. Richard Tonson had

---

[2] Land Commission, Dublin, EC1332.
[3] Durell, P., Discover Dursey, Beara, 1996, p.39.

probably owned Rock Island as he "had greatly extended the family estates in Carbery"[4]. The family seat was at Lisnegar near Rathcormac, Co. Cork. He had also been a founder in 1768 of Warren's Bank along with Sir Robert Warren, Sir James St John Jefferyes and James Bernard. Between them they had wealth of £80,000. However the bank collapsed in 1784 as a result of the "electioneering follies" of the partners the previous year[5]. The Tonson family were nearly bankrupted by the collapse[6].

William Hull/Richard Tonson married Rose Bernard (1758–1810) in 1773. They had seven sons and one daughter. After his death she married Captain Millerd, of the 55th Foot[7]. The first Lord Riversdale was succeeded by his eldest son, also William (1775-1818), upon his death in 1787. He married Charlotte Theodosia, daughter of Lord Doneraile. It appears they may not have had any offspring. The second Lord sold Rock Island in March 1816. In the sale indenture he and his two brothers, Charles Ludlon Tonson (1783-1861) and the Reverend Ludlon Tonson[8] are mentioned. It appears that Charles succeeded his brother to the title in 1818 until his death in 1861 when the title was extinguished.

Rock Island is presently accessed from the main Goleen to Crookhaven road. The turn-off is to the left, 1.5 km from Goleen, at Coppinger's Cross[9]. This exit is in fact the continuation of the old main road. A petition was sent to Lord Lieutenant Wellesley in early summer 1822 by clergy and gentlemen of the area for a new road to be built linking Crookhaven and Skibbereen. The road was laid out and built by Richard Griffith, civil engineer for Munster, later made

---

[4] Dickson, D., Old World Colony: Cork and South Munster, Cork, 2005, p.90.
[5] Dickson, Old World Colony, 164.
[6] Dickson, Old World Colony, 79.
[7] www.paulturner.ca/Ireland/Cork/HOB/HOB-12.htm
[8] Hon. Ludlow Tonson, D.D., appointed Protestant Bishop of Killaloe 1839. He remained Bishop at Killaloe until his death in 1862 - www.clarelibrary.ie/eolas/coclare/history/frost/chap10_killaloe_protestant_bishops.htm
[9] The Coppingers were significant landowners on the Mizen Peninsula in the 17th Century. It is possible they retained land in the area until more recent times.

famous for Griffith's Valuation, the closest surviving approximation to a mid-nineteenth century census. He commenced work on the road on the 29th of July 1822. The road ran from three km west of Skibbereen at New Court to the slipway at the western end of Rock Island, a distance of 37 km (23 miles). For a lot of the route he avoided the old coastal road and went inland over more boggy terrain. Over 3,000 men were employed who he regarded as "of wild and turbulent habits". The road was 6.4 metres (21 feet) wide and was similarly constructed to MacAdam's with layers of small stones and gravel and well drained. The total cost, which included 14 bridges, was £9,439[10]. Although not built directly by local government it became known as a Grand Jury road[11]. The slipway at the road end was "used by the Crookhaven Ferry man and parties landing from ships"[12]. At the two causeway crossings on Rock Island, Griffith left gaps in the wall, presumably to allow locals to collect and load sea-weed, a very important fertiliser, onto horse drawn carts. Samuel Lewis provided the following description in 1837:

> **ROCK ISLAND**, a village, in the parish of KILMOE, Western Division of the barony of WEST CARBERY, county of CORK, and province of MUNSTER, 19 miles (S. W.) from Skibbereen: the population is returned with the parish. It is advantageously situated on a peninsulated rock opposite Crookhaven, on the south-western coast, and has risen into a flourishing state through the spirited exertions of its proprietor, R. Notter, Esq. A new line of road has been recently opened between this place and Skibbereen, and the post-office has been removed hither from Crookhaven: there is a mail to Skibbereen every second day. Immediately off the village, which contains some well-built houses, is the entrance to the spacious and well-sheltered harbour of Crookhaven, noticed in the

---

[10] Hickey, P., Famine in West Cork: The Mizen Peninsula: Land and People, 1800 – 1852, Cork, 2002, pp. 50-55.
[11] Until 1899, with the establishment of County Councils, local government was controlled by a Grand Jury made up primarily of large landowners.
[12] Williams, A.T., Office of Public Works Coast Guard file, National Archives, Dublin, OPW5/47019/80.

article on that place. Here is a coast-guard station (usually called the Crookhaven station), being one of the nine included in the Skibbereen district. A dispensary has been established in the village.

He described the parish of Kilmoe as follows

> **KILMOE**, a parish, in the Western division of the barony of WEST CARBERY, county of CORK, and province of MUNSTER; containing, with the villages of Rock Island and Crookhaven (both of which are described under their respective heads), 6889 inhabitants. It forms a peninsula on the southern coast, bounded by Dunmanus bay and Crookhaven; and comprises 10,738 statute acres, as applotted under the tithe act. About one-third of the land is under tillage, chiefly by spade-husbandry, and the remainder is bog and mountain land, but the base of the mountains affords good pasturage; the highest mountain is Cahir, near Mizen Head... Within the limits of the parish are numerous bays and creeks, the principal of which are Ballydevlin bay, Crookhaven, and Barley cove, in each of which there is good anchorage. Petty sessions are held at Tourmore (*sic.*) on alternate Wednesdays, and there is a constabulary police station at Goleen. The principal seats are Rockview, the residence of Florence. McCarty, Esq.; Seaview, of D. Coghlan, Esq.; Rock Island House, of J. Notter, Esq.; Ballydevlin, of L. J. Fleming, Esq.; Crookhaven House, of R. Doe, Esq.; Ballynaule, of J. Baker, Esq.; Goleen House, of J. McCarthy, Esq.; and Tourmore, of R. Bailie, Esq[13].

The 1843-44 Parliamentary Gazetteer referred to Rock Island as a "hamlet in the parish of Kilmoe...it stands on a rocky peninsula adjacent to Crookhaven". Crookhaven and the harbour were described as follows

> Crookhaven proper is a narrow inlet from the west side of this [Ballydevlin] bay; strikes off from it at right angles almost immediately within the entrance; and runs 1½ mile westward to a

---

[13] Lewis, S., A Topographical Dictionary of Ireland, Vol. II. H-Z, 1837.

narrow isthmus which divides it from Barley Cove. At its head it has a depth of 18 or 20 feet; and further out, an average depth of 20 fathoms. It offers clean anchorage, and completely landlocked shelter; but, in consequence of the remoteness of its situation, and the rocky rudeness of its shores, it serves little other purpose than that of an asylum from adverse winds. In 1841, a lighthouse was erected on Rock Island...It was once a place of considerable note, but is now an obscure fishing village[14].

Rock Island from British Admiralty Chart 1848

The present continuation of the road to Crookhaven around the harbour was undertaken during the Great Famine. Through Fr. Barrett, the people of Crookhaven applied to the Board of Works to build a new road between Rock Island and Crookhaven. On the 15th of September 1846, the county surveyor provided an estimate of £1,857 to build the new road with a total length of 1,280 perches[15]. This was the most expensive piece of roadway approved by the Presentment Sessions for the barony of West Carbery, West Division

---

[14] The Parliamentary Gazetteer of Ireland, Dublin, 1844, p.546.
[15] A perch is equal to 5.5 yards; 320 perches are equal to a mile. Therefore the length was estimated at 4 miles or 6.4 km.

that day in Ballydehob[16]. Richard Notter was at the meeting and can be assumed to have supported the building of the road[17]. It is not clear when the work was commenced or completed.

The significance of Crookhaven harbour as a port of refuge and for provisioning is demonstrated in a petition requesting a new pier at Crookhaven sent to the Office of Public Works in 1846. It was signed by over 100 local men and stated that there were "upwards of eighty foreign vessels" in the harbour at any one time during the previous year. This significance, although reduced, carried on into the early twentieth century. Constable John Reilly undertook the census in 1901. He reported a total of 20 ships in the harbour with 377 men on board on the 31st of March. There was one British steamer, the *Agate* from Glasgow weighing 66 tonnes. There was also an Italian barque, the *Enricon* from Genoa weighing 601 tonnes. She was "on foreign trade". Sixteen French fishing boats and two from Yarmouth were also in the harbour. The harbour was also popular with Isle of Man fishermen
Jermyn, in her recollections, stated

> Early this century the mackerel fleet from the Isle of Man called regularly, and Manx boats anchored here by the score. They would arrive in March and leave for the Shetlands in June after the herrings. Mr. O'Driscoll, who is over 80 remembers when 'you couldn't drag your feet for sailors!'[18]

The population of the townland since 1841, as per the various censuses, was as follows:

	1841	1851	1861	1871	1881	1901	1911	2002
Rock Island	119	111	88	84	79	75	63	7

---

[16] Hickey, Famine in West Cork, 152.
[17] Hickey,P., A Survey of Four Peninsular Parishes in West Cork 1796-1855, MA Thesis, UCC, 1980, p. 335.
[18] Jermyn, N. My Parish, Schull, 2000.

The male and female breakdown was as follows for Rock Island:

	1841	1851	1861	1871	1881	1901	1911	2002
Male	62	50		37	43	36	33	2
Female	57	61		47	36	39	30	5

The numbers of houses were:

	1841	1851	1861	1871	1881	1901	1911	2002
Occupied	18	19		16				3
Unoccupied	4	5		1				19
Total	22	24	18	19	17	22		22

We have been left with a number of names for various parts of the townland, when it was a much more populous place:

Trawnabirrea – Sruthán Trá na mBiorar (strand of the watercress)
Sheamon Point – Rinn na Páirce Sighe (headland of the field of the fairies)
Coosnablaha– Cuas na Blátha (cave of the flowers)
Coosnafranca – Cuas na Franca/Francach (cove of the Rats/Frenchmen)
Coosnasoldad – Cuas na Sulchoid (cove of the willow/sallow)
Station Point – named after the Coast Guard Station
Lamb's Island- tenants on Rock Island during the 19th century
Ellis's Island
Piper's Rock
Snug Harbour – aptly named as it is here that local fishermen moor their boats prior to the worst of forecasted storms.

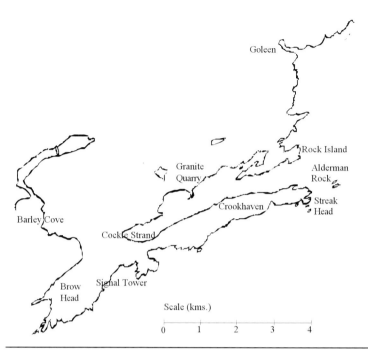

Rock Island

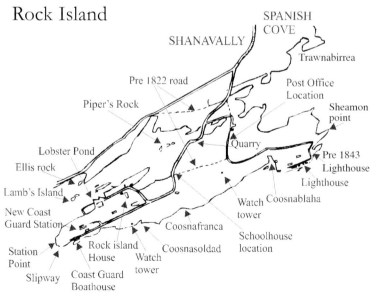

CROOKHAVEN LIGHTHOUSE

The first reference to a lighthouse on Rock Island is a British Admiralty Chart of 1817 which locates it at Sheamon Point. A small mark on the chart is located to the east of the present lighthouse. However another chart drawn at the same time by the same Captain Martin White records no lighthouse. There is also no reference to this lighthouse in any of Irish Light's correspondence. A few courses of stone remain of what could have been a square lighthouse tower just outside the boundary wall of the lighthouse property. It is unknown as to who may have been responsible for building this tower and for how long it functioned as a lighthouse. It is possible that it was maintained by the local revenue officer as the Customs Board was responsible for lighthouses in Ireland in 1800. This function was transferred to the Ballast Board of Dublin in 1810 by an Act of the British Parliament.

Remnants of tower, possibly early lighthouse

It may be assumed that this light was no longer maintained, or possibly regarded as inadequate, by the 1830s as Daniel Coughlan, Lloyds' Agent in Crookhaven, wrote to the Dublin Port Ballast Board (the Commissioners of Irish Lights' predecessor until 1867) on the 6th of January 1838

> Having considered the subject we talked of yesterday, respecting the utility of erecting a lighthouse or beacon at the entrance of this harbour, I take leave to say that humanity, as well as the mercantile public good of the U.K., much require a beacon or light at the entrance of this port, which if placed there long since, would have saved many lives and valuable property. Indeed many men of rank

in the navy with whom I often conversed on this subject, said it was a shame that a lighthouse was not long since placed there[1].

Coughlan apparently included a list of 20 vessels lost in his lifetime. The list would have included the *Darthula* of Newfoundland, which was on a voyage from Liverpool to St John's, Newfoundland in 1822. She was wrecked "on the rocks at the mouth of Crookhaven harbour". Also the brig *Mary*, which had come from the West Indies with a cargo of sugar and coffee, was wrecked on the Barrell's Reef in Crookhaven harbour. The list would have included the *Thomas Worthington* of St John, New Brunswick, Canada which was lost in the harbour in 1836. Its cargo of timber and the hull were auctioned[2].

Four days later on the 10th of January 1838, 49 residents of Crookhaven signed a letter which they delivered to Richard B. Hungerford, the Crookhaven Coast Guard Chief Officer:

> You will please forward through the department of Coast Guard the views we the undersigned persons being inhabitants of Crookhaven entertain relative to the very great necessity there is and always has been of having a light established at the entrance of this very valuable and safe harbour, the resort of several of Her Majesty's Ships of War and which large fleets of Merchant Ships & the coasting trade and also the vessels employed in the fishery frequently & we may say always continually have occasion to seek safety and shelter in…nothing but a strong feeling of humanity urges us to make this application[3].

---

[1] House of Commons Parliamentary Papers 1861, National Archives, London, 67.461.
[2] Hickey, Famine in West Cork, 127. There is no known Barrell's Reef near Crookhaven harbour. There is however the Barrell Sound to the west of Long Island Sound.
[3] Journal No.8, Corporation for Preservation & Improving The Port of Dublin & Co., p.172.

Rock Island

This letter was forwarded by the Coast Guard to the Ballast Board. Included with the letter was a list of 16 ships[4] which had been lost near the harbour entrance.

George Halpin Snr., the Ballast Board's Inspector, prepared a report on the 26th of September 1838 after visiting the area. He wrote "Crookhaven a good harbour in most winds is much resorted to in Easterly gales and a small light house there would be very useful". He dismissed the Alderman Rock's, which the locals proposed, as unsuitable. He believed it was not "practicable" to build a lighthouse there at "a reasonable cost" due to the "slaty unsound structure of the rock and its extreme exposure to the heavy stroke of the sea". He recommended a "small harbour light" on the "outer point of land on the North or Starboard side of the entrance". This location, Sheamon Point on Rock Island, is some 800 meters north of Alderman Rocks. He believed a lighthouse here "cannot be mistaken in thick weather for that of Cape Clear"[5].

The Ballast Office approved Halpin's proposal with the Secretary H. Vereker writing to Trinity House, London (who had to approve any major capital projects) on the 21st of October 1838 "it appears a small lighthouse at the northern entrance of the harbour, would be of great advantage to the many vessels which frequently seek shelter here". The Elder Brethren of Trinity House gave their statutory sanction to the lighthouse on the 31st of October 1838. They believed that the Alderman was the most suitable site, but due to the "great difficulties" of erecting a lighthouse there, "the Board approves the erection of a small harbour lighthouse (to be maintained by a toll upon vessels resorting to the place) on the outer point of the land on the north or starboard side of the entrance".

Richard Notter, the Rock Island landlord, wrote to the Ballast Board on the 25th of June 1839. He stated that he was willing to make the necessary land available for a "nominal rent of 40/ per annum" on a "fee farm lease". Ending the letter he stated "I need hardly premise

---

[4] No list of their names could be located.
[5] Journal No.8, 172.

that I hold the land in fee"[6]. William Goddard, Law Agent, wrote to Irish Lights in December 1839 stating that Mr. Notter considered it a "hardship" to have to supply the necessary title documents to allow the lease at his own expense. Goddard strongly recommended the need for a search regarding any interest on the land. The Board agreed and accepted the related costs[7].

William Goddard wrote on the 15th of July 1840 "in the presence of Messrs Drevor, Codd & Hamilton the Commissioners in Bantry determined that the land been acquired for the Rock island lighthouse was worth £140"[8]. This was apportioned as follows:

To Richard Notter proprietor	£0/ 1/0
Mesrs Thos Deane & Alex G Deane Mortgagees	£132/ 9/0
Five Tenants at will at £1.10. each	£7/ 10/0
	£140/ 0/0

The total cost of purchasing the land including legal expenses was £219/12/5[9].

Amongst those submitting quotes for the building work was Richard Howard of Limerick. His quotation was £450 for the dwelling and £250 for the tower. The Board thought his price for the house was "high" but the tower price was "moderate". They asked if he would be willing to only build the tower, to which he indicated he would not. John Notter of nearby Ballydevlin[10], brother of landlord Richard Notter, won the contract[11]. The Board noted "considering all the circumstances and the facilities which Mr. John Notter another of the persons proposing has he residing at and being connected with this neighbourhood as also his general character as a builder" His tender,

---

[6] Journal No.8, 306. "In fee" means that he had the freehold title over the land.
[7] Journal No.8, 393.
[8] Journal No.9, Corporation for Preservation & Improving The Port of Dublin & Co., p. 70.
[9] The pre-decimal pounds currency was divided into pounds/shillings/pence. There were 12 pence in a shilling and 20 shillings in a pound.
[10] John Notter's house later became the parish priest's house – Notter, I., Crookhaven – Past & Present, typed notes, p. 9.
[11] Journal No.9, 108.

which did not include any of the fitting out of the lighthouse, was as follows:

Tower £390
Residence £397
Total £787

He was also paid £3/16/0 per perch (16.5 feet/5 metres) of roadway which is around 900 metres long. George Halpin, the Inspector and designer of the lighthouse, wrote in his annual report of November 1841:

> the tower and residence so far as advanced have been executed in a substantial workmanlike manner much to the credit of Mr Notter the contractor for the building, considerable progress has also been made with the road of approach to this light house, and the light house will be ready for lighting in course of next summer probably in the month of June.

Locals believe, however, that the road was not built until later and was part of famine relief work.

In March 1842 Halpin wrote "I remained at the Crookhaven Light house works for three days, the works have been carried on satisfactorily the outer iron work of the lantern has been set up and is ready for the copper top covering".

Progress however did not go to plan as Halpin reported in November 1842 that "Crookhaven light house works were in forward state as well as the road leading to the premises, the lantern has been put up & glazed & may be lighted in May next a form of notice will be shortly submitted to the Board".

Halpin, in December 1842, informed the Board that the foreman of works at Crookhaven had been accused of various charges by a painter on site, Richard Roycroft. A local magistrate had investigated the charges finding that he was guilty of only one – he had lent some paint and "paint oil" to the contractor. As a result he was reprimanded and removed from the station[12].

---

[12] Journal No.9, 426.

Notter received a total of £1,943/9/4, paid as follows:
23.07.41	£400 for lighthouse
26.08.41	£100 for road
14.10.41	£100 for road & lighthouse
18.11.41	£100 for road
23.12.41	£197 second & final instalment on residence
30.06.42	£535/4 for masonry
12.01.43	£100 for road
09.02.43	£411/5/4 for masonry

According to the Ballast Board Audit Board, Notter was overpaid £100 which he refused to acknowledge and the Board had to accept the cost[13].

The total cost of building the lighthouse, dwelling and the road was £9,151/7/0 according to Callwell; however an analysis of the payments approved by the Board provide a total cost of £7,701/8/10. The principle costs, other than Notter's, from this analysis were: labour £2,620; metals (iron, steel, lead and copper) £520; flagstones & granite £367; and freight £276.

On the 30th of March 1843 a Notice to Mariners was issued:

> The Corporation for Preserving & Improving the Port of Dublin do hereby give notice that a lighthouse will be shown at sunset on the 1st of August 1843 and which will thereafter be exhibited every night from sunset to sunrise.
> The light house is erected on Rock Island Point at the northern side of the entrance to Crookhaven.
> The Light will be a fixed White Light. The lantern is open to seaward and to the Haven from E by S to W by N and is
> Elevated 62 feet above the level of high water spring tides
> Elevated 67 feet above the mean level of the sea

---

[13] Journal No.10, Corporation for Preservation & Improving The Port of Dublin & Co., 31st July 1844.

Rock Island

Mariners were informed that the lighthouse was located at latitude 51°28'35" N, longitude 9°42'31" W.
It does not appear to have been first lit until the 4th of August 1843 – no explanation for the delay is available[14].

Entrance to Crookhaven Harbour with Lighthouse, as depicted on 1848 Admiralty Chart

Griffith's Valuation of 1851

Griffith did not record the actual residents at the lighthouse but recorded the occupier as the "Ballast Board" who owned the land "in fee". The area was recorded as two acres, one rood and six perch i.e. 0.93 hectares[15]. The buildings were given an annual valuation of £10/10/0 and the land 10/ giving a total of £11/0/0. The land however appeared to be exempt from rates.

Improvements & Changes to the Lighthouse & Pier

Trinity House agreed with the Ballast Board in March 1859 "as to the propriety of colouring the Crookhaven Light as proposed [red over an arc passing across Alderman Rock] and of erecting a beacon on the Alderman Rocks". Halpin submitted an estimate of £25 for "red panes to define eastern limit of red light, ruby cylinders, expense of lamp fitter etc". In November 1859 Mariners were notified that the part of Crookhaven light showing over the Aldermen was now

---

[14] There are two mentions of an operational light at Rock Island, Crookhaven in 1841: Hickey, Famine in West Cork, 128, who refers to the "Parliamentary Gazetteer for Ireland"; Murphy, S., "Rock Island and Its Families", *Mizen Journal*, no.5, 1997, p. 167.

[15] 1 acre = 4 roods; 1 rood = 40 perches; 1 acre = .405 hectares.

coloured: "the catoptric[16] illuminating apparatus is as yet retained; its focal plane 72 feet above the mean level of the sea, and the coloured light should be visible in clear weather from a distance of about 10 miles"[17].

It appears that to improve Crookhaven lighthouse as a navigational aid, the exterior walls were whitewashed annually as reported by the keeper, James Doyle, in June 1865. W. McMahon reported, also in June 1865, that he had completed the painting on Rock Island and was "proceeding to Fastnet". In 1867 Doyle reported that he had sufficient lime in store and requested the "outside face of sea-wall be done".

C. J. Day (Doyle's temporary replacement) wrote on the 14th of November 1865 acknowledging receipt of eight new burners. I. Thullier, a lamp fitter, arrived at Crookhaven on the 17th and had "nearly completed" their fitting on the 23rd[18]. The Secretary requested that a Notice to Mariners be issued concerning the new burners.

In July 1866 Trinity House stated that the present catadiptric light should be replaced with a "third order Lenticular Apparatus"[19]. John S. Sloane[20] reported on the 28th of August 1867 that the new "dioptric light" at Crookhaven "works well". J. S. Sloane sent drawings to the Board in March 1867 "showing [the] position of red light to shine across Alderman Rocks". In May Sloane requested a fitter and glazier.

James Doyle reported in January 1867 that a lantern pane of glass had broken. He thought it was caused by "serious smoke [?] pattern", presumably from the oil burned for the light.

---

[16] A catoptric light operates by concentrating the light's rays using reflectors into a beam visible at a distance. They contrast with catadioptric systems which use both mirrors and lenses and with pure dioptric systems which use only lenses.

[17] Journal No.18, Corporation for Preservation & Improving The Port of Dublin & Co., 10th November 1859.

[18] Lighthouse Register 1865, Corporation for Preservation & Improving The Port of Dublin & Co.

[19] Lenticular is defined as having the form of a double-convex lens.

[20] Engineer-in-Chief, 1868-1877.

Rock Island

In December Gardiner was indicating that ten crossbars were required for the "lantern sash". These and plate glass arrived in January 1869. The tradesmen were working on installation throughout January. However Gardiner was not happy with the fitter, Doyle, who he said was "neglecting his duty while at station". The lantern sash was however completed on the 1st of February.

Henry Gardiner, in March 1869, reported that "three Ruby Glasses" were cracked and he needed a "fresh supply". A few days later he sent one of the brass cases that held the Ruby Glass by "morning car".

Henry Stocker, the keeper in June 1872, was allowed to employ a man for three days "to assist in receiving oil cisterns". Stocker in September 1872 was requesting instructions as to the colour of the glass in the lantern. He was told the painter would replace the glass. Thomas Doyle informed head office on the 12th of November 1873 that the "ruby sectors" had not arrived at the station. Stocker wrote a week later saying the glass had arrived at Skibbereen. They were fitted by late November.

In April 1873 Stocker got approval to employ someone to whitewash the wall as it was "very dirty after severe winter". In November 1873 he sent a proposal for erecting a gate at the lighthouse entrance. He was directed to have a gate made in early December.

In July 1903 Trinity House sanctioned the replacement of the catadiptric apparatus with a six-wick burner. It was also agreed that the area showing towards Alderman Rock should have red glass installed. The cost of these works was sanctioned at £150[21]. The new light was first exhibited on the 21st of December 1904. With the changing of the light, the Engineer proposed that Crookhaven Lighthouse could be looked after by the off-duty Fastnet keepers. Sometime between 1904 and 1909 the lighthouse stopped being a full-time position for a keeper living in house no.1 and became the responsibility of off duty Fastnet keepers.

---

[21] Journal No.42, Commissioners of Irish Lights, p.140.

Crookhaven Lighthouse

In 1909 the Board requested approval from the Board of Trade to convert the lighthouse to an "unwatched acetylene light" which would stop the need for a keeper and a new dwelling. This proposal appears to have been initiated by a petition sent to the Commissioners by the assistant keepers (AK's) living on Rock Island. The petition was dated the 17th of February 1909 and signed by J.J. Sweeny, E.J. Smith, E. Sullivan, R. Blakely, W.J. Martin and Wm. Snow. It stated

> on relief days keepers coming on [Fastnet] Rock and going on shore leave have to perform sixteen and twenty hours continuous duty, as the man on the four to eight morning watch on Fastnet resumes the eight to midnight at Crookhaven, and vice-versa, and working hard without any rest in the intervals which comprises twenty hours.

They related that over the previous 12 months the average period they spent each on Fastnet, without relief, was 6½ weeks. Due to regular storm conditions on Fastnet, for three to five of these weeks they were confined to the tower. The asked "pray that you will exempt us, the Fastnet keepers from all duties ashore except such as pertain to our own station"[22].

R. Deane, Irish Lights Inspector, was asked to investigate the accuracy of the petition and he did this in April questioning James Twohig, Fastnet Principal Keeper (PK) as to the work schedules. As a result of this petition, the Secretary of Irish Lights wrote in June to the Board of Trade "to obviate the expense attendant upon increasing the staff and building a new dwelling" they proposed substituting the fixed light for an unwatched. Trinity House suggested that the light should have a different character to prevent it being confused with Fastnet whose character was 1/6 second white flash every 5 seconds. Charles W. Scott[23] replied that such a mistake could not happen because "The Crookhaven light shows red from

---

[22] Irish Lights Work File 1909/204.
[23] Engineer-in-Chief, 1900-1930.

seaward to any vessel coming from the West until it bears North 59° West. Coming from the Eastward, inside of Cape Clear, the Mariner must know where he is, and cannot possibly be misled"[24].
Scott was given the job of designing the unwatched lamp which would require no keeper to be on duty throughout the night. He proposed a burner consisting of seven jets which would produce a light about "5% more powerful that the two outer rings of the six wick burner at present in use". He believed that if the light was fixed (i.e. on continuously) the seven burners would consume a total of $5\frac{1}{4}$ cubic feet of gas an hour at a cost of £34 - £40 per annum. However if it was occulted to the adopted character the cost would be reduced to £12 - £14 per annum. As a result both the Board of Trade and Trinity House had by September 1909 agreed to an unwatched occulting acetylene light. Its character was agreed as "$2\frac{1}{2}$ seconds light and 5 seconds dark". They approved a cost of £230 for part-automating the light[25].
The work of converting the light included an acetylene generator house measuring 2.4m by 2.4m which was built to the south-west of the lighthouse in 1910. An oil store was also converted to a carbide store. M. Lynch was transferred from Skellig to Crookhaven to undertake this work. Twohig wrote to Deane on the 18th of November 1910 telling him that the generator house was completed but "none of the Generating Plant has as yet been delivered"[26]. Mess'rs Pintsch's Patent Lighting Co. Ltd.'s tender of £20 each for the two flashers required for the group of seven $\frac{3}{4}$ cubic feet burners was accepted[27]. The Board was informed that as the Commissioner's ship, the *Alexandra*, was not available before the 30th of December 1910 the new Crookhaven light would not yet be exhibited. The unwatched light, "the first automatic flashing light of any size in the Commissioners' service"[28] was first exhibited on the 17th of February

---

[24] Irish Lights Work File 1909/204.
[25] Journal No.44, Commissioners of Irish Lights, 24th September 1909.
[26] Irish Lights Work File 1910/396.
[27] Journal No.44, 29th April 1910.
[28] Wilson, T.G., The Irish Lighthouse Service, Dublin, 1968, p. 128.

1911[29]. However an explosion occurred that night which resulted in the light being extinguished for 20 minutes. Twohig wrote "everything worked satisfactorily until 11.00 p.m. when Generator in use made a violent charge blowing the seal and emptying all the Carbide (a full charge) from the Hopper". As a result he extinguished the light for 20 minutes to allow the gas to escape from the lantern area. Twohig asked Scott, in his report on the explosion, "would there not be danger of this gas getting into lantern through ventilators or into Crookhaven dwelling [No.1] close by with its small rooms and windows of same open where there is both fire & light?". Scott wrote on the 20th of February to allay Twohig's fears "you need not be afraid of danger from a generator blowing its seal. Consider what happened the other night – you had a charge of 56lbs in the generator and you subsequently recovered 40lbs of good carbide, therefore less than 20lbs of carbide had been converted into gas and lime". He went on to say "25 c ft in 1,500 c ft [area of lantern] are equivalent to a mixture of 1 2/3% which is perfectly safe as it is necessary to have 3 1/3% of acetylene present to obtain an explosive mixture. You need not be afraid that a blow off in the generator will cause danger of a serious explosion in the lantern or dwellings"[30]. The following year, the Board of Trade approved £20 expenditure to install a new ventilator which may have been as a result of the initial explosion.

On the 18th of February 1911 a Notice to Mariners was issued. It stated "the Character of this Light has been altered from a Fixed to an Acetylene Flashing Light of about the same candle power, exhibiting one flash every 7½ seconds thus: Flash, 2½ seconds, eclipse, 5 seconds. The Light when exhibited is unattended".

When the new light was being tested in January, Twohig was given the job of training the "other Keepers now in Fastnet and Mizen". The final cost of the light was £354/3/1 which included £21/12/6 spent on wages and allowances while instructing keepers on

---

[29] Irish Lights Work File 1912/642.
[30] Irish Lights Work File 1911/183.

Rock Island

operating it. At this time the majority of lighthouses around the coast were lit by oil (69); only three were acetylene lights (Crookhaven, Valentia and Sligo); three more were lit by coal gas; and one (Muggins) by "oil gas".

The Engineer in March 1918 requested approval for the demolition of two old storehouses, presumably dating from the Fastnet construction of 1899-1904. He also wanted the removal of the *Irene's* gear from the upper-storey of the pier storehouse to allow storage of lighthouse material. The Board approved both requests.

Murphy & O'Connor of Bantry had the contract for supplying "fresh burned unslaked lime" presumably for whitewashing the walls in 1918 and 1919. They supplied four drums in 1918 at 3/- per drum and also four barrels of lime putty at 7/2 per barrel. The cost increased significantly in 1919 to 3/6 and 8/6 respectively.

A proposal by the Inspector and Assistant Engineer in 1932 to replace the Crookhaven acetylene gas generators with larger ones seems to have been accepted. The benefit was that they could discontinue the £10 supervision allowance per annum paid to the Fastnet PK[31]. In future, the PK would get 10d per hour when working single-handed or 6½d per hour when assisting a tradesman[32]. Later, in March 1937, a proposal from the Inspecting Committee to replace the acetylene generators at an estimated cost of £130 was sanctioned by the British Board of Trade[33]. The Engineer in June 1946 decided that "considerable repairs" were required to the Generator house. Also a new sludge pit for the carbide residue was required and replacement of the flagstones around the generator house.

The character of the light was changed on the 10th of December 1964 to two seconds flash and six seconds eclipse. Crookhaven Lighthouse was converted from the acetylene generator to electricity in 1976. A back-up diesel engine was also put in place. The diesel engine was replaced "by duplicated chargers and 24 volt ampere hour batteries"

---

[31] Irish Lights Work File 1932/115.
[32] Irish Lights Work File 1932/115.
[33] Irish Lights Work File 1936/577.

in 2004. A new light arrangement was also put in place in March 2004 with a cluster of four 12 volt 35 watt tungsten halogen lamps. Also a telephone landline was installed allowing remote control and monitoring from the Dun Laoghaire monitoring centre.[34]

Relocating Crookhaven Lighthouse

On the 10th of November 1847, the *Stephen Whitney*, an American liner, in heavy fog, apparently not being able to see the Cape Clear Light due to its high elevation, mistook the Crookhaven Light for the Old Head of Kinsale Light. Captain Popham had sailed from New York on the 18th of October bound for Liverpool. The ship was 1,034 ton, had 27 crew and 83 passengers and a cargo of corn, cotton, cheese, raisins and 20 boxes of clocks. The crew were not aware that there was a light at Crookhaven. It therefore steered a course which resulted in it being wrecked at 9.45 p.m. on the west tip of Western Calf Island with the loss of 92 lives. The surviving 18 managed to scramble up the rocks[35].

Only five weeks after the destruction of the *Stephen Whitney*, on the 17th of December 1847, the *Lady Charlotte*, "a splendid sailing ship" from Liverpool, was destroyed on the Dromadda rocks on the western entrance of Long Island channel after the captain mistook the Crookhaven Light for the Old Head of Kinsale Light. No-one died but one man was rescued by Henry Baldwin of the Coast Guard. The Coast Guard also recovered $36,000 worth of silver plate.

As a result of both of these incidents, Captain Thomas, the manager of Coosheen Mine near Schull, and others sent a memorial to the Admiralty. They blamed the problem on the positions of the Cape Clear and Crookhaven Lighthouses; they "are useless and that Fastnet Rock is the only eligible spot for a real lighthouse". Major

---

[34] Ruttle, Stuart, "Innovative Technology", *Beam: The Journal of the Irish Lighthouse Service*, Vol. 33, 2004, p. 6.
[35] Washington, State of the Harbours and Lighthouses on the South and South-west coasts of Ireland, Dublin, 1849.

Rock Island

Beamish also sent a memorial to the Admiralty where he said that "three other vessels were also lost in Roaringwater Bay in 1839". In an Admiralty report to the House of Commons in 1849, they agreed with the memorial saying that the Crookhaven Lighthouse was on the wrong side of the harbour "alluring vessels to their destruction"[36].

In March 1859 Lord Bandon took up the case for relocating Crookhaven lighthouse and suggested that a fog bell be established on Fastnet. Bandon wrote to W. Lees, Secretary of the Ballast Board

> I have the honour to request you to call the attention of the Ballast Board to the necessity of changing the lighthouse at Crookhaven to the opposite side of the Harbour and also to the importance of a fog bell on the Fastnet Rock for the protection of vessels in foggy weather[37].

The issue was obviously given consideration as E. J. Roberts of the Ballast Board reported in October on whether there should be a buoy on the Black Horse, the most northerly of the Alderman Rocks. He believed, as it was always above water, all mariners would "give it a berth of at least half a cable"[38]. His advice was not taken as the Board, the following month, gave approval for the erection of an iron beacon on the Alderman Rocks. The cost of this was to be £305[39]. This was calculated as follows:

Rock cutting	£ 45
Metal casing, freight	£ 150
Masonry, erection, etc	£ 80
Sub-total	£ 275
Contingencies @ 10%	£ 27/10
Total	£ 302/10

---

[36] Washington, State of the Harbours.
[37] Journal No.17, Corporation for Preservation & Improving The Port of Dublin & Co., 3rd March 1859.
[38] Journal No.18, 14th October 1859.
[39] Journal No.18, 246.

The Marine Department of the Office of the Committee of Privy Council for Trade did not sanction the building of a beacon tower "that later could be converted to Harbour Light" on the Alderman Rocks. They believed "the work will only benefit the local trade". The Inspecting Committee of the Ballast Board responded in April 1859 stating that it was a worthwhile beacon as "during the prevalence of easterly winds, the harbour of Crookhaven is thronged with vessels from foreign countries, frequently more than 100 sail being there at the same time and it is the principal port in Ireland for the resort of vessels in such circumstances" As a result of this plea, the Board of Trade agreed to a beacon and asked "that, in preparing a plan [for the beacon], the object of providing a refuge for wrecked men may be kept in view"[40].

The Marine Department of the Office of the Committee of Privy Council for Trade wrote to the Ballast Board in February 1860 asking for an update on the beacon's progress. They added that the report on the stranding of the *Irish Lily* of Limerick on the 10th of February close in to the Alderman Rocks stated that it could have been avoided if there had been a "Buoy, Perch or Beacon …on the Rock". The Inspecting Commander of the Coast Guard also believed the Alderman Rocks were most in need of a buoy or perch. Halpin replied that the beacon had not yet been built but he hoped to have the work done during the summer. Tenders were due to be received by the 26th of April 1860 with work to be undertaken during the summer months of that year[41].

Lord Bandon was not satisfied with the proposed beacon and took the issue up with T. M. Gibson, M.P. and President of the Board of Trade, in October 1860 stating that the relocation "could be easily done at a trifling cost". He included a memorial signed by the Mayor of Cork and 75 leading Cork traders requesting the "removal" of Crookhaven lighthouse. The Board of Trade informed the Ballast

---

[40] House of Commons Parliamentary Papers 1861, National Archives, London, 67.461.
[41] Journal No.18., 24th February 1860.

Rock Island

Board the same month that they had no intention of demanding a change of location. They stated that the present plans would "answer every purpose" and removing Crookhaven Lighthouse would be "very expensive work"[42].

Bandon, however remained persistent, and in November 1860 he sent a further Memorial to Gibson signed by 29 captains in Crookhaven Harbour. In the same month, Lieutenant Colonel William Bernard M.P. of Bandon also wrote to Gibson urging the relocation and stated that "as many as 130 [vessels] having been there at any one time". Also Robert Singfield of Merrion Square, Dublin wrote on the matter to Gibson.

The next party to take up the issue of relocating the lighthouse was Vincent Scully[43] M.P. for Cork. He indicated in December 1860 that a number of "influential constituents" were concerned. Lord Pelham Clinton[44] had asked him to raise the issue, regarding the present location as "mischievous"[45]. The Board met Scully on the 6th of December 1860 but showed no interest in moving the lighthouse. He wrote again on the 7th asking the Board to forward his objection to the Board of Trade. He was obviously very frustrated after the meeting, writing "your Board did not favour me with any of their views. On the contrary they civilly declined to answer any questions, unless through the Board of Trade, whereupon some mutual pleasantries passed respecting circumlocution and Red Tapeism, Garibaldi and Cavour[46]". On the 14th he enclosed a Memorial signed

---

[42] Journal No.19, Corporation for Preservation & Improving The Port of Dublin & Co., p. 125.
[43] Vincent Scully (1810-1871), TCD & Trinity College, Cambridge, Irish Bar 1833, QC 1840, MP for Cork 1852-57 & 1859-65.
[44] Lord Charles Pelham Clinton (1813-1894), eldest twin son of Fourth Duke of Newcastle upon Lyne, Capt First Life Guards and Member of Parliament for Sandwich 1852-57. He was listed as a magistrate in Kilmoe parish in 1861 – Thom's Almanac and Official Directory, 1861.
[45] Journal No.19, 4th December 1860.
[46] Giusseppe Garibaldi, 1807-82, widely regarded as the father of modern Italy invaded Sicily in 1860 and marched on Rome. He gave the whole of Southern

by 250 people which included the Earl of Shannon, merchants, traders, gentry and clergy connected with the south-west of Ireland. They requested that consideration be given to the question of relocating[47]. The Board of Trade in reply to this Memorial stated that relocating would be "very expensive work" and annual costs would be "greatly increased" as it would now be a rock station.

Scully sent a second Memorial from 19 ships masters stating "that it would be highly expedient to have the present light removed from where it now stands to the Alderman Rock"[48]. A third Memorial followed from "Ship Agents, Shopkeepers, Inhabitants of the town and townland of Crookhaven, Ballynaule, Ballyvogue, Malavogue and others interested in the Harbour of Crookhaven". It stated "that as soon as this railroad [Bandon-Skibbereen] is completed, the Harbour of Crookhaven will be connected with the City of Cork by telegraph wire, for the greater convenience of homeward bound ships, who will receive their orders in Crookhaven" thus resulting in increased use of the harbour. This Memorial said that "as many as 6 and 80 vessels have been at several times anchored within its shelter".

As a result of the Board's intransigence, Scully, through the House of Commons, raised the question of relocating the light. The Port of Dublin Corporation received a demand on the 15th of February 1861 from the House of Commons for "a copy of all correspondence between the Board of Trade, The Trinity House and the Port of Dublin Corporation respectively relating to the original erection upon Rock Island of the present Light House for Crookhaven Harbour or to the proposed erection either of a new Light House or of a Beacon Tower upon the Alderman Rock"[49].

The Board of the Port of Dublin Corporation had on the 31st of December 1860 accepted the tender of Head, Ashby & Co to build the beacon for £995, a sum much larger than the Board's estimate

---

Italy to Count Camillo Benso di Cavour, 1810-61, the Piedmontese Prime Minister.
[47] Journal No.19, 125.
[48] Journal No.19, 172.
[49] Journal No.19, 165.

the previous year of £305. However in April 1861 Head, Ashby & Co.[50] were requesting an increase in their accepted tender for the erection of the beacon. This was refused on Halpin's recommendation. In August the Port of Dublin Corporation paid £300 to Head, Ashby & Co. as a result of the beacon arriving safely in Crookhaven. By the 24th of October 1861, there had been two unsuccessful attempts to erect the beacon. It was decided later that month that they would have to wait until the following year. In January a request by Head, Ashby & Co. to be allowed relocate the beacon due to "damage to metal work" was denied by the Board. In February they were promising to undertake the work "in early spring". They were worried about "the fearful seas that may attack it"[51].

The foreman of the new shore dwellings, I. Connolly, wrote in July 1862 "Alderman Rock foundation bolt holes finished, metals expected shortly"[52]. On the 26th of August he stated "Beacon Tower finished – chasing around base of tower requires to be done with stone and cement. Contractor refuses to do it, it not being specified". He wrote again on the 4th of September, saying that the beacon was now finished and he had borrowed cement from the shore dwelling contractor to complete. He had used one cask of "Modena cement" to fill the groove around the base of the beacon. The following day, Isaac Notter of Crookhaven also wrote to say the beacon was finished. He asked that an Inspector be sent. As a result a Mr Kirwin was sent; he later wrote that the work was completed. On the 25th of September 1862, Head, Ashby & Co. indicated that the beacon was completed and requested their final payment including a payment for the location being moved. The request for additional payment was refused as the relocation was due to the contractors' bolts being

---

[50] A Teesside, England engineering company formed in 1840.
[51] Journal No.20, Corporation for Preservation & Improving The Port of Dublin & Co., p. 170.
[52] Lighthouse Register 1862, Corporation for Preservation & Improving The Port of Dublin & Co., 19th July 1862.

washed away "caused by their not being properly supported with Masonry"[53].

In May 1863 Isaac Notter and John Blake submitted tenders for painting the Alderman Rock Beacon. Blake's tender was accepted. In June, the Crookhaven keeper wrote that painting of the beacon had started. He also said that "two plates of balcony carried away". By the 9th of July, the painting had been completed.

J. Leahy of Crookhaven offered to scrape and paint the Alderman Beacon the following year for £15. Isaac Notter, in July 1864, offered also to paint the beacon for £15. Neither got the job as the Crookhaven keeper reported that Blake was painting the beacon in August. It was finished on the 19th of September.

William Douglass appears to have inspected the Alderman Rock while on a visit to Fastnet in March 1865[54]. In May E. F. Roberts, the Inspector of Lights, following an inspection on the 22nd of April, suggested the Alderman Rock Beacon "be taken down". This was due to it being "30° out of perpendicular occasioned by the storm in January last" (James Doyle had reported on the 20th of March that the beacon had been damaged)[55]. Roberts believed that "this Beacon should never been placed where it is". If "practicable" it should be replaced with one on Black Rock (part of the Alderman Rocks)[56]. The Board however deferred any decision on this. C. J. Day (Doyle's temporary replacement) reported on the 14th of November that the beacon "had disappeared"[57]. In December T. Notter of Crookhaven

---

[53] Journal No.21, Corporation for Preservation & Improving The Port of Dublin & Co., 9th October 1862.

[54] William Douglass (1831 – 1923). In 1865 he was the Construction Engineer of Trinity House, the UK Lighthouse Authority. In 1878 he was appointed Engineer to Irish Lights – Pelly, F. "William Douglass: Designer of Fastnet Lighthouse", *Beam*, Vol. 33, 2004, p. 24.

[55] Lighthouse Register 1864, Corporation for Preservation & Improving The Port of Dublin & Co.

[56] Journal No.23, Corporation for Preservation & Improving The Port of Dublin & Co., 11th May 1865.

[57] Lighthouse Register 1865, Corporation for Preservation & Improving The Port of Dublin & Co.

was requesting payment of £82/12/8 for work on the Alderman Beacon, presumably before its disappearance.

In July 1866, Trinity House again refused to consider relocating the lighthouse. They stated "its value [of relocating] would rather consist in its applicability as a Coast Light to lead vessels from the Westward but as the anchorage is used mostly in Easterly winds and the Fastnet Light is only at a distance of 6 miles and abreast of the entrance". They however approved a new beacon located at the "lowest part to Seaward" on the Black Horse Rocks. These suggestions were accepted by the Board of Trade[58]. In September J. S. Sloane appears to have submitted plans and specifications for a new beacon on Alderman Rock. This was approved by the Port of Dublin Corporation and forwarded to the Board of Trade.

Work on the new beacon was started the following year. In March 1867 Sloane, while on Fastnet, requested a labourer and three coils of rope for Blackhorse Beacon[59]. In June, he reported the arrival of the Black Horse Beacon "Iron Work". In late October he stated that he would have the Black Horse Beacon coloured red. He also sent the Board further drawings of the Beacon at this time.

The Earl of Bandon again raised the question of relocation in June 1871. In a further request for relocation in August 1872 he indicated that some 40,000 tons of vessels used Crookhaven in 1871. His demands, or those of others interested in the issue, had some impact as the Board of Trade in the same month asked Irish Lights for the cost of a) removing Crookhaven Lighthouse, erecting and annual maintenance of same on the Alderman Rocks, and b) maintaining Crookhaven Lighthouse, erecting new light at Streak Head and the annual maintenance. They also asked when was the Black Horse Beacon erected, and the dioptric apparatus erected at Crookhaven,

---

[58] Journal No.24, Corporation for Preservation & Improving The Port of Dublin & Co., p. 37.
[59] Lighthouse Register 1867, Commissioners of Irish Lights, 30th March 1867.

Crookhaven Lighthouse

both of these having been sanctioned by the Board of Trade in 1866[60].

In November 1872 the 259 ton *Leonara* hit Castle Island in Roaringwater Bay. She was on her way to Liverpool from Wilmington (Delaware or North Carolina), with a cargo of cotton, turpentine and resin, and a crew of 11. At 6.15 on the 4th of November a light was seen for about two minutes through the fog to the northward. The captain and the mate assumed it was the Fastnet and steered accordingly. However what they had seen was Crookhaven Light. Shortly afterwards they hit Castle Island with the crew managing to land safely[61].

As a result of the Board of Trade request in August 1872 and probably the *Leonara's* destruction, the Elder Brethren of Trinity House along with the Commissioners Inspecting Committee visited Crookhaven on the 12th of June 1873. The Elder Brethren arrived with William Douglass aboard the *Argus*. They "satisfied themselves that there was space on the inner rock [of the Alderman] to erect a lighthouse". However neither group believed that the cost of removing the lighthouse on Rock Island should come from the Mercantile Marine Fund. This was due to the Alderman Light being of no use as a "passing light" as it would be blocked by Streak Head. Also "the Fastnet Light gives any vessel heading for Crookhaven sufficient lead while the Red Sector from the Crookhaven Light keeps her clear of the Alderman Rocks". They went on to say that Crookhaven was "principally used by Vessels as a refuge from in East Winds". This function of the harbour was, according to them, of less significance due to the replacement of the sailing ships with steamers. They suggested that the tonnage anchoring in the harbour "was very considerably less in 1872 than in previous years". Also, to support not relocating the lighthouse, they suggested that with a light on the Alderman Rock, shipping would potentially hit the Black

---

[60] Journal No.26, Commissioners of Irish Lights, 30th August 1872.
[61] Lankford, E., Cape Clear Island: Its People and Landscape, Dublin, 1999.

Rock Island

Horse rocks and as a result they would need a second light to "guide them to their anchorage"[62].
This was however not the end of the matter as a Colonel Percival wrote in January 1874 requesting a decision on the relocation.
On the 9th of October 1893 the 68 ton schooner *Sir Richard* was wrecked between the Alderman Rocks and Streak Head. She was travelling to Newport, Wales with pyrites. The three aboard survived.

Annual Inspections

George Halpin, reporting on the annual inspection conducted in late 1844, wrote "Crookhaven light house, lightroom, residence and premises throughout were in very satisfactory order".
The General Inspection of 1876 stated "found the lighthouse clean and in good order, also the Fastnet Shore Dwellings clean, but some of the buildings require repairs and painting, which should be done at once, having been ordered last year". As a result £593/9/0 was sanctioned for repairs[63].

One of the Commissioners near the Coast Guard Station on the annual inspection ca. 1903

---

[62] Journal No.26, 1st August 1873.
[63] Journal No.30, Commissioners of Irish Lights, p. 48.

Crookhaven Lighthouse

The Inspection of 1910 found the "station in very good order and the keepers very smart and business like in appearance". The report recommended "a parapet or fence was required at the end of the concrete platform to the westward of the Mizen head dwellings"[64]. This fence is still in place.

On the 7th of June 1947 Crookhaven was inspected with the property receiving a "very good" report.

The Cast Iron Fastnet Lighthouse[65]

As a result of Cape Clear Lighthouse being "very frequently obscured by fog" and the number of ship wrecks in Roaringwater Bay, Trinity House sanctioned the building of a lighthouse at Fastnet Rock in January 1848 and the decommissioning of Cape Clear light[66]. They accepted George Halpin, Snr's design for a cast iron lighthouse as it "would much lessen the difficulty and time of erecting a lighthouse and thus prove more economical"[67]. There is no indication that Rock Island was used as a base for the construction from 1849-1853. The "metal castings" were however described as being "conveyed to Crookhaven" in 1849[68]. The new light on Fastnet was first lit on the 1st of January 1854[69].

Within ten years of the erection of the first Fastnet Lighthouse it was evident that it was "not strong enough to compete with the Atlantic". The Board was informed in February 1862 by I. Connolly, foreman,

---

[64] Journal No.45, Commissioners of Irish Lights.
[65] For the history of the Fastnet Lighthouses: Scott, C.W., History of the Fastnet Rock Lighthouses, Schull, 1993; Morrissey, J., A History of the Fastnet Lighthouse, Dublin, 2004.
[66] Scott, History of the Fastnet Rock Lighthouses, p. 1.
[67] Journal No.11, Corporation for Preservation & Improving The Port of Dublin & Co., p. 392.
[68] Washington, State of the Harbours and Lighthouses on the South and Southwest coasts of Ireland, Dublin, 1849.
[69] Journal No.14, Corporation for Preservation & Improving The Port of Dublin & Co., p. 161.

Rock Island

of damage to the Flagstaff and dwelling on "Fastness"[70] due to a gale on 20 February. Various efforts were made from 1865 to improve the structure[71]. J. S. Sloane was responsible for repairs that year. On the 14th of August the Fastnet PK James Healy reported that two stonecutters, Noble and Maguire had landed on the rock. Two weeks later a bricklayer and a labourer, Nagle, arrived. On the 30th of September J.S. Sloane, oversaw the landing of the first metal plates. The same day he requested 50 casks of cement from Cork. A week later he was requesting a fitter from Calf Rock. In late October he reported that 31 of the 52 "plates casting had been landed". He also reported on the progress of the "Iron House" and requested permission to depart from Rock Island. It seems Sloane's place was taken by the foreman, Cunningham who was at Rock Island on the 2nd of November and landed on Fastnet the following day. He wrote on the 9th that he was "setting plates". He returned to Rock Island on the 1st of December. That same month T. Notter of Crookhaven was requesting payment of £15/12/0 for Fastnet works, possibly delivering supplies.

Work seems to have re-commenced on the 3rd of April 1866 with the arrival of two carpenters on the rock. Cunningham reported on the 9th that "workmen, provisions, bricks, cement and sand landed". A week later he reported on progress to the "Iron House". Maguire, the stonecutter, was back on the rock on the 4th of May. Healy, the Fastnet PK, requested that the painters be allowed overtime which was accepted. Also in May, Cunningham was reporting on the chimney pots on the cast iron dwelling. On the 11th of June, J. S. Sloane reported that the "Fastnet Iron Dwelling" was finished[72]. On the 19th all the men had been discharged by Cunningham except for a labourer. However Healy reported on the progress of the carpenters'

---

[70] The present name Fastnet may be derived from Fastness meaning "a secure place well protected by natural features" – Oxford English Dictionary.
[71] Wilson, The Irish Lighthouse Service, 37.
[72] The "Fastnet Iron Dwelling" and The "Iron House" would refer to the two storey addition made to the east end of the keeper's iron dwelling - Scott, History of the Fastnet Rock Lighthouses, 5.

work on the 2nd of July. On the 22nd of July, the Crookhaven keeper reported that E. Keogh, a fitter, had not paid his hotel bill to Mr. Downing of Goleen. The painters had left on the 20th of July and commenced painting the shore dwellings the following day.

J. S. Sloane sent an estimate of £3,451/15/0 for the Fastnet works in August 1866. The following March Sloane was back on Fastnet. He requested a stove for cooking there. Again on the 3rd of April he was on Fastnet with workmen who commenced work that day. He also requested, that day, 40 fathoms[73] of 5/8-inch chain, and roofing felt. The foreman this year was James Tocker.

Sloane employed men on Rock Island in June 1867 to remove granite blocks presumably for Fastnet. In August he reported that he had "ordered Messrs Edmundson to forward part of casing now ready for". Messrs Edmundson & Co. was a Dublin lighthouse equipment manufacturer and supplier. In September Sloane reported that the *Shark* had landed stores on Fastnet. Work on Fastnet for 1867 ended in November.

In January 1868 Sloane was ordering "granite stones" for the chasm on Fastnet. The foreman Tocker had arrived on Fastnet on the 21st of March 1868. In April Tocker received a pay increase to seven shillings (per day?). Sloane reported from Fastnet on the 11th of May that the cranes and sheds had been erected. Also the plate and chasm works had commenced. The following day he informed the Secretary "a gale of wind obliged cutter to run for Crookhaven with two boats which after broke adrift". By the 14th the drifting boats had been recovered[74]. In August Sloane submitted details of the expected expense of "filling chasm at south-western end of rock". Work for the year appears to have ended on the 26th of October. The efforts to reinforce the Fastnet tower do not seem to have been successful as W. Williams PK reported on the 31st of December 1868 that the "tower vibrates now as much as formerly"[75].

---

[73] A fathom is 6 feet in length equal to 1.8 metres.
[74] Lighthouse Register 1868, Commissioners of Irish Lights.
[75] Lighthouse Register 1869, Commissioners of Irish Lights.

James Tocker was requested, in May 1869, to report on the quantity of stone required to fill the chasm so as to present a smooth surface to the seas. He appears to have waited a month for the arrival of Sloane. At the end of May he was requesting two fitters and two quarrymen to work on Fastnet. On the 19th of June he reported that all the paint and stone had been landed on Fastnet. By the 22nd of November 1869 Tocker was reporting that work at Fastnet was finished. However in December, the Fastnet keeper Williams was querying why the Inspector had ordered two helpers to remain on the rock during the winter months.

In November 1870 Williams reported details of the work done by the stone cutters. Tenders were received in June 1871 for conveying cement to Fastnet. In October 1872, R. Shakespeare was reporting on the progress of work at Fastnet. He was requested to have a derrick made by the carpenter on site and to clear out the old store relocating the materials to the new store.

Keepers Rules & Regulations

The position of lightkeeper was sought after throughout the era of manned lighthouses (until the 1980s). Keepers benefited from a salary and a pension but conditions at many stations were hard and primitive. Keepers were also subject to many rules but the principle one was deference to those in authority at all times.

Instructions to keepers were detailed and distributed in book form. In 1905 the Commissioners published their *Instructions to Light Keepers*[76]. Potential keepers were required to be a minimum of 5'4" (163cm) and had to undertake exams in Mathematics, Dictation, English Composition, Geography, Reading and Writing. If successful, they started as Probationary Keepers usually at the Bailey Lighthouse and progressed to Supernumerary Keepers. Their initial pay as Probationary Keepers was 2/6 per day which was to cover their cost of board and lodging. If available, they were allowed to stay

---

[76] Commissioners of Irish Lights, Instructions to Light Keepers, Dublin, 1905.

Crookhaven Lighthouse

on spare Light Vessels in Kingstown (Dun Laoghaire) Harbour. Probationary Keepers, before being promoted, had to demonstrate that

> they have acquired a practical knowledge in the management and cleaning of lamps, lenses and reflectors, and the duties keepers have to attend to in the lantern of a lighthouse, that they are clean and neat in their habits and appearance, and can wash and mend their clothes, but above all that they are strictly obedient, respectful to superiors and of good manners[77].

They also had to "be able to read and make signals correctly with the International and lighthouse codes, Morse system, Semaphore and Signal Lamp".
Stations were categorised as rock, island and land stations with keepers divided into Principal Keepers, Assistant Keepers, Gunners (who only appear to have been employed at Hook Head and Kinsale) and Gasmakers. Gunners were selected from "pensioners in the Royal Navy, are permanent in their employment at a station, and are not allowed retiring pensions". Keepers based on Rocks, such as Fastnet, were to "reside at the dwellings on the mainland…where they are to occupy themselves keeping a look out for, and replying to any signals that may be made from the Lighthouse or the Commissioners' Steamers". Keepers were required to hoist the Commissioners Ensign on "Sundays, State Days, Public Holidays, Inspection Days" and whenever any of the Steamers of the General Lighthouse Authority are in sight of the station. In winter watches were not to exceed four hours.
Every year keepers had to paint the lantern inside and out, the gallery, gates, iron fences, gutters and downpipes, oil tanks and flagstaffs. The annual whitewashing, cleaning out of "ashpits, cesspools, etc" was to be carried out as soon as possible after the 1st of April. Where labour was required for these jobs it had to be approved annually in advance. All other painting was done by the

---

[77] Commissioners, Instructions to Light Keepers, 7.

Rock Island

Commissioners' painters. The dwellings and the station were to also "be kept neat and free from weeds". Any provisions supplied were charged to the keepers. An allowance of eight tons of Scotch coal or seven tons of English coal was made to each keeper every year. Each keeper got three tables, chairs, a chest of drawers and kitchen utensils. Bed clothes and bedding were only supplied to relieving stations such as Fastnet i.e. where there were separate shore dwellings.

Whilst working at stations, tradesmen and labourers were expected to work a 54 hour week over six days. From March to October on Monday to Friday they started at 6.30 a.m., had a break for breakfast 8.30-9.30, break for lunch 1.30-2.30, and finished at 6.00 p.m. Saturday also started at 6.30 a.m., breakfast 8.30-9.30 and finished at 2.00 p.m. In the winter months they started at 7.00 a.m., lunched from 12.00 p.m.–1.00 p.m. and finished at 5.00 p.m. Overtime was only to be done in exceptional cases with the first two hours at $1\frac{1}{4}$ times normal pay, the next four at $1\frac{1}{2}$ time.

The following pay rates applied in 1905:

	Per Day	Per Annum
Supernumerary Keeper unqualified	2/6	£45/12/6
Supernumerary Keeper qualified at Rock Station	3/0	£54/15/0
Assistant Keeper	3/0	£54/15/0
Assistant Keeper after 5 years service	3/3	£59/6/3
Assistant Keeper after 10 years service	3/6	£63/17/6
Assistant Keeper after 15 years service	3/9	£68/9/9
Principal Keeper	4/3	£77/11/3
Principal Keeper after 5 years service	4/6	£82/2/6

Annual leave for keepers was not to exceed 14 days. A uniform was supplied annually and a top coat triennially. From the 1st of May to the 1st of September a white cover was worn on the cap which was removed for the winter months[78].

---

[78] Scanlon, D., Memoirs of an Islander: A Life on Scattery and Beyond, Ennis, 2003.

Lightkeepers

Irish Lights' records gave us a flavour of some of the keepers, and their families', time on Rock Island. Unfortunately they usually came to the attention of head office for the wrong reasons with the many men who gave excellent service never getting any mention.

George Halpin, as Superintendent, was required to go to Crookhaven in April 1859 as a result of charges been brought against the Fastnet keepers and the crew of the attending boat by a William John Mahony. Statements relating to the matter were taken under oath in Crookhaven in front of a Justice of the Peace[79]. Unfortunately there is no further information on the incident.

In September 1861, Higginbotham, the Crookhaven lightkeeper was admonished by the Board "on the subject of wreck sold there". Higginbotham stated that he was "not aware that his son had sold the Iron at the time"[80].

Manus Ward, a keeper on Fastnet, was unhappy in 1862 with the house rented for him on shore. He said it was "out of repair". The Board insisted he live in the house and demand any repairs necessary from the landlord[81]. At this stage there was no purpose-built housing for Fastnet keepers on Rock Island. Dr McCormick, the local doctor, submitted a medical certificate for him in February 1863 indicating that he was in good health. Ward requested a month off in April 1864 to allow him to get married to Eliza Hamilton of Rock Island[82] – he said he had no-one on shore to help him with the preparations. In August 1864, Ward was on shore due to "illness". In September he was asking for "removal to a more favourable station" on account

---

[79] Journal No.18, Corporation for Preservation & Improving The Port of Dublin & Co., p. 21.
[80] Journal No.20, Corporation for Preservation & Improving The Port of Dublin & Co., p. 12.
[81] Lighthouse Register 1862, Corporation for Preservation & Improving The Port of Dublin & Co., 25th June 1862.
[82] Manus Ward was from Rosses, Co. Donegal - Murphy, "Rock Island and Its Families", 170.

of his ill-health. He was finally transferred in January 1865 with William Doherty replacing him. Ward was later required to provide an explanation for his wife's travelling expenses from Fastnet to Howth Bailey.

In March 1862 the Fastnet PK John McKenna requested an additional third assistant. The request was referred to the Inspecting Committee[83]. He also requested a transfer from Fastnet in December 1862 as he "had been on rock stations since he was appointed lightkeeper"[84]. McKenna was in trouble in mid-January 1863 as he informed head office that there was a warrant out for his arrest over a debt. He requested that a replacement keeper be sent because he was obliged to leave the rock. The Crookhaven keeper was told to send Manus Ward in his place. By the 25th of January McKenna had settled the debt and was told to remain on Fastnet as Principal Keeper[85]. McKenna expressed a preference in February 1864 to be transferred to Balbriggan[86] (this appears unusual as the Balbriggan lighthouse was downgraded to a minor harbour light, not in Irish Lights' care, from the commencement of the Rockabill light on 1 July 1860). It appears that the intention was to transfer him to Tory Island which he was opposed to, due to his children's schooling needs. His schooling concerns were obviously of little interest to the Board as he was transferred to Skellig Lower in March. His family would have lived on Skellig with him as the shore dwellings for the families were only completed on Valentia Island in 1901. He was replaced on Fastnet by James Healy[87]. Prior to McKenna's departure, he wrote in February 1864 that J. Maginn AK, had not returned from his leave on time; he had been absent from the 25th of January to the 24th of February. None of Maginn's explanations for not returning

---

[83] Lighthouse Register 1862, 31st March 1862.
[84] Lighthouse Register 1863, Corporation for Preservation & Improving The Port of Dublin & Co.
[85] Lighthouse Register 1862, 12th & 25th January 1863.
[86] Lighthouse Register 1864, Corporation for Preservation & Improving The Port of Dublin & Co., 19th February 1864.
[87] Lighthouse Register 1864, March 1864.

were deemed satisfactory. It appears that J. Maginn was transferred to Balbriggan in May 1864 with James Doyle, previously based on Tory Island, taking his position.

In September 1864 Daniel Coughlan, Fastnet "watchman" forwarded an explanation for not carrying out the instructions of an assistant keeper[88]. Coughlan requested in January 1866 that keepers get their clothing allowance annually. This may have been due to the particularly difficult conditions on Fastnet at the time. He later asked, in September 1871, for his son to be appointed an AK. He was informed by the Board in an unusually frank letter "that his son is considered a lazy idle good for nothing lad". J.S. Sloane had indicated that previously he had employed the son and "found him next to useless"[89]. Coughlan in July 1873, now an AK on Fastnet, requested a pay increase as he had been a lightkeeper for 25 years. In August 1883 Coughlan was "superannuated owing to failing health"[90]. He was awarded an annual pension of £33/6/6. Later that year, his son, also Daniel Coughlan had his request to take his father's position refused "as it appears that he is the man who assaulted the Principal Keeper"[91].

The Inspector in December 1866 submitted newspaper reports of the "disgraceful conduct" of William Doherty, Fastnet AK. Captain Roberts was instructed by the Secretary to give Doherty a copy of the newspaper and inform him that he would have been dismissed "had he not been punished by the Magistrates". He was warned that similar misconduct in the future would lead to dismissal[92].

Thomas Fortune, Fastnet AK, forwarded a doctor's certificate for measles which kept him off work for five days in February 1867. He returned to the Fastnet on the 27th of February. In November 1881

---

[88] Lighthouse Register 1864, 2nd September 1864.
[89] Lighthouse Register 1871, Commissioners of Irish Lights, 1st September 1871.
[90] Journal No.33, Commissioners of Irish Lights, 17th August 1883.
[91] Journal No.33, 14th December 1883.
[92] Lighthouse Register 1866, Corporation for Preservation & Improving The Port of Dublin & Co., 26th December 1866.

Thomas Fortune was Principal Keeper on the Calf Rock, off Beara Peninsula when it was destroyed in a storm. He and five other men were rescued twelve days later[93].

W. Williams, the Fastnet PK, was ill on shore in August 1869 so James McCormick was in charge on Fastnet. Williams was again ill in August 1870 having been given a medical certificate by Dr. McCormick. Williams, in November 1870, forwarded an application from J. Brownell AK for a PK position. Brownell again applied to be promoted in May 1871. He stated he had been an AK for almost 12 years[94]. He was finally promoted to PK Calf Rock in November 1871. He took responsibility there on the 17th from Henry Stocker. Stocker took over, in November 1871, from Henry Gardiner as Crookhaven keeper with Gardiner transferred to Ballycotton. Gardiner's wife had been paid since August 1868 for her lighthouse duties at Crookhaven.

In April 1872 W. Wilson, Fastnet PK, requested the appointment of his son as a keeper. In August he forwarded a certificate proving his son's age. Wilson regularly asked when his son would be called up for the entrance exam; on one occasion in December 1873 he was told "when his time comes".

Wilson was requested to explain in October 1872 why he had not reported the charging before a magistrate of Francis Cooper AK for a dispute with Isaac Notter. Wilson replied that as the case was dismissed and was "not for drunkenness" he saw no reason to forward a report. There is no indication as to the nature of the dispute[95].

Charges also appear to have been brought against George Dunleavy, AK Fastnet, as Wilson sent an explanation to Dublin in November 1872[96]. Dunleavy left Fastnet the same month, having hired a hooker to take himself and his family to Skellig Rock.

---

[93] Harrington, G., "The Harringtons and Calf Rock", *Beam: The Journal of the Irish Lighthouse Service*, Vol. 29, 2000, p. 36.
[94] Lighthouse Register 1871, 11th May 1871.
[95] Lighthouse Register 1872, 15th October 1872.
[96] Lighthouse Register 1872, 6th November 1872.

Dr. McCormick, on the 31st of December 1880, sent a bill for attending to John Stapleton AK based on Fastnet[97]. The same Stapleton was reprimanded in June 1881 "for unsatisfactory state of his dwellings and his absence from the station"[98]. In December that year the Fastnet staff were one PK, three 1st class AK's and two 2nd class AK's.

On the 29th of July 1893 Dr. R.F. Brideoake (residing at Rock Island House), who was retained by Irish Lights as doctor for keepers at Crookhaven and Fastnet, wrote that George Brownell PK was suffering from "Cnychia in left foot" and needed at least two weeks off. Brownell was released from duty from the 3rd to the 15th of August[99].

In March 1900 Dr. John Twohig, Cape View House, Goleen wrote "John Wills Lt Keeper Fastnet Rock is suffering from Capillary naevus [enlarged capillaries] on point of elbow which requires immediate treatment". Wills himself wrote the following day, 7th of March "since I came ashore 28th inst I have been doing duty at Crookhaven Lt House so cannot relinquish until relieved". Edward Rohu PK wrote later that he relieved Wills, and Twohig the "Board's doctor" had operated on him[100]. Rohu, of the Malahide Coast Guard Station, had applied for an assistant keeper posting in January 1867. In October 1900 Rohu was writing to the Cashier, Irish Lights Office that he had received no wages when he had gone to "Rockisland" Post Office to collect them on the 30th of September. The Post Mistress informed him that she was not holding any mail. As a result the Bank Post Bill for his September pay of £6/4/1 was cancelled and re-issued[101].

On the 20th of April 1901 Rickard Hamilton, PK at Rathlin O'Birne Lighthouse, wrote that "the lands of Rock Island, Co. Cork belong to me, a few years since". He said he gave Irish Lights permission to

---

[97] Journal No.32, Commissioners of Irish Lights, p. 52.
[98] Journal No.32, 158.
[99] Irish Lights Work File 1893/848.
[100] Irish Lights Work File 1900/278.
[101] Irish Lights Work File 1900/1042.

Rock Island

[handwritten note: Nollaig's great great grandfather. Father of Alexander whose photographic portrait sits in the dining room]

"erect poles for the Fastnet new works free of any charge". He however stated that the landlord was looking for compensation and enquired whether any payment had been made. He was informed that no payment was made to the landlord. He also added "the land is now in the courts… I am also the Executor of the 'will' of these lands"[102].

Hamilton was born on Rock Island on the 28th of January 1845. He joined Irish Lights on the 16th of August 1866 after having served in the Royal Navy. He appears to have been based on Fastnet in 1868 as he was reported as sick in September. On the 1st of March 1880 he was promoted to PK. In 1900 he was moved from Dunmore East Lighthouse to Rathlin as punishment for cutting fishermen's nets which he denied. He was also accused by John and Michael Power, fishermen from Dunmore, of using the "lighthouse at Dunmore [as] a lodging house for Cape Clear fishermen"[103]. R. Deane, Irish Lights' Inspector, wrote on the 25th of June 1901 that Hamilton "appears from correspondence dated back to 25th December 1883, to be unreliable, and in consequence unsuitable for taking charge of any lighthouse"[104].

Due to illness Rickard Hamilton requested a transfer "to any station on the South Coast" in March 1902. He was admitted to Mercer's Hospital, Dublin on the 2nd of April 1902 by Dr. Lunnesden who wrote that he had "Incipient Brights Disease", a kidney disease causing back pain, vomiting and oedema. Lunnesden requested that Hamilton be transferred to a land station "within easy reach of medical aid"[105].

It appears he was relocated to Wicklow Head as he wrote from there to head office in September 1902 requesting a transfer to Rock Island. He stated "the lands of Rockisland are in the possession of my family for the last 80 years. The Post Office there for the last 47 years I will now have to give both up on account of my wife's

---

[102] Irish Lights Work File 1901/460.
[103] Irish Lights Work File 1901/557.
[104] Irish Lights Work File 1901/628.
[105] Irish Lights Work File 1902/369.

health…though the picture of health she could drop any day". He said that his daughter, who was presently with him, could take charge of the lands and the post office after "being instructed by her mother". Deane wrote "during my recent visit to Crookhaven I accidentally heard that one of the Hamilton's sons was residing there, and that Mrs Hamilton continued to attend to the duties of the Post Office". Hamilton's request was refused[106]. The following month Hamilton asked Irish Lights to remove the poles on his land which were located near the stone storage area. He had decided to sell his land to his brother, Alexander, as he was refused the relocation[107]. Irish Lights agreed to move the poles but asked if they could wait until the following June[108].

Dr. Thomas Neville[109] of Goleen requested that William J. Martin AK be given additional sick leave in December 1904 as he had injured himself on Fastnet while "rolling up lantern curtains". He fell and received bruising "causing slight concussion of the brain"[110]. Neville wrote to the Board in June 1906 to say he was resigning as Medical Officer for Crookhaven lightkeepers but would continue to look after the lightkeepers and their families "at his usual visiting rates, payable in advance". It appears his temporary resignation was due to an argument over fees. Irish Lights wanted to pay a monthly capitation fee of 10d per head while Dr. Neville wanted 2/6 per head (not including midwifery) which was eventually accepted in October[111]. Later it was noted that he had agreed to an annual fee of £45 with an additional £5 per annum once Mizen was established[112].

---

[106] Irish Lights Work File 1902/806.
[107] Rickard and family later settled in Cobh/Queenstown where he lived until 1932 – Murphy, S., "Kevin Murphy, Principal Keeper", *Beam*, Vol. 32, 2003, p. 19.
[108] Irish Lights Work File 1901/993.
[109] Dr Thomas Neville was the Goleen doctor from 1903-46. He previously had served in the Boer War, 1899-1902. For most of his time in Goleen he lived in Cape View House. He died in 1957 and is buried in Goleen Catholic Graveyard.
[110] Irish Lights Work File 1904/1292.
[111] Journal No.43, Commissioners of Irish Lights, 5th October 1906.
[112] Journal No.44, Commissioners of Irish Lights, p. 2.

He was also getting 5/- for every certificate furnished and 1/8 per month for every workman employed (of which 10d was paid by the worker), presumably on the Mizen Head works. Dr Neville was still employed by Irish Lights in December 1950.

J. Twohig PK wrote in 1907 that he spent "232 days yearly average on [Fastnet] Rock". Twohig asked in 1909 if he could be relieved altogether from spending time on Fastnet. He asked to be given responsibility, along with the Female Assistant Keeper, for Crookhaven Light and to only visit Fastnet and Mizen Head on relief days. He was informed by the Irish Lights Secretary that they did not intend to increase the number of Fastnet keepers and he would go back on duty there once the Mizen Head dwellings were completed. He was also told that the Female Assistant's allowance would only continue until the Mizen Head was operational. Once operational, the Fastnet PK would receive an additional allowance of £20 per annum as he would also have responsibility for the Mizen Head[113]. Twohig also informed head office that a relief of Fastnet was successfully undertaken that day, the 15th of February 1909, with three keepers coming off as the last relief had been six weeks earlier on the 6th of January.

In December 1908 Edward Rohu, a "pensioned light keeper" submitted to the Board receipts to the value of £12/7/0 for doctors and hospital fees paid as a result of his son accidentally shooting himself in the head at Crookhaven Lighthouse. Initially the Board refused his request but later they sanctioned payment of half the costs from the Donations Fund[114].

---

[113] Pay & Allowances: In 1910, the Fastnet Principal Keeper received a monthly wage of £6/15 (4/6 a day). He also received £5/1/6 rock allowance; £5 special allowance; £2/18 Lloyds allowance; 15/9 fog allowance. He presumably was given garden space at Crookhaven Lighthouse as the other keepers were given 10s garden allowance. The senior Assistant Keeper, who looked after Mizen Head, received £5/5 per month wage (3/6 per day). The other Assistant Keepers received a monthly wage of £4/1/6 (3/3 per day).

[114] Journal No.44, Commissioners of Irish Lights, 11th December 1908.

In December 1910, James Twohig PK informed the Board that a "Lifesaving Company" had been set up at Mizen Head, made up of three AK's and seven "villagers". The Board allowed their cliff ladders to be stored at the fog station.

T.P. Murphy[115], the Fastnet PK, wrote on the 8th of November 1912 that AK Martin "Kennedy's child has been ill for the past few days and the Doctor on visiting her yesterday evening pronounced her illness to be a case of Scarlet Fever". The Doctor demanded that the child be isolated to prevent the other children at the station contacting it. Mrs Kennedy was "worn out" from single-handedly looking after the child and requested Murphy to have her husband taken from the Fastnet, by the Irish Lights steamer, to assist her. The Inspector agreed that a local boat could be hired to take him off at a cost not greater than 30/-. On the 9th he was successfully removed and James Glanville, a temporary keeper, was landed in his place. The child recovered and J. Devaney AK informed head office "rooms disinfected, walls of same scraped, painted and distempered". In January the following year Kennedy wrote "I had to burn a lot of my household effects bedding etc. by order of the Doctor with the object of stamping out the disease and preventing it spreading to the other families". His request for compensation of £13/1/3 was agreed to[116].

In 1917, during World War One, the Fastnet lighthouse keepers requested an allowance for the risk of being hit by a mine while going to and from the rock. They complained of the "indiscriminate sowing of mines by many submarines"[117].

In 1924 the Inspector proposed that the Fastnet and Mizen keepers would work ten weeks on, then four weeks "liberty". He stated that

---

[115] T. P. Murphy (1872–1940) was Fastnet PK 1911–1919. His wife was Mary Hamilton, daughter of Rickard Hamilton – Murphy, "Kevin Murphy, Principal Keeper", 19.

[116] Irish Lights Work File 1917/450.

[117] The German navy had started an unrestricted campaign of U-boat attacks and mine laying on the 1st of February 1917 having reduced attacks after the outrage caused by the sinking of the *Lusitania* in May 1915.

the Fastnet PK's rota should include a period at Mizen Head thus "saving cost of periodical inspections by him of Mizen"[118].
In September 1929 the Board refused the Engineer's recommendation for a telephone line linking Rock Island and Goleen[119]. As a result, urgent messages were sent by telegram from Goleen Post Office. Keepers were paid 1½d per mile in 1944 to carry telegrams to the post office.

Coast Guard Gun Practice

James Doyle, Crookhaven lightkeeper, reported to the Secretary that on the 23rd of September 1867 a large outer pane of green glass was "broken from exercising of gun". For some reason it was not until the 30th of October that the Irish Lights' Board was informed. It was, according to Doyle, as a result of the Coast Guard exercising nearby in the gunboat *Bruiser*. When questioned about the incident, the Admiralty replied "on no occasion were the guns of *HM Ship Bruiser* fired in the vicinity of Crookhaven and on the 23rd inst. the day the glass was broke she was at anchor in Castletownsend but that *HMS Blazer* on that date was firing at a mark about a mile from the Lighthouse in the direction of the village of Glun [Goleen?]". The Admiralty however denied responsibility for breaking the glass. Later James Doyle wrote to say that J.S. Sloane, Superintendent of Works, told him the glass breakage was "caused by the heat of the sun"[120]. Doyle reported in November that another pane of green glass was broken on the 5th. He added that the gunboat *Bruiser* was "practising on that day"[121].

---

[118] Journal No.50, 15th June 1924.
[119] Rock Island lighthouse was connected by telephone at some stage as the Commissioners requested the G.P.O., in November 1962, to "withdraw" the telephone (No.4 Goleen) as part of the property sale - Irish Lights Work File 1959/146.
[120] Journal No.24, Commissioners of Irish Lights, p. 376.
[121] Lighthouse Register 1867, Commissioners of Irish Lights, 8th November 1868.

Fog Records

In 1883 an explosive fog signal was established on Fastnet at a cost of £250. Fog Signals were to commence when objects at three miles (5 km) "become obscured". A gun cotton charge was "electrically" fired every five minutes[122]. The gun cotton rockets were stored on Rock Island. In 1903 the following hours and minutes of fog per quarter were recorded for Fastnet[123]:

Quarter ended 31/03/03	135.30
Quarter ended 30/06/03	117.40
Quarter ended 30/09/03	211.25
Quarter ended 31/12/03	91.30
Total	556.50

It was the third highest of the 22 stations which measured fog hours, with Coninbeg Lightship the highest at 970.59.

For 1906 Irish Lights produced the following information for the total number of hours & minutes of fog in the month:

	Crookhaven	Fastnet
January	19.00	25.45
February	13.50	10.45
March	43.20	47.00
April	7.40	12.30
May	118.48	133.20
June	54.20	60.35
July	69.25	101.30
August	187.40	176.35
September	10.05	18.55
October	3.30	7.55
November	63.50	85.00
December	17.40	23.05
Total	609.08	702.55

Again Coninbeg Lightship was the worst for fog that year with 1,386.48.

---

[122] Scott, History of the Fastnet Rock Lighthouses, 8.
[123] Irish Lights Work File 1904/400.

Fastnet Reliefs

Fastnet keepers were taken out to the Rock from Rock Island by private contractors until 1890. Reliefs, until 1886, were undertaken monthly, often leading to extended stays on Fastnet Rock due to weather conditions. Contractors also had responsibility for providing various supplies to Fastnet. In a remote area, like the Mizen Peninsula, there were few parties who had suitable boats and crew to undertake the often hazardous journey. One individual, Isaac Notter of Crookhaven, had a near monopoly on the reliefs. This lead to considerable frustration within Irish Lights.
In February 1862 Isaac Notter wrote to Irish Lights to enquire whether his tender for boat attendance of Fastnet was accepted. The Board replied that it was under consideration. Later the same month he asked the Board that "preference" would be given to his tender[124]. It appears his tender that year was not successful as John Blake wrote in April 1862 acknowledging acceptance of his tender[125]. Relations between Blake and Notter were poor. In October 1862 Notter wrote that he would not risk his vessel to bring stores from Queenstown to Dursey Sound. This was probably material for the cast-iron lighthouse being built on Calf Rock, later destroyed as a result of a storm in 1881. Blake wrote that he knew of two boats which would do the job: one for £30 and the other for £40[126]. Blake apparently was in financial trouble by mid-November 1862 as J.S. Sloane, Engineer-in-Chief, wrote from Schull to say Blake was a bankrupt and his boats had been sold. An enquiry from the Board's Secretary to the Crookhaven keeper followed to see if attendances on Fastnet were continuing. He replied that they were "going on as usual".
Tender documents for relieving Fastnet in 1863 were sent to two Blakes (W. & J. – most likely the proprietors of Blake's Hotel,

---

[124] Lighthouse Register 1862, Corporation for Preservation & Improving The Port of Dublin & Co., 14th & 17th February 1862.
[125] Lighthouse Register 1862, 14th April 1862.
[126] Lighthouse Register 1862, 27th October 1862.

Crookhaven, presently O'Sullivan's Bar), and I. Notter. All three, in December 1862, were referred to as having "good boats".
On the 5th of May 1864 the Inspector of Lights was on Rock Island. He reported that the crew of Blake's hooker had not received their pay for the quarter ended the 1st of April. The Secretary replied that Blake had been paid £41/12/0, presumably the quarterly relief payment, on the 21st of April[127].
Isaac Notter wrote in June 1864 to inform the Board that the hooker attending Fastnet had "near been lost, her jib and foresail been blown away and mainsail in very bad condition". Seemingly, as a result of this damage, the keeper J. Maginn almost died.
In July 1864 C. Sullivan was the boat contractor as Robert Blake, AK Fastnet, received his pay from him. By October 1864 Isaac Notter had the boat attendance contract again. The following April he was requesting payment of £52/4/0 for boat attendance.
In November 1865 E. A. O'Brien of the Telegraph Company, London wrote offering their steamer should Irish Lights be tendering for Fastnet attendances. He was informed that "none will be called for".
Isaac Notter wrote in October 1867 that his cutter *Kate Dawson* which undertook Fastnet reliefs was "in want of repairs" and he would be substituting the cutter *Osprey* to do the work[128]. Notter was required in December 1869 to explain why his tender for boat attendance to Fastnet was so high. The same month however the Board of Trade accepted "Mr [Isaac?] Notter's" tender for Fastnet "attendance", presumably for 1870. However they were unhappy with his "monopoly" situation[129]. This dissatisfaction obviously resulted in T. Harrington being awarded the tender in June 1871[130]. R. Driscoll of Crookhaven, who may have been employed by Harrington, asked for

---

[127] Lighthouse Register 1864, Corporation for Preservation & Improving The Port of Dublin & Co.
[128] Lighthouse Register 1867, Commissioners of Irish Lights, 14th October 1867.
[129] Journal No.26, Commissioners of Irish Lights, 31st December 1869.
[130] Journal No.26, 23rd June 1871.

an increase in wages for himself and the crew of the boat attending Fastnet in September 1872. The Board declined to interfere[131].
Isaac Notter was awarded the boat attendance contract in July 1873. In October W. Wilson, the Fastnet PK wrote that Isaac Notter would "not allow boat crew land stores, coal at Lthouse". The Secretary wrote to Notter to say he was "bound to have stores brought up to lighthouse"[132]. In 1874 Notter was being paid £2/5/0 per trip.
Relations between the relief contractor and the Fastnet keepers were occasionally fractious. In November 1874 a Fastnet keeper, Tyrell, was "cautioned to conduct himself quietly and properly if he wishes to retain his situation leaving Mr. Notter to employ his own men"[133].
In February 1878 Isaac Notter's request to transfer the contract for provisioning the Fastnet to his brother Richard was approved by the Board. The Board noted a complaint from Mr. Notter in April 1879 that French luggers[134] had prevented him leaving Crookhaven harbour to service Fastnet. To assist him he said that the Coast Guard had twice sent *HMS Orwell*. It was noted however that Notter had caused "the Admiral at Queenstown much trouble" and added "if Mr Notter's moorings were in a proper place and not in the fairway of the Harbour, no inconvenience would be caused"[135].
In April 1881, the Inspector submitted a letter and telegram from Isaac Notter of Crookhaven who was referred to as the "Boat Attendant" to Fastnet. Notter stated he was unable to leave Crookhaven to get to the Fastnet "in consequence to the entrance to Crookhaven Harbour being blocked up by French"[136]. A few days later, Irish Lights had received a report from Crookhaven Coast Guard via the Naval Commander in Chief at Queenstown (Cobh)

---

[131] Lighthouse Register 1867, 7th September 1872.
[132] Lighthouse Register 1873, Commissioners of Irish Lights, 6th October 1873.
[133] Journal No.26, 27th November 1874.
[134] "A small ship with two or three masts and a four-sided sail on each" – Oxford English Dictionary.
[135] Journal No.31, Commissioners of Irish Lights, 18th April 1879.
[136] Journal No.32, Commissioners of Irish Lights, 1st April 1881.

stating that the harbour was not blocked. This report was forwarded to Notter.

Isaac Notter, in December 1885, was unable to service the Fastnet as he was boycotted by the Land League and as a result his crew were prohibited from working for him. To deal with this problem the British Navy provided a gunboat. Later Notter wrote that he was "ready to proceed to Fastnet aided by the Coast Guard as soon as weather permitted". To service the Fastnet the Board approved his temporary charter of the 34 ton sailing schooner *Heroine*, two yawls and a whale boat at a quarterly cost of £26. The Lord Justices of the Privy Council refused to act concerning Isaac Notter's boycott as he was being "meddled with" and there was "not sufficient intimidation"[137]. In February 1886 Notter's crew returned to work and it appears the Irish Lights' crew returned to Dublin. Later the same year the Board approved fortnightly Fastnet reliefs rather than the previous monthly.

In August 1887 Notter was being paid 1/- per man per trip and 2/- for the use of the boat due to a drought. In February 1890 the crew of the *Halycon* wrote to say they had left Notter's boat and were now working for Mr. McCarthy on the *Self Reliance* which had been hired by the Fastnet PK to service the Fastnet. Notter stated that the crew had been intimidated by the Goleen Roman Catholic Curate. As a result the *Alert* was sent to Crookhaven and Notter was informed that he was not required "for the present"[138]. McCarthy was paid 36/9 per trip for two reliefs of the Fastnet in January 1890. In March Notter wrote, as did his son Thomas D. Notter, that he had hired a new crew for the *Halycon* and he claimed wages for them. Captain McCrombie, of Irish Lights, asked if Notter could be re-used. The former crew of *Halycon* asked Irish Lights to have them re-instated but they refused to interfere[139]. The issue of servicing Fastnet was raised in the House of Commons by Mr. Gilhooly MP in March

---

[137] Journal No.34, Commissioners of Irish Lights, p. 202.
[138] Journal No.36, Commissioners of Irish Lights, p. 176.
[139] Journal No.36, 7th March 1890.

1890. This resulted in the Board of Trade raising the matter with Irish Lights.

It appears, that as a result of the problems with independent contractors, principally Isaac Notter, Irish Lights decided to undertake the reliefs themselves from August 1890. The *SS Flying Foam* under M. Langan, based in Castletownbere was the first Irish Lights captained ship to provide the service. She provided supplies such as oil and water, and undertook the lightkeepers' relief of the Fastnet as well as Bull Island, Tearaght, the Skelligs, Valentia and Roancarrig. The tug was however not seen as very satisfactory due to its slow speed. It appears to have been owned by the Union Steam Co[140].

Edward Kearon was the Master of *SS Flying Foam* from late 1890. He sent extensive reports to Dublin of his reliefs of the south-west lighthouses[141]. On the 13th of November he took the Irish Lights' Inspector on board at Schull, bringing him to Crookhaven on the 16th. The same day he successfully relieved the Fastnet. On the 19th he placed R. Ward, seaman of the *Flying Foam* on Fastnet "to relieve R. Lyons, keeper who was sick". Successful reliefs were also conducted on the 4th and the 16th of December.

On the 6th of February 1891 William Maginn PK reported that Edward Donovan arrived on Fastnet Rock, replacing R. Lyons who was transferred to the Baily[142]. Kearon wrote of this relief indicating that he also landed water and charges and took off keeper Harris and sick keeper Coghlan. He wrote "I was obliged to put [Thomas] Aspinal AB [able-bodied seaman] on the rock in lieu of Coghlan. I proceeded to Castletown after landing the keepers at Dwellings". Later the same month, on the 18th, he carried out a relief also landing a Mr. Rochford and a Mr. Rodgers (fitter) on the Rock. He returned

---

[140] Journal No.36, 12th September 1890.
[141] Irish Lights Work File 1891/954.
[142] Irish Lights Work File 1891. E. Donovan was born on the 9th of April 1864 at Mourne Co. Down; his father was the Chief Officer, Kingstown Coastguard. He was appointed a supernumerary keeper on the 3rd August 1890 and was unmarried when appointed to the Fastnet.

to Castletown with Mr. Rochford on board the same day. In March he wrote that J. Coghlan AK relieved T. Aspinal AB on the 8th. However Aspinal was back on the Rock on the 20th of March as Maginn PK remained on shore sick. That day Kearon also landed 144 gallons of fresh water, one case of lamp glasses, a "Dynamo" received from Dublin, guncotton charges, and took off AK Donovan." On arrival at Crookhaven, I had the Wreck buoy removed from Isaac Notter's yard and left at Fastnet dwellings". Again on the 14th of April, Aspinal was landed on Fastnet as Harris AK was absent on leave, Kennedy AK was taken back to Rock Island.

On the 13th of May he wrote how the Master of the schooner *Agnes* refused to go alongside the Fastnet stores on Rock Island as he had been chartered for Crookhaven. He did later agree as Kearon on the 15th "hired a store the property of Mr. C. Scully of Goleen and landed 27 tons (being the balance of the *Agnes* cargo) into this store at Rock Island (North quay). I got a written agreement from Mr. Scully for to store and keep safe the coals at 15/- per month to cover all charges". On the 16th he finished unloading the *Agnes* having hired two boats at 5/- per day and 8 labourers at 3/- per day to help with the task.

On the 8th of July, Maginn was again sick and had to be landed at Rock Island while a sailor was left in his place on Fastnet. Maginn was replaced as PK in September 1891 by Francis Ryan. On the 4th Maginn, his family and luggage, were taken aboard the *Flying Foam* to the Old Head of Kinsale station and on the 5th Ryan was brought to Rock Island.

Later that month (the 21st and 22nd) Kearon "took on board what coals the Steamer *Alert* left remaining at Fastnet Stores Rock Island viz 28 tons". On the 25th he took on board provisions for Fastnet from the steam yacht *Princess Alexandra*. He was back in Crookhaven on the 16th of October carrying out a Fastnet relief and removing "planks and deals from Mr. J. Skully Store on Rock Island". On the 25th of November 1891 Kearon wrote of landing keepers and

Rock Island

provisions on the 20th of November, also "all the empty casks & c were taken on shore & stored in Fastnet Stores Rock Island".
In March 1895 Kearon was carrying out reliefs on the *S.S. Moya*. He carried out one such relief on the evening of the 4th of March. That day he also took off the Fastnet six empty heavy mineral oil casks which he forwarded to the appropriately named Messr's Light & Sons, Liverpool[143].
In March 1899 the Irish Lights' Accountant sent a note to the Secretary indicating the following pay for 1899-1900[144]:

Master *SS Moya*.	Wages	£142/4/7	
	Victualling[145]	£41/1/3	£185/5/10
Master of steamer attending Fastnet Works.	Wages	£90/0/0	
	Victualling	£41/1/3	£131/1/3
Superintendent, District Stores.			£251/7/9

In February 1900 Kearon, Master of the *SS Moya*, got quotes for coal required by the ship; amongst them were ones from Murphy's of Bantry and Biggs of Bantry but none from Crookhaven. He ended up buying coal from J. Shanahan of Castletownbere at 25/ per ton[146]. Around this time, the intention was to relieve rock stations on the 1st and 15th of each month[147].
In 1905 the *Moya* was sold and the *Ierne*[148] (which had been specially built for servicing the building of the new Fastnet, now completed) took over its responsibilities for the "Southern Rock Stations". Kearon took over charge of the *Ierne* on the 14th of February from Brady.

---

[143] Irish Lights Work File 1895/263.
[144] Irish Lights Work File 1899/232.
[145] Food & Provisions.
[146] Irish Lights Work File 1899/570.
[147] Irish Lights Work File 1902/390.
[148] The *Ierne* stayed in Irish Lights Service until 1954 - Wilson, The Irish Lighthouse Service, 38.

William Allen of Ballydevlin, Goleen (born 23rd May 1880) was appointed a permanent Fireman aboard the *Ierne* on the 1st of June 1906 by William Davis, the new Commander of the *Ierne*. Previous to this he also worked on board the *Ierne* for Brady (1904) who described him as "most hardworking, sober". Brady was annoyed in September of that year as Kearon of the *Moya* tried to poach Allen[149]. Whilst in Glasgow with the *Ierne* in November 1906 Allen was admitted to the Royal Infirmary Glasgow where he was diagnosed as suffering from "inflammation of the spinal cord with paralysis of the lower part of the body". The following year, Dr. Neville wrote that Allen needed three to four weeks rest as a result of a "severe nervous breakdown"[150]. Allen is again mentioned in July 1907 when he refused to accept his wages after insurance had been deducted from then[151].

James Twohig PK wrote that the *SS Ierne* had arrived in Crookhaven Harbour on the night of the 5th of January 1907. The captain informed him that the keepers and provisions were to be ready to leave Rock Island at 7.00 a.m. the following morning "an hour and a quarter before sunrise to enable him to get on Derrick, water etc in Fastnet while landing was good". As a result Twohig could not go out to the Fastnet as he had to maintain the Crookhaven light until sunrise. He added that "since E. Rohu late Principal Keeper was pensioned – there was always the possibility of all keepers being left on Rock on relief days through landing getting bad". On this particular relief, "the *Ierne* brought off derrick and case containing Marconi Receiver, but landing getting too bad she did not land same; reliefs effected; water & provisions landed"[152].

The winter of 1924/25 was obviously very bad as the Fastnet was not relieved between the 17th of October and the 2nd of February. It is uncertain whether the *Alexandra* was successful on that date and it

---

[149] Irish Lights Work File 1904/1066.
[150] Irish Lights Work File 1906/1491.
[151] Irish Lights Work File 1907/618.
[152] Irish Lights Work File 1909/204.

may have been the 16th of February before they were relieved. Apparently the keepers were down to four days food on the 31st of January[153].
In 1926 it was estimated that it would cost £270 to provide oil storage facilities at Berehaven and Crookhaven for the new motor tender *Moya* based at Berehaven[154]. These facilities were provided and still in place 40 years later. On Rock Island, the tank was placed on concrete supports at the south-end of the main pier.

Two keepers on their way from Rock Island to undertake a Fastnet relief in the early 1960s

---

[153] Journal No.51, Commissioners of Irish Lights, p. 31.
[154] Journal No.51, 297.

Keepers on Fastnet were paid an additional 1/10 an hour in 1958 for assisting in the discharge of oil, water, coal and tonite[155]. Supplies at this time were delivered by the Irish Lights ships *Valonia*[156] and *Isolda*[157]. In November 1962, Martin Kennedy PK, John Sugrue AK, G. B. O'Connell Supernumerary Assistant Keeper (SAK) were paid 2/6 per hour for five hours to "erect pump and pump to oil store 400 gallons paraffin". The following year Martin Kennedy, Thomas Walsh, John Coughlan, John Sugrue and Supernumerary Assistant Keeper O'Driscoll worked four hours on the 10th of June to "erect pump and pump to oil store 35 casks [1,575 gallons/7,160 litres] from *Atlanta*[158]".

Fastnet reliefs, from the 1st Of April, 1962, were carried out from Castletownbere, where the Irish Lights' ships were based. Up to this date reliefs were carried out from Rock Island but by this time none of the keepers lived there anymore.

In the 1960s Jack Harrington of Goleen had the contract for supplying coal to Fastnet. He delivered the coal from Crookhaven or Goleen on Sean Flynn of Crookhaven's boat, the *Britannia*, and was required to bring the coal up to the lighthouse. One of his crew was Michael Donovan of Ballydevlin[159].

In 1969 supplies were brought to Fastnet from Dun Laoghaire by the *Atlanta* to build a new helipad. This was completed in September with the first Fastnet helicopter relief undertaken on the 29th of October 1969. Undertaking reliefs by helicopter was deemed a great

---

[155] Tonite is a blasting explosive made from guncotton and barium nitrate - D3 Book Fastnet 1956-68, Inspectors Dept, Commissioners of Irish Lights.

[156] "[The *Valonia*] would have looked well on the Cumbrian lakes but was not suited to the toughest coast off Europe" - O'Briain, "Epilogue", 36.

[157] The *Isolda* was bombed and sunk on the 19th of December 1940 off the Wexford coast by a German plane. Six crew lost their lives.

[158] The tender *Atlanta* commenced service with Irish Lights in November 1959. She was sold in 1988.

[159] O'Sullivan, Stephen, conversation with, 16th October 2005.

success. No longer would the Fastnet keepers be forced to wait, often for weeks, for their relief.

Communicating with the Fastnet

A Mr. Wright/Knight of Rockview House, Crookhaven, Lord Charles Pelham Clinton's Agent, wrote to the Board of the Port of Dublin Corporation in September 1863 requesting permission to lay down a telegraph cable between Crookhaven and Fastnet Rock. This interest in a telegraph cable obviously tied in with the South Western Telegraph Co.'s (of which Julius Reuter was a shareholder) opening of the Crookhaven-Cork telegraph in December 1863. The Board however declined his request and informed him we "regret it is impossible to give this accommodation"[160].

The British & Irish Magnetic Telegraph Co., which had laid telegraph cables connecting Ireland to Scotland, asked "relative to sighting steamers from Cape Clear, request permission to have them signalised from Fastnet Island"[161].

J. S. Sloane, Engineer-in-Chief, wrote from Fastnet on the 25th of September 1865 that there was the "exhibition of a very bright light from Brow Head by Telegraphic people when mail boat are (*sic*) expected from America"[162]. James Healy later added that this Brow Head light was first exhibited on the 13th of September. The Fastnet keeper wrote in November that he had not "seen light on Brow Head recently".

Isaac Notter asked in October 1879 if the Port of Dublin Corporation could accommodate two clerks and the "instrument" on Fastnet "relative to the proposed Establishment of Telegraphic Communication". In 1883 Lloyds were paying the salary of one of

---

[160] Journal No.21, Corporation for Preservation & Improving The Port of Dublin & Co., p. 214.
[161] Lighthouse Register 1863, Corporation for Preservation & Improving The Port of Dublin & Co., 2nd December 1863.
[162] Lighthouse Register 1865, Corporation for Preservation & Improving The Port of Dublin & Co.

Fastnet's AK's. In January 1885 a foreshore licence was issued to Lloyds by the Harbour Department of the Board of Trade. The licence allowed a cable to be laid from Fastnet to Galley Cove, 1.5 km west of Crookhaven village. A map attached to the application indicated that the cable would run from the south-east of Fastnet and then in a straight line into the beach at Galley Cove, an area owned by Lord Clinton. The licence gave

> permission to use the said cable and land wires for the purpose of transmitting to the Postal Telegraph Office at Crookhaven aforesaid telegrams reporting the passing of vessels receiving by signals from the owners or Masters of vessels passing the [Fastnet] Rock or from passengers on board the same also telegrams from persons on the Rock.

The General Post Office (G.P.O.) agreed to "work day and night Sundays included" to transmit messages received. Lloyds would pay £70 per annum to the Post Office for "services rendered …at Crookhaven"; £10 per annum for the use of a "Morse Telegraph Instrument and Battery at the Crookhaven Post office; £1/10 per annum for the licence to lay the cable plus the normal telegram transmission rates. The Crookhaven sub-postmaster, James Guilfoyle, was paid 12/6 per week by Lloyd's and 10/6 by the postal authorities. It was due to Guilfoyle's complaints about the arduous nature of his duties that the £70 charge was included as they envisaged providing him with an assistant[163].

The ship to lay the cable was due to arrive on the 6th or 7th of January 1885. The cable laying appears to have been done by the Telegraph Construction and Maintenance Co[164]. In May 1887, the Postmaster-General noted "in 1885 the Corporation of Lloyds having endeavoured unsuccessfully to induce the Department to establish

---

[163] Ireland Reports & Minutes, Vol. 42, 22nd December 1884, Royal Mail Heritage.

[164] The Telegraph Construction and Maintenance Co. was formed in 1864. In 1866 it successfully laid the transatlantic cable using the *Great Eastern*. It was a dominant force in submarine cable manufacturing and laying.

telegraphic communication with the Fastnet Rock had a cable laid at their own expense". The intention was "to replace Brow Head with Fastnet". As a result of the cable being laid in 1885, signalling from Brow Head to shipping was transferred to Fastnet with onward telegrams now going transmitted via Crookhaven Post Office. Guilfoyle was paid £60 per annum to provide himself with an assistant due to his increased work load[165]. However "the cable proved a failure, as had been anticipated by the Department and was finally removed on the 1st of November 1886 when the Brow Head Station was re-opened[166]". Guilfoyle continued to claim the right to the cost of an assistant but the Postmaster-General refused to pay him the allowance. Later a Board of Trade memorandum in 1893 noted "this cable seems to have been done away with some time since, the experiment having been abandoned in 1886"[167]. Irish Lights also noted in 1894 that Lloyds had made unsuccessful attempts in 1885 and 1886 "to establish electrical communications with the Fastnet"[168].

On the 12th of February 1895 Francis Ryan PK wrote from Rock Island "I received a semaphore from Rock yesterday saying that landing mast was carried away"[169]. This was the only means of communicating until the 12th of July 1895 when the Board of Trade wrote to Irish Lights to tell them that Fastnet was "about to be electrically connected with the mainland"[170]. The G.P.O. London wrote to Irish Lights on the 16th of July telling them that the District Superintending Engineer would provide detailed training to the keepers on using the "telegraph apparatus". On the 17th of July the Board of Trade gave permission to the "Postmaster General" to lay a

---

[165] Ireland Reports & Minutes, Vol. 48, Royal Mail Heritage.
[166] Ireland Reports & Minutes, Vol. 47, 10th May 1887, Royal Mail Heritage.
[167] Fastnet Foreshore Cable Licence, National Archives, London, MT10/615.
[168] Journal No.38, Commissioners of Irish Lights, p. 72.
[169] Irish Lights Work File 1895/263.
[170] Journal No.38, 81.

cable from Fastnet to Galley Cove. They were given three years to complete or the "assent…shall be void"[171].

Edward Rohu, the Fastnet PK wrote to head office on the 9th of June 1896 informing them that Le Grand & Sutcliff Boring Engineers had commenced boring a hole 2½ inches (6.35cm) diameter on Fastnet. An employee of the Telegraph Maintenance Company accompanied them. In August he wrote again "the telegraph people have succeeded in boring the south-side hole and have come out at a depth of twenty four feet six…they are speaking of endeavouring to blast out the bottom of the north hole with dynamite". Their desire to blast was based on having bored to a depth of 38 feet (11.6m) without coming out.

William Douglass[172] ordered, on the 20th of September 1896, that the Telegraph Construction Company was not to do any blasting on Fastnet to connect the telegraph line, as it would damage the rock. He also wrote "boring operations [for telegraph] have taken much longer than I expected and have delayed the placing of men on the rock to commence the cutting of the foundation for the new tower". Five days later, John Moore wrote to Irish Lights, Dublin from Rock Island stating "the men belonging to the Telegraph Construction Company left here yesterday for London".

On the 12th of October 1896 Rohu stated that he had received a semaphore message from Fastnet indicating that the "telegraph cable was broken on the south of rock" during a storm. Communicating by the old method of semaphore was only possible when the weather was "favourable"[173].

On the 26th of May 1897 Douglass wrote to Irish Lights Secretary Owen Armstrong indicating that the steamboat *Monarch* had arrived at Crookhaven "with appliances for restoring communication between the Fastnet and Crookhaven". The following day Willoughby Smith "the inventor of the system of electrical signalling"

---

[171] Map of Mizen Head to Kinsale with proposed Fastnet Cable, National Archives, Dublin, BT/5155.
[172] Engineer-in-Chief, 1878-1900.
[173] Irish Lights Work File 1896/824.

of Gutta Percha Company Patentees, London asked that a Mr. Granville be allowed stay on the Rock and that the keepers would assist him[174].

A. W. Preece, of the Office of the Engineer-in-Chief of the G.P.O., London wrote to Irish Lights about the fact that the keepers trained to use the telegraph system in 1895 "have left for duty elsewhere".

In July 1898 the Engineer recommended that a wireless communication system be put in place between Fastnet Rock and Crookhaven[175]. This was followed up in January 1899 when the Wireless Telegraph & Signal Co. requested communication with the Fastnet to be via the "Marconi system". Records for October 1899 indicate that Fastnet was "electrically connected with Crookhaven P.O.". However a Notice to Mariners issued 20th September 1899 stated "that the working of the Electrical Communication with Fastnet Rock is uncertain cannot be relied upon"[176]. This appears to have been caused by the new Fastnet building works.

Lloyds of London wrote to Irish Lights on the 3rd of September 1902 offering homing pigeons which they kept at Brow Head for communicating between ship and shore. They were no longer needed and Lloyds wanted to see if Irish Lights would use them for communicating between Brow Head and Fastnet. Irish Lights declined the offer[177].

On the 6th of January 1903 Lloyds asked Irish Lights' permission to set up a wireless telegraphy operation on Fastnet. For this work they asked that an "extra keeper might be attached to the station to transmit reports of passing vessels to Brow Head". They agreed to pay 6d per keeper for this service[178]. On the 25th of January 1904 Kearon landed a Marconi official, a carpenter and fitters on Fastnet to install new wireless equipment. On the 28th of January, Irish Lights were informed that the Marconi equipment had been installed on

---

[174] Irish Lights Work File 1897/854 & 1897/692.
[175] Journal No.39, Commissioners of Irish Lights, 15th July 1898.
[176] Irish Lights Work File 1899/971.
[177] Irish Lights Work File 1902/804.
[178] Irish Lights Work File 1907/999.

Fastnet. It was agreed that Francis Periera, in charge of the Marconi International Marine Communication Co. Ltd. "Browhead" Crookhaven Station, would provide training to the keepers in operating the equipment. Lloyds would pay 6% (£48 p.a.) for the additional dwelling required on Rock Island. Also the keepers were paid 3/- everyday they attended training at Brow Head. They walked from Rock Island to Brow Head, a distance of four miles, to start classes at 9.30 a.m. which finished at 1.30. J.W. Wright asked that Irish Lights sanction the 5/- cost of daily horse and car hire. He was however informed that the 3/- allowance was to cover this[179]. On the 24th of March 1904 Deane wrote that he had visited Brow Head to check on progress[180]. While Periera was training the keepers on land, Mr. Richard of the Marconi Co. was looking after the Fastnet.

Lloyds issued a Notice to Mariners in March 1904 stating that "signalling of vessels at the Fastnet Lighthouse will commence on the 1st of April"[181]. These would be transmitted by Marconi Wireless Telegraphy to Brow Head Signal Station. Daytime signalling with shipping from Fastnet was with flags. Jibs for exhibiting the flags were supported from the lantern dome. In March Lloyds supplied a lamp for night signalling.

In May 1904 the Irish Lights' Secretary wrote to Lloyds indicating that the keepers were now competent in working the "Marconi Apparatus without any further help from the officials at Brow Head"[182]. The annual cost of maintaining the signalling operation was estimated to cost £198/8/1 according to an Irish Lights memo to the Board of Trade[183].

T. P. Murphy PK in 1904 said that telegraphs for Fastnet were being sent to Rock Island where "in hazy or foggy weather may be lying ashore for 3 or 4 days before they can be signalled to the Rock",

---

[179] Irish Lights Work File 1904/180.
[180] Irish Lights Work File 1904/347.
[181] Irish Lights Work File 1904/347.
[182] Irish Lights Work File 1904/490.
[183] Irish Lights Work File 1904/180.

presumably by semaphore flags. He asked that instead the messages could be "sent direct to Fastnet via Brow Hd by wireless"[184].

The Fastnet keepers supplied details of shipping communicated with, at night, by Morse lamp in July and August 1907[185]:

Day	Time	Ship	Message
3 July	12.40 a.m.	*Montcalm*	"Montcalm for Liverpool"
7 July	2.30 a.m.	*Micmac*	"Micmac"
7 July	11.00 p.m.	*Potomac*	"NDPW Potomac please report me"
25 July	9.50 p.m.	*Cedric*	"Cedric"
31 July	1.50 a.m.	*Innishowen Head*	"Innishowen Head"
6 Aug	10.45 p.m.	*Haverford*	"Haverford"
10 Aug	3.40 a.m.	White Star Line	"Cevic" – apparently
15 Aug	11.05 p.m.	*Potomac*	"NDPW Potomac"
22 Aug	1.55 a.m.	*Dictator*	"Dictator for Liverpool"
22 Aug	9.55 p.m.	White Star Liner	Morse signals unreadable

In January 1908 Twohig wrote that they experienced considerable difficulty transmitting messages to shipping at night using the flashing lamp. This was due to the ships being unable to differentiate the flashing lamp from the lighthouse light above. The acting Irish Lights Secretary wrote to Lloyds the following month stating that for the previous two years, ships had been using a Morse flashing lamp for night signalling which "entails considerable hardship on the keepers in bad weather, the man on watch being kept in the Signal gallery without shelter of any kind".

Deane, the Irish Lights' Inspector, supported Twohig's request that he continue to receive the Lloyds allowance[186]. He had been given the position of work overseer for the new houses being built on Rock Island for the Mizen keepers. On relief days however he was expected to visit the Fastnet and "satisfy yourself that all is in order, and return to Crookhaven with the relieved keepers". Stephen McMahon SAK was sent to Fastnet in his place. The Board of Irish

---

[184] Irish Lights Work File 1904/1104.
[185] Irish Lights Work File 1907/999.
[186] Irish Lights Work File 1907/999.

Lights however in May 1908 wrote to Twohig telling him he was not entitled to the Lloyds allowance as he was being paid 2/6 a day "in lieu of rock and signalling allowances".

In July 1908 Twohig sent a letter from J. J. Sweeney AK to head office requesting that the Lloyd's allowance to the Keeper in Charge of 1/- a day be paid to him during the Principal Keeper's absence. The Board agreed to this.

Responsibility for the Brow Head Station transferred from Lloyds to the G.P.O. in 1909[187]. The G.P.O. wrote to Irish Lights in October 1914 asking if the wireless station could be relocated to Rock Island from Brow Head. It appears that the buildings at Brow Head were very "unsatisfactory" and needed replacing. At that time, there was an overseer and four operators working there. The G. P.O. proposed that the keepers and/or their wives and daughters could do the work on Rock Island. The G.P.O. would pay for building the new station and would pay all the wages. Irish Lights would be paid a fee of £208 per annum whereas in 1914 they were getting "about £230". At that time, there were 1,100 messages per annum transmitted between Fastnet Rock and the mainland. The G.P.O. no longer needed Brow Head for its purposes as they had opened a station at Valentia. However they were legally required, by their agreement with Lloyds, to maintain the Fastnet connection until 1924. In that year they would be willing to transfer the station ownership to Irish Lights. The Irish Lights' Board however decided they could not agree to the proposal. In February 1915 a Captain Loring of the G.P.O. asked the Board to reconsider saying as an alternative "we are deciding to close Crookhaven and erect a temporary station at Schull or Baltimore to take the Fastnet Rock work for the next few years". He said that the G.P.O. would pay the rent on any capital outlay made by the Board [of Irish Lights] as a result of their anticipated need to hire additional keepers and therefore build additional housing. The Board again refused the offer[188].

---

[187] Irish Lights Work File 1907/510.
[188] Irish Lights Work File 1914/987.

T. P. Murphy PK informed head office in November 1914 that "nearly all the night signalling now, is done by Morse lamp, Pyrotechnic signalling having almost discontinued". The following year, he was looking for a more powerful Morse lamp as the lighthouse light was still blinding vessels when transmitting messages. He said that the volume of messages they had to transmit to Brow Head from shipping had increased a lot since the outbreak of the war "we have long messages to signal, owner orders and admiralty instructions". Lloyds wrote, a few weeks later, that "use by the Lightkeepers of Flashing Morse Signals for long messages is only temporary"[189]. It was due to the Admiralty Intelligence Officer ordering "the discontinuance of the signals made at the Fastnet directing Merchant Ships to proceed to Brow Head or the Old Head of Kinsale for instructions"[190].

In April 1915, J. E. Clague AK of Fastnet was not permitted to leave the station even though he had resigned. This was because he knew the telegraph code of Lloyds which they agreed to change. Once the code was changed he was allowed to leave[191].

Communication by telephone between Mizen Head Fog Station, Brow Head Signal Station and Rock Island Coast Guard station was put in place in February 1916[192]. Rock Island Lighthouse however was not connected.

In April 1919 J. J. Treeby was sent to Crookhaven (presumably Brow Head Wireless Station) for wireless training prior to taking over the position of Fastnet PK from T.P. Murphy[193].

The Principal Keeper on Fastnet was informed "by wireless through Brow Head" of the IRA raiding Mizen Head Station on the 16th of May 1920. In the same year the General Post Office quoted a cost of

---

[189] Irish Lights Work File 1915/55.
[190] Irish Lights Work File 1915/55.
[191] Journal No.47, Commissioners of Irish Lights, 30th April 1915.
[192] Journal No.47, 14th February 1916.
[193] Journal No.49, Commissioners of Irish Lights, 9th April 1919, J. J. Treeby was Fastnet PK 2/11/1919 to 17/4/1924 - Treeby, Craig, email, 8th of Mar 2006.

£75 to connect the Rock Island dwellings to the telephone exchange through the Coast Guard station. The annual rental would be £13/5/0. The Board of Trade refused to sanction the expense but agreed to pay 6d per message for urgent messages conveyed by off-duty Coast Guards to the lighthouse station[194].

In December 1921 the British Admiralty wrote to Irish Lights saying that as a result of the withdrawal of the Coast Guards from Crookhaven they could no longer assist in maintaining the wireless communication with Fastnet. Irish Lights wrote to Lloyds saying that they had no use for the "Wireless Telegraph Apparatus" and enquired about its disposal[195].

However in February 1936 the Board approved a request from the Irish Light House Keepers Association for a wireless telephone on the Fastnet[196].

In 1945 and 1946 a J. or S. Camier of Schull was been paid 15/- for charging four 12V batteries needed for an Aldis lamp. This lamp, which had a sight on it, was used, by means of shutters, to transmit Morse code.

Rock Island Dwellings

In September 1848, George Halpin raised the question of shore dwellings for Fastnet Rock. He said that the Commissioners of Customs had offered for sale, their houses on Rock Island. "The premises are extensive, there are twelve houses of two stories each and a store & office, the premises are subject to a rent of sixty three pounds sterling per year and at present four of the houses are set to tenants at will". He believed the premises were too large for lighthouse needs and wondered whether they could negotiate to take part of the station. The owner of Rock Island was also offering land ("141 foot frontage by 190 feet in depth to rear") for a shore station at £5 per year. Halpin also raised the rather dubious suggestion that

---

[194] Irish Lights Work File 1929/583.
[195] Journal No.50, Commissioners of Irish Lights, 30th December 1921.
[196] Journal No.54, Commissioners of Irish Lights, 19th February 1936.

they may not need a shore station as the keepers and their families could live permanently on the Fastnet "as is the case at the Tuskar and Roancarrig". The Board decided not to take any action at that time[197].

William Prendergast wrote on behalf of Lord Charles Clinton in January 1855 indicating that he would be happy to provide any land needed for a shore base for Fastnet. "Lord Charles Clinton is the owner of the land surrounding the Harbour of Crookhaven (with the exception of Rock Island)"[198].

It was not until January 1861 that the decision was taken to seek quotations to build the necessary shore dwellings for Fastnet station on Rock Island[199]. The contract was awarded to a T. H. Limerick. The Irish Lights' foreman I. Connolly wrote in March 1862 to say "little can be done to the dwellings in consequence of bad weather"[200]. In May 1862 a progress report was sent to head office indicating that "cut stone being repaired, no carpenters at work". A further update was sent on the 24th of May. He wrote "carpenters putting in trimming of doors and windows of south dwelling [no.2] also Hall and Kitchen nearly tiled – North Dwellings (no.8 & 9) progressing also stone cutters work". On the 9th of June he wrote "South, doors hung – North, first set of doors & window frames put in". Two weeks later "North are up to level of arches over the doors - Contractor has sent to Cork for materials to finish South Dwellings". On the 5th of July the foreman reported that the floor joints and sash window frames were in the "south dwellings"[201]. On the 28th of August 1862 "a letter was read from Mr. T.H. Limerick

---

[197] Journal No.12, Corporation for Preservation & Improving The Port of Dublin & Co., p. 71.

[198] Journal No.14, Corporation for Preservation & Improving The Port of Dublin & Co., p. 55.

[199] Journal No.19, Corporation for Preservation & Improving The Port of Dublin & Co., p. 165.

[200] Lighthouse Register 1862, Corporation for Preservation & Improving The Port of Dublin & Co., 31st March 1862.

[201] Lighthouse Register 1862, Corporation for Preservation & Improving The Port of Dublin & Co.

soliciting payment on foot of his contract for Fastnet Rock shore dwellings". The request was referred to Captain E. F. Roberts[202]. J.S. Sloane had recommended full payment of the second instalment two weeks previously.

Connolly had purchased lime at 4/- per barrel from the contractor to put in grates, kitchen ranges, chimneys and cisterns. For the cisterns he had hired a mason to build the foundations. He had also used four casks of Portland cement to build steps for the shore dwellings. Work continued on the dwellings throughout 1862. A stone cutter, Daniel Maguire was recovering from an injury in October. His injury was obviously quite serious as he did not leave hospital until February[203].

In mid-November Connolly reported that the "north dwellings" (the houses north of the lighthouse known as the "valley houses") were roofed and almost floored. The kitchen range had been put up, as well as two cisterns and the "landing steps". Also the contractor had started the drains at the rear of these dwellings.

A little later the walls of the privy (outside toilet) and an ash pit had been built. Annually from 1865 the Board sanctioned a labourer to clean the ash pit. A stone cutter named Hanlon had finished his work and left for Dublin on the 29th of November. The contractor Limerick wrote that he had completed the sewers in mid-December and a few days later he submitted his third and last bill for the shore dwellings of £380[204].

In January 1863 Limerick submitted an invoice for £503/3/0 for additional work done. Connolly reported at the same time that that the woodwork for the three dwellings was now ready for painting. On the 29th of January this painting was "nearly finished" while a coal store was completed. Connolly took full possession of the new

---

[202] Journal No.20, Corporation for Preservation & Improving The Port of Dublin & Co., p. 170.

[203] Lighthouse Register 1863, Corporation for Preservation & Improving The Port of Dublin & Co., 10th February 1863.

[204] Lighthouse Register 1862, Corporation for Preservation & Improving The Port of Dublin & Co., 12th December 1862.

houses from the contractor on Thursday, the 19th of February 1863. He had taken down some old sheds by the end of February, presumably used during construction. After the Inspector's visit in mid-March, Connolly reported that he would return to Dublin in late March.

In December 1863, the Crookhaven keeper wrote to say that the walls "on top of rock" were finished. We may presume this was the properties sea-front wall.

James Tocker, foreman, arrived on Rock Island in September 1864. He was supervising work on the dwellings. The plasterers working for him were dispatched to Calf Rock when the work was finished. All the work was completed by the 5th of November.

The Fastnet PK reported in July 1870 that the plaster was falling off the walls of the AK's dwelling which would have been one of the valley houses.

In November 1871 the Assistant Inspector proposed "that on account of the Crookhaven Dwellings, an additional storey be built, thereby converting the lower storey or present Dwelling into a store, which would also afford storage accommodation for the Fastnet Station"[205]. The Engineer was asked to provide a cost estimate but it would not appear that the proposal was acted upon as house no.1 & 2 remain single-storey and no.8 & 9 were designed and built originally as two storey dwellings.

W. Wilson Fastnet PK stated in July 1872 that he could employ Henry Lamb to clean out the water closet for £3. He was told that "there must be plenty of labourers in Rock island who would gladly do this work for £1"[206].

The Board of Trade sanctioned £593/9/0 as a result of a recommendation made during the annual inspection of 1876 to have repairs and painting done to the Fastnet Shore Dwellings. In September 1876, the board had received the following tenders for Fastnet Shore Dwellings:

---

[205] Journal No.26, Commissioners of Irish Lights, 15th December 1871.
[206] Lighthouse Register 1871, Commissioners of Irish Lights, 6th July 1872.

R. Sullivan   £630
W. Murphy   £621
R. Notter   £525

Richard Henry Notter's tender was accepted[207]. By January of the next year, Sloane was recommending a part payment to Notter for work done. However, on the 22nd of June, Notter's work was described as unsatisfactory and as a result they decided to retain the balance owing.

On the 5th of February 1895 an easterly gale took off slates from the dwellings and outhouses, "the coal house being the worst as the leading is lifted up". George Brownell PK Fastnet said it would take a mason and labourer two days and cost 17 shillings for labour and 2/6 for slates. He wrote later saying that they had to wait until the 27th of February to get the repairs done "owing to the severity of weather"[208].

In August 1897, the Irish Lights Engineer submitted an estimate of £601/11/4 for new dwellings for the Fastnet keepers. The Board of Trade initially questioned the need for these houses but obviously later agreed[209]. While unable to work on the new Fastnet Lighthouse and during the winter months, the Fastnet workers built three new houses for the Fastnet keepers. House no.3, the principal keeper's house was built first and completed in 1901. Houses no. 4 & 5 were built together alongside no.3 and completed in 1904. The total cost of these and the pier powder magazine was £1,518. Head office was informed in April 1905 that the new shore dwellings were now occupied[210]. A second smaller magazine was also built at some time

---

[207] Journal No.30, Commissioners of Irish Lights, p. 88.
[208] Irish Lights Work File 1895/233.
[209] Journal No.39, Commissioners of Irish Lights, 13th August 1897.
[210] A number of orders for the materials needed to build these new houses survive. In January 1902, the following was ordered for the "New Double Dwellings":
1. Messr's T & C Martin, North Wall, Dublin
1,250 24" * 12" best blue Bangor Slates
50 feet Blue Staffordshire ridge tiles 90°

Rock Island

in the valley garden. The detonators for the Fastnet fog signal were stored in the valley and the charges in the pier magazine[211].

In May 1906 the Board of Trade sanctioned £7,850 for the Mizen Head works and the new houses required on Rock Island. The Mizen Head keepers would be under the authority of the Fastnet Principal Keeper[212]. Quotes for building the houses and improving the pier were received by the 24th of July 1907. One came from Robert Calwell of Belfast who quoted £3,005/6/9 and eight months to complete. Robert Kelly, Builder and Contractor of Bantry, quoted £3,213/3/4. The contract however was awarded to Alexander Hull of Ringsend Road, Dublin[213] who quoted £2,237 of which £180 referred to pier improvements. The flat roofed houses had been designed by Charles Scott, Irish Lights Engineer, and as a result would become known locally as "Scott's houses". Scott got them to agree to reduce their quote to £2,107 saying that they could get all the stone required for building from the excavations necessary before the foundations could be laid. However upon excavation the rock was found to be unsuitable. George L. Johnston, the contracted Engineer for the Mizen Head and Rock Island construction, and

---

50 feet 4" cast iron sewer pipe
2. Henshaw & Co., Abbey Street, Dublin
Two sets of fittings for R.W. [rain water] Tanks
10 9" * 6" ? ventilators @ 4/6 each
6 9" * 3" galvanised ventilators @ 7/- each
3. Messr's Edmundson & Co., Capel Street, Dublin
3 Moules patent earth closets pattern no. IV pull up action @ £2/1/0 each
3 galvanised pails fn Do @ 6/- each
3 Sieves @ 4/6 each
4. Messr's Curtin & Sons, Abbey Street, Dublin
3 lengths heavy lead waste pipe with 4" ? for scullery @ 6/6 each
5. Brooks Thomas, Abbey Street, Dublin
5 casings for earth closets @ 30/- each

[211] Griffin, Dermot, conversation with, Goleen, 30th October 2005.
[212] Journal No.43, Commissioners of Irish Lights, 4th May 1906.
[213] In 1924 Alexander Hull & Co. Building Contractors were awarded the contract to re-build Dublin's G.P.O.

previously the draughtsman for the works[214], wrote to Scott "I condemned all the stone on site of said dwellings for concrete, as it is altogether too slatey"[215]. Scott stated that the excavations necessary were "the most expensive stone to break that I have ever come across".

Scott provided the following cost breakdown[216]:

Foundation/excavation work	£195
Two houses @ £596 each	£1,192
Two water tanks @ £30 each	£60
Fixed furniture for two houses	£72
General store & office	£125
Ladder shed	£11
Levelling site, drains etc.	£242
Preliminary expenses	£30
Pier improvements	£180
Total	£2,107

He added that the Commissioners would spend an additional £90 on ironmongers, around £75 on a clerk of works and some £50 for drawings, etc. The complete costs would be about £2,322. The excavation costs were not set by Hull but based on the amount of material removed. Their quote included a charge of 4/2 per cubic yard of shale and 6/10 per cubic yard of rock.

Johnston later requested an allowance to keep a horse and trap. He said that he had to go to Schull on a Thursday or Skibbereen on other days to "draw the weeks pay for Mizen Heads works". Also he estimated he was going to Rock Island from Mizen Head three times a week a distance of about 8.5 miles "and the road is not well kept that part which runs along the edge of the lake is often covered with water". When he had to bring his "level or some other tool" to Rock Island he could not do so on his bicycle and had to hire a car which

---

[214] Irish Lights Work File 1910/561.
[215] Irish Lights Work File 1909/496.
[216] Irish Lights Work File 1907/710.

cost him 10/-. Scott recommended and the Board approved a weekly allowance of 25/-.[217]

In October 1907 the Irish Lights' Board refused Hull's request to ship materials on Irish Lights *SS Tearaght*[218]. Hull ended up bringing the sand for internal plastering and other building materials from Dublin. He bought the stone from Alexander Hamilton who presumably quarried it at his Rock Island quarry. The total cost for stone bought from Hamilton was:

April to Sept 1908	£26/14/6
Cartage of same	£15/19/6
Total	£42/14/0

Johnston, by the end of 1907, was finding it difficult to properly oversee the two projects and Scott wrote on his behalf to the Board "He [Johnston] will be at Rockisland… two or three times a week and will not require a regular clerk of works and it would be sufficient if he had a man of fair intelligence who could look round the work once an hour or so". Scott recommended J. Twohig, the Fastnet PK, for this position of Overseer which was accepted. In lieu of his Rock and Signalling Allowance he received 2/6 per day[219].

Upon completion of the houses in 1909, Hull claimed £157/10/3 for "extra cost of stone & c. used in the work". Receipts were produced for this additional amount but the Irish Lights' Board only approved £80. For the six months ending the 31st of March 1909, the Board of Trade sanctioned £606/9/4 and £135 to furnish the two new houses built for the Mizen keepers[220]. The £135 was as follows: three houses at £40 each i.e. shore dwellings & lighthouse living room; other costs £15 of which "linseed oil[221] etc £7/18/4"[222]. The following month,

---

[217] Irish Lights Work File 1907/1027.
[218] Irish Lights Work File 1907/1050.
[219] Irish Lights Work File 1908/122.
[220] Irish Lights Work File 1907/1099.
[221] The linseed oil was used for coating and protecting all the internal woodwork.
[222] Irish Lights Work File 1907/973.

on the 3rd of May 1909, the fog signal at Mizen Head started operation.

In August 1910 R. Spense, a Dublin plasterer, who was working on Rock Island, was diagnosed by Dr. Neville as suffering from Tuberculosis. He was sent back to Dublin accompanied by the Rock Island Foreman Lynch. The Chief Clerk of Works Doherty had written on the 13th of August that upon arriving at Crookhaven at 8.30 a.m. he "noticed that R. Spense was looking rather pale and on making enquiries I found that he had been spitting up blood immediately before my arrival". His landlord also told Doherty that "he had been unwell the whole of the previous night". For his examination and report Dr. Neville charged £2/2/0[223].

"Special repairs" to the Rock Island dwellings in 1911-12 cost £371/18/9: £321/18/9 for repairs to dwellings approved in October 1910; and £50 for water tanks at the Fastnet keepers' dwellings. The sum of £33 was approved for new windows in the Fastnet dwellings in 1914[224].

To allow for the airing of "the unoccupied houses" in 1924, James Johnson, the Fastnet PK requested a half a ton of coal. He was sent one ton for this purpose. In a note written around the same time, possibly by C. W. Scott, it was stated "no.2 dwelling, the old Fastnet PK house, has been badly neglected and left shut up…no.8 dwelling in the valley has been singularly neglected". The note demanded that keepers on shore would get house no.2 cleaned and aired "without delay". When this was done, the keeper living in no.7 was to move into no.2. "The two valley houses numbers 7 & 8 are to be the unoccupied ones".

The Inspector also wrote a detailed note on the accommodation at Rock Island in April 1924. He stated that as there were nine houses and only seven keepers, there were now two "redundant or spare houses". House no.1 was referred to as the "Crookhaven house"

---

[223] Irish Lights Work File 1910/737.
[224] Journal No.47, Commissioners of Irish Lights, 10th October 1913.

although by this time the lighthouse was automated and managed by the off-duty Fastnet and Mizen keepers (it appears from details below that it was being lived in by one of the Mizen AK's). House no.2 was referred to as the old Fastnet PK's house; no.3 as the new Fastnet PK's house; no.4 & 5 were the "two single houses"; no.6 & 7 the "new Mizen Head houses"; and the two valley houses as no.8 & 9, which differs from the above numbering but agrees with the present numbering. He agreed with the above note in saying that no.2 and no.8 were unoccupied with "the former for several years and the latter since I think last summer". He believed that "it would be much better to house all the keepers on the upper level" thus leaving the Valley houses unoccupied. However he said that no.2 was "in a shocking state due to neglect. The walls of the kitchen and practically all the other apartments are covered with a minute black fungus". This was after it being last painted in 1921. With regard to the valley houses he stated "the floor joists and flooring of these two parlours are practically destroyed by dry rot…the halls and kitchens are tiled". He also referred to a new station gate[225]. This is known locally as "Foot's gate" presumably after F.R. Foot engineer of Irish Lights[226]. It was moved in nearer to the lighthouse than the old gate.

Following on the issue of the two vacant houses, W. H. Davis, Inspector and Marine Superintendent, wrote to the skipper of the Irish Lights ship *Deirdre* (which was based in Crookhaven) in June 1924. He asked whether any of his crew "would like to take over the two houses in the valley for a nominal rent". He said that a keeper was presently staying in one of them but would be asked to move to "one of the houses at present vacant in the block of buildings near the lighthouse". The captain replied the following month that none of his men wanted the houses[227].

In 1929 the Secretary requested approval from the Board of Trade to spend £100 on repairs to the Fastnet PK's house. It was stated "the floors of two of the bedrooms have recently given way consequent

---

[225] Irish Lights Work File 1929/440.
[226] O'Meara, Denis, conversation with, 21st of November 2005.
[227] Irish Lights Work File 1924/484.

on the decay of the joists and boards owing to the absence of under ventilation". There was a need for new floors, three new fireplaces, new eve gutters "to be flashed with lead", two new external doors and one new door frame. Also replastering of some walls and ceilings was required[228].

In 1931 Mr J.W. Tonkin[229] recommended a separate Principle Keeper for Mizen Head which the Irish Lights' Board approved. It was estimated that the additional cost would only be £3/19/9 as the Fastnet PK would lose his £20 supervision allowance. The first Mizen PK was the former Fastnet PK, Andrew Kilgallon[230]. He stayed in house no.3, the Fastnet PK's house. Benjamin Godkin was appointed Fastnet PK and moved into house no.6. He was also given a garden allowance as Kilgallon presumably retained the garden plot[231].

In 1935 the Fastnet PK, Eugene Fortune requested an additional ton for each of the four Fastnet houses as the "houses are very damp"[232]. The same was also requested for the Mizen keepers. The Irish Lights' Board agreed to half a ton stating that it was "in consequence of wet winter". Supporting this opinion, C. Beecher, Master of the *M.T. Nabro*[233] which had replaced the *Deirdre* in 1926/27, wrote in April

---

[228] Irish Lights Work File 1929/440.
[229] Engineer-in-Chief, 1930-1945.
[230] In 1930 Andrew Kilgallon PK received £2/10/0 per month to oversee Mizen Head.
[231] Lighthouse Wages & Allowances 1930-31, Commissioners of Irish Lights.
[232] Irish Lights Work File 1935/205.
[233] The *Nabro* (Inish na Bró, island of the quernstone, anglicised Inishnabro, one of the islands in the Blasket group) was launched in Arklow on 9th September 1926. She was 18.8 metres long and based at Castletownbere carrying out the Keeper reliefs, fuelling, watering and storing of rock stations off the West Cork and Kerry coasts. The Captain and the majority of her crew were permanently resident in Castletownbere. In April 1950 the *Nabro* was sold. At the time of her sale the crew of the *Nabro* was - J. Moran – Master; J. McLoughlin – Mate; P. Sheehan – Engineman; T. Driscoll - Assistant Engineman; P. Sullivan – Seaman; Denis Driscoll – Seaman; Daniel Driscoll – Seaman; M. O'Shea – Seaman. The assistant engine man, T. Driscoll, and the seamen P. Sullivan, Denis Driscoll and Daniel Driscoll had been with the boat during her entire

Rock Island

1935 "we had a lot more rain and damp weather in the district for sometime past". As a result James Wardie & Sons of Glasgow shipped 26 tons of coal for the Fastnet dwellings (instead of 24 tons) and 19.5 tons for the Mizen dwellings (instead of 18 tons) to Crookhaven[234].

A request was made in November 1938 to the Board of Trade to undertake £500 of repairs. The letter stated "Mizen Shore Dwellings and the stores and Buoy Yard at Rockisland have become very dilapidated and it is necessary to carry out immediate repairs. The roofs, ceilings, doors, windows, grates, floors and water tanks all require attention. The floors are badly affected with worm". The estimated cost breakdown was as follows:

No.1 Dwelling, Mizen Head	£117/ 0/0	
No.3 Dwelling, Mizen Head	£24/ 0/0	
No.6/7 Dwellings, Mizen Head	£62/10/0	
Sub-total		£203/10/0
No.2 Dwelling, Fastnet	£78/ 0/0	
No.4 Dwelling, Fastnet	£13/ 0/0	
No.5 Dwelling, Fastnet	£17/ 0/0	
No.6/7 Dwellings, Fastnet	£62/10/0	
Sub-total		£170/10/0
No. 8 & 9 Dwellings (unoccupied)		£10/ 0/0
Crookhaven Stores		£37/ 0/0
Crookhaven Generator House		£15/ 0/0
Buoy Yard, platform & store		£37/ 0/0
Boundary walls (common)		£10/ 0/0
Travelling & transport		£17/ 0/0
Total		£500/ 0/0

---

service with the Commissioners of Irish Lights - Gore-Grimes, J., "A Labour of Love", *Beam*, Vol. 24, 1995. "An uglier and worse seaboat it would be hard to imagine" - O'Briain, "Epilogue", 36.
[234] Irish Lights Work File 1935/205.

The cost of the actual work was lower at £432/1/3. In a letter from Irish Lights to the Board of Trade dated 17 November 1939 concerning the above repairs on Rock Island they wrote "practically nothing was obtained locally, except broken stone, and for this there happens to be a first rate quarry fronting on the sea, about 1½ miles up the creek from the dwellings"[235]. This would appear to refer to the quarry at Castlemeighan in Crookhaven Harbour which started operations in the early 1920s and terminated with the outbreak of the Second World War.

In 1941 the Fastnet PK wrote to the Irish Lights' Board asking for the garden allowance rather the garden plot he had at Rock Island, as it was "useless". His "potatoes were all eaten by rats and all the other vegetables were destroyed"[236]. Rats were a continuous problem at Rock Island. An amusing account of the keepers' efforts to keep them under control in the 1950s was recounted by the former attendant Dermot Griffin. Keepers would place explosive fog signal charges on the rocks in front of the Fastnet PK's house and place bread around them. A wire would be taken away some distance. When the rats gathered around the charges to feed, the wire would be connected to a battery thus blowing the rats to smithereens!

The Engineer in June 1946 requested that repairs be undertaken to dwelling numbers 2, 3, 4 and 5. They required new roof slates, guttering and replacement of interior plaster where it had fallen down. He specified that the kitchen of house no.2 required a "new oval flue pipe to Tarbert range". Two Truburn cookers with a left hand oven were later delivered to the dwellings in December 1953 from Skibbereen. They cost £24/1/5 each and were charged to the Fastnet Shore account.

A local man, Patrick (Patsy) McCarthy provided a delivery service from the 1940s (F. McCarthy, possibly his father, provided the same service in the 1920s charging 10 shillings for conveying keepers from

---

[235] Irish Lights Work File 1929/440.
[236] Irish Lights Work File 1941/2900.

Mizen Head to Rock Island). He received six shillings per trip (two trips were needed) for delivering one ton of carbide and a ½ cwt (25 kg) of Puritol (an anti-corrosive paint especially for water tanks) from Schull in February 1942[237]. It is not apparent whether the delivery was sent by rail or ship to Schull. In May of the same year he brought the "annual stores" from Schull railway station to Rock Island. McCarthy delivered a wireless telephone to Mizen Head from Rock Island in November 1945. It had been delivered to Rock Island by the *SS Discover*[238]. In May 1956 he was paid eight shillings to deliver a "hamper etc" from Goleen to Rock Island. In March 1957 he did two trips from Goleen to Rock Island conveying 20 drums of carbide. His charge for delivering from Goleen went up to 10/6 in 1960. Tim Coughlan of Goleen (owner of the Lobster Pot) appears to taken over the deliveries and was charging eight shillings from Goleen to Rock Island from 1962 to 1967.

In 1951 Kevin Murphy was appointed PK of Mizen where he was based until his transfer to the Baily in 1957. He had spent from 1911 to 1919 growing up on Rock Island while his father T. P. Murphy was PK of Fastnet. He was taken to and from Rock Island to Mizen by side-car, presumably by P. McCarthy[239].

On a visit to the Rock Island dwellings on the 1st of October 1959, the Inspector noted: house no.1, J. Power's showed no sign of occupation; no.2, J. Walshe's also showed no sign of occupation; no.3, M. Crowley's was "obviously occupied"; no.4, B. O'Regan's was not occupied with O'Regan living in Goleen; no.5, P. J. Coughlan's – "this keeper has been sick for a considerable time"; no.6, J. Hegarty's – only sometimes occupied; no.7, D. Gaughan's not occupied; and no.8, J. Sugrue, not occupied – living in Castletownbere. The Inspector also stated that no. 4 & 5 were originally one house but were later divided into two with one room

---

[237] D3 Book Crookhaven 1936-55, Inspectors Dept, Commissioners of Irish Lights.
[238] D3 Book Mizen 1936-55, Inspectors Dept, Commissioners of Irish Lights.
[239] Kevin Murphy (1907-2003) - Murphy, "Kevin Murphy, Principal Keeper", 19.

downstairs and two upstairs in each, which does not agree with other accounts which indicate it was built as two houses.

Renting of Store from Notters

On the 21st of April 1863 Thomas Notter of Rock Island wrote acknowledging receipt of rent[240]. It appears this was for a store. He was paid rent again in October 1863. The following April, Thomas Notter requested payment "for rent of cottage". His wife, Eliza, requested payment of the rent for a "store at Rock Island for the use of Fastnet Rock" in October 1864. J. S. Sloane submitted Notter's bill for "Crookhaven storage" in May 1867. The Engineer reported in November 1872 that the new store was complete and there was no need to continue renting the store. As a result a notice of surrender was sent.

The *Wolverine* Wreck

In June 1872 the Assistant Inspector drew attention to the wreck of the *Wolverine* in Crookhaven harbour which had been there since March 1867 (for the rescue of the crew see the Coast Guard section). He asked that the owner remove it or drop his ownership claim.
In June 1877 a Mr. Heilbury wrote abandoning all claims to the wreck *Wolverine*[241] which had sank in Crookhaven Harbour. Richard Notter stated that he would remove the wreck provided he was given possession of it[242]. In July, his brother Isaac wrote to Irish Lights indicating that he had not yet removed the wreck "owing to the difficulty of obtaining the services of a diver". The Irish Lights' Board indicated that they would supply their diver provided Notter

---

[240] Lighthouse Register 1863, Corporation for Preservation & Improving The Port of Dublin & Co.
[241] The crew of the barque *Wolverine* were rescued by the Coast Guard using the Rocket Apparatus on the 17th of March 1867 at Crookhaven Lighthouse.
[242] Journal No.30, Commissioners of Irish Lights, p. 298.

Rock Island

paid the cost[243]. Later Notter indicated he would not remove the wreck due to the cost of the diver. Mess'rs Dineen then asked what they would be paid for removal as well as taking ownership of the wreck. The Board decided to tender for the removal. Amongst those who tendered were Isaac Notter, a Mr. Levis, a Mr. Powell and William Armstrong whose tender for £450 was accepted[244]. It was however not until the 14th of February 1879 that the Board was informed by the Inspector that the wreck had been removed, 12 years after it had been abandoned.

Coal & Supplies

Isaac Notter was given the contract to supply coal to Fastnet in September 1863. He also supplied coal to Ballycotton and Youghal. Six hundred gallons of oil, for the light, were landed on Fastnet on the 9th of May 1864.

It appears that the Rock Island dwellings and Fastnet had run out of coal in July 1872, as Timothy Dwyer, Boat Contractor of Castletownbere, was instructed to get a temporary supply to both places as soon as possible. This was done by early August[245].

Isaac Notter notified the board in July 1873 that he would "supply coal to Fastnet, Skelligs & c. immediately".

In 1905, James Waldie of Glasgow had the contract for supplying coal. They wrote that the annual supply had "been shipped by *June Rose* and will be delivered by W. Camier". Fifty tons were delivered: forty two tons for the shore dwellings and eight for Fastnet. With seven houses on Rock Island at the time, this would equate with six tons per house[246].

---

[243] Journal No.30, 328.
[244] Journal No.31, Commissioners of Irish Lights, 13th Sept 1878.
[245] Lighthouse Register 1872, Commissioners of Irish Lights, 5 August 1872.
[246] Morrissey, A History of the Fastnet Lighthouse, 46.

Rock Island as a base for the new Fastnet Lighthouse

As outlined above, the original Fastnet Lighthouse, even after considerable efforts to strengthen it, proved unsatisfactory. When a hurricane on 26th November 1881 smashed the lantern, and swept away a similarly constructed cast-iron tower on Calf Rock off the Beara Peninsula nearby, Fastnet's replacement became an obvious priority. In December 1891 Trinity House approved Irish Lights proposal for a new lighthouse[247]. As a result the decision was taken to build a larger lighthouse constructed from granite which was sanctioned in November 1895[248]. The structure was designed by the Irish Lights' Engineer William Douglass.

Initially the Commissioners looked for a site in Schull Harbour, the terminus of the Skibbereen-Schull tramline, to act as a base for the new lighthouse. Renting land there proved too costly, so the decision was taken to use Crookhaven Lighthouse as the shore base.

Fastnet granite blocks at Rock Island awaiting shipment

Work on shore commenced in 1896. Within the next two years a 38 metre long pier, formed by facing up the existing rock, was built. The

---

[247] Scott, History of the Fastnet Rock Lighthouses, 8.
[248] Scott, History of the Fastnet Rock Lighthouses, 9.

pier has a three fathom (5.4m) depth at spring low tide. Where the rock for facing up was quarried, an office, stores, a timber barracks for workers, carpenter's and blacksmith's shops were built. A steam wharf crane for loading and unloading the granite blocks, a tramway connecting the wharf with the stone-yard and a gantry with hand-powered overhead crane were also installed. The cost of this work amounted to £2,060.

In 1898 work commenced on the powder magazine at the southern extremity of the pier. In the same year, construction of the first of two additional houses required for the Fastnet keepers commenced. One of these would become the principle keeper's home, while the other was a double house with two separate entrances, each house accommodating two single keepers.

The ketch Kobah unloading stone alongside Rock Island lighthouse wharf

Dr Twohig of Goleen was paid a fee a 1/8 per month for every man employed on the Fastnet new works. The men had half this amount deducted from their pay. A Jeremiah Coughlan who was employed on the Fastnet works injured one of his eyes in August 1898. I. Travers Wolfe, his solicitor, claimed £90; he was however paid £35/18/0[249].

---

[249] Journal No. 40, Commissioners of Irish Lights, 27th January 1899.

On the 1ˢᵗ of March 1899 William Douglass, Irish Lights Chief Engineer, requested the Secretary, Owen Armstong, to approve Delaware P. Fleming as Master of the *Ierne*. Fleming had previously had charge of the *Alert* and the *Princess Alexandra*. During the construction of the Bull Rock Lighthouse he had charge of the *Lady Ombrasine* which acted as the tender.

Fleming wanted the following crew: Mate – P. Newland of Kingstown; Seamen – M. Sullivan of Bere Island, Timothy Sullivan of Bere Island (replaced D. Donovan of Ballyrisode, Goleen whose name was crossed out), M. Callahan of Bere Island, D. Flynn and R. Driscoll of Crookhaven[250].

Fleming's appointment was approved and he wrote from the *Ierne* at Rock Island on the 12ᵗʰ of April 1899 "I proceeded [from Queenstown] and arrived here at 5 p.m. that day [10ᵗʰ of April 1899], I reported arrival to Resident Engineer, under whose instructions I have placed myself".

William Douglass was forced to retire due to ill health in September 1900 and he was replaced by C. W. Scott who completed the project and later wrote *Fastnet Rock Lighthouses*[251].

The *Ierne* resumed attendance in 1900 in early March[252]. The Commissioners requested approval for insurance cover from the Board of Trade in April 1900. They wanted to cover the building on Rock Island used to accommodate the Fastnet workers and also a nearby store. "These buildings are of timber, with tarred felt roofs and if burned down would cost about £500 to rebuild". The best insurance quote they received was £1/10/2 from the North British and Mercantile Insurance Company. However the Board of Trade refused to sanction the cover.

---

[250] Irish Lights Work File 1899/232.
[251] Pelly, "William Douglass", 25.
[252] Irish Lights Work File 1900/236

Rock Island

Captain Deane (middle) and Captain Flemming (right) on board the S.S. *Alexandra*

Fleming took a week off from the 7th of April 1900 due to an inflamed eye "caused I [Castletownbere doctor] believe by exposure during this inclement weather". He was replaced by Kearon[253].

Scott informed head office that the *Ierne* had left Crookhaven on the 5th of October 1900, arrived in Kingstown on the 6th and went into dock on the 10th[254]. She would not return to work on the Fastnet until the following spring.

Frederick Foot, the Superintendent of the Fastnet works based on Rock Island rented one of the Coast Guard houses during the project. In the 1901 Census, Frederick Foot, civil engineer aged 47 was living there. He lived there with his wife Catherine (aged 48), sons Harold (14) and Rob (13). They also had a servant Sarah Wilbank (25). Another house was rented from the Coast Guard for William Moore (32), blacksmith, Patrick Sheehan (60), accountant, John O'Connor (26) and John O'Driscoll (24), labourers. Foot requested a month's leave after the Fastnet work was completed for the year 1901, about the 15th of October. This was approved and prior to his departure he wrote "I will make all arrangement for

---
[253] Irish Lights Work File 1900/392.
[254] Irish Lights Work File 1900/1057.

carrying on shore Dwelling and unloading cargoes of store, before I leave here, and intend to place R. Spencer in charge"[255].

Crookhaven Lighthouse around 1900

In March 1902 Scott requested Fleming to bring the *Princess Alexandra* to Kingstown and then take the *Ierne* to Crookhaven to be ready to start stone setting on the Fastnet beginning on the 1st of April. Foot was requested "to proceed to Rockisland to take charge of the Fastnet Works on the 1st April"[256].

In May 1903, the following medicines were delivered to Rock Island from The Apothecaries Hall, Mary Street, [Cork?] for the "Fastnet New Works"[257]:

    2 * 1 doz bottles Antibilious Pills
    3 * 8 oz bottles Castor Oil
    1 * 4 oz bottles Friars Balsam
    8 * 1 pint tins Carbolic Acid

---

[255] Irish Lights Work File 1901/994.
[256] Irish Lights Work File 1902/209.
[257] Order Book, Commissioners of Irish Lights, 13th May 1903.

4 * 2 oz tins vaseline
1 * 8 oz bottle Elimans Embrocation
4 * 1 lb packages linseed meal
1 doz calico bandages
12 yards lint

All 2,074 granite bocks for the new lighthouse, totalling 4,370 tons were cut and numbered at Penryn, Cornwall (the stone was cut so well that not one piece was rejected). They were shipped from Cornwall to Rock Island over the course of construction and taken out to Fastnet Rock as required by the specially constructed 38 metre long steamer, *Ierne* which was capable of carrying over 90 tonnes of cargo. The first stone was landed on Fastnet Rock on the 9th of June 1899. Due to the vagaries of the weather, it was 1903 before all the stone had been landed.

James Kavanagh, from Wicklow, was the foreman on Fastnet during construction. He showed incredible dedication to the project, remaining on the Rock during all the construction period. Having completed the 89th and last granite course of the tower he was taken ill and brought to the shore dwellings on Rock Island on the 3rd of July 1903. He died of "apoplexy" (a stroke) on the 6th of July 1903 at the age of 47. He had been administered the last rites on Rock Island by Fr. McSweeney. His body was taken on the *Ierne* from Rock Island to Wicklow[258].

Foot, in April 1904, wrote from Rock Island asking for sick leave and treatment in Cork. He said "I have been spitting blood and feel that it is imperative I should seek further advice and treatment". He was suffering from laryngitis which he said was due to long fog on Fastnet. He was given sick leave from the 16th of April to the 9th of May[259]. At the same time the poor weather was preventing Fleming from landing optical gear for the new lighthouse on Fastnet.

---

[258] Fastnet Lighthouse Centenary 1903-2003, Commissioners of Irish Lights, 2003.
[259] Irish Lights Work File 1904/400.

On the 27th of June 1904, the new light was exhibited. William Douglass was invited by the Commissioners to join their 1904 inspection of Fastnet. He wrote back from Penzance, from where he had retired to, accepting the invitation and joined the Commissioners at Valentia on the 19th of July[260]. On the 21st of July, Sir Robert Ball, Scientific Advisor to the Commissioners, reported

> It was about eleven o'clock when the *Alexandra* was headed round to return to Crookhaven. By this time the night had become much darker, for the moonlight had disappeared and there was occasional rain as well as haze.
>
> As to the beams of the Fastnet during all the time of our return to harbour, I cannot describe them otherwise than by saying they were magnificent. At ten miles' distance the great revolving spokes of light, succeeding each other at intervals of five seconds, gave the most distinctive character possible. Almost before one spoke {of light] had disappeared the next came into view, but the effect was doubtless in part attributable to the haze. It was a most beautiful optical phenomenon. Each great flash, as it swept past, lighted up the ship and the rigging like a searchlight. After the ship entered Crookhaven harbour, and the direct light from Fastnet was, of course, cut off, the glow of each successive beam showed in a striking manner over the high land that bounds the harbour[261].

Foot, in September, returned £150 of the £400 float he had for the new Fastnet works "as work is now drawing to a close" Also in September, the Commissioners approved a payment of £4/2/0 to Dr. Neville of Goleen for amputating the little finger of J. Sullivan. Sullivan of the *Ierne* got his finger jammed between the "gunwale and ship's side when he was returning from leave"[262].

On the 1st of October Captain Louis Brady of the *Ierne* was informed that he would be required to stay at Crookhaven with his ship until Scott had decided that all the Fastnet work requiring the *Ierne* was

---

[260] Irish Lights Work File 1904/718.
[261] Wilson, The Irish Lighthouse Service.
[262] Irish Lights Work File 1904/1109.

Rock Island

completed[263]. On the 24th of November Scott wrote "I have now no further use for the *SS Ierne* on work for the Fastnet"[264].

Whilst working at Rock Island, labourers earned 2/6 (15p/20c) a day. Two men lost eyes on Rock Island: one while building the tram line; another when quarrying.

When the *Ierne* replaced the *Moya* in servicing "Southern Rock Stations" from 1905, half the initial cost of the *Ierne* (£11,800 * 50%) was credited to the Fastnet new works project[265].

Once operational the new Fastnet had a complement of six keepers with four on the rock on any one time, and two ashore. Two men were changed at each relief by steamer. Due to the difficulty of landing and removing the keepers from Fastnet many changeovers were delayed, often for weeks.

1901 & 1911 Census Records

The 1901 Census, taken on the 31st of March, records three men on the Fastnet that night:

Name	Religion	Age	Born	Occupation
James Twohig	R.C.[266]	34	Co. Dublin	Principal Keeper
Jonathan Wright	C.I	27	Co. Sligo	Assistant Keeper
Alfred Rohu	R.C.	21	Dundalk	Assistant Keeper

The records for Rock Island lighthouse property were:

House Name		Religion	Age	Born	Occupation
1.[267]	John Wills	R.C.	29	Antrim	Assistant Keeper
2	Margaret Twohig	R.C.	32	Cork	
	Margaret Twohig	R.C	7	Cork	

---

[263] Irish Lights Work File 1904/1066.
[264] Irish Lights Work File 1904/1362.
[265] Irish Lights Work File 1905/1099.
[266] R.I. Roman Catholic; C.I. Church of Ireland (Protestant)
[267] The house numbers placed beside each household for both censuses are guesses. The 1901 census recorded the number of windows at the front of each house as a means of classifying the house. The number of windows given for the above houses equates except for number three which had eight windows but Rohu's house was recorded as having only two.

House	Name	Religion	Age	Born	Occupation
	Elizabeth Walsh	R.C.	23	Cork	Seamstress (sister)
3.	Edward Rohu	C.I.	52	Donegal	Principal Keeper
	Anastatia Rohu	R.C.	48	Dublin	
	Elizabeth Rohu	R.C.	17	Down	
	Edward Rohu	R.C.	9	Down	
	Kathleen Hamilton	R.C.	23	Louth	Lighthouse keeper's wife
	Patrick Hamilton	R.C.	5	Down	Nephew
8.	Charles Nicholls[268]	C.I.	24	England	Stone Mason
	Elizabeth Nicholls	C.I.	28	Cork	
	Annie Nicholls	C.I.	1	Cork	
9.	Charles Harcourt	C.I.	68	England	Navy pensioner (widower)
	Edith Harcourt	C.I.	22	Cork	Housekeeper (daughter)

Ten years later, in the 1911 census we have the following information for Fastnet:

Name	Religion	Age	Born	Occupation
William Martin	R.C.	26	Cork	Assistant Keeper
William Snow	C.I	30	Dublin	Assistant Keeper
Robert Blakely	Presbyterian	32	Down	Assistant Keeper
James Glanville	R.C	41	Cork	Navy pensioner

On Rock Island lighthouse property, the following people were listed:

House	Name	Religion	Age	Born	Occupation
1.	Bridget Sullivan	R.C.	33	Mayo	Wife
	Daniel Sullivan	R.C	5	Cork	Son
	David Sullivan	R.C.	3	Cork	Son
	Ellen Sullivan	R.C.	1	Cork	Daughter
2.	Patrick Brennan	R.C.	29	Clare	Assistant Keeper
3.	James Twohig	R.C.	44	Dublin	Principal Keeper
	Margaret Twohig	R.C.	43	Cork	Wife
	Margaret Twohig	R.C.	17	Cork	Daughter
6.	Joseph Sweeny	R.C.	36	Down	Assistant Keeper
	Kathleen Sweeny	R.C.	30	Mayo	Wife
	Mary Sweeny	R.C.	5	Mayo	Daughter

---

[268] Charles Nicholls was born in 1877 in Penzance, Cornwall. He was employed at the time of the 1901 census by John Albert Freeman who supplied all the granite for the Fastnet Lighthouse from his quarry at Penryn, Cornwall. Nicholls' job was to assist in the erection of the tower.

Rock Island

	House Name	Religion	Age	Born	Occupation
	Thomas Sweeny	R.C.	4	Mayo	Son
	John Sweeny	R.C.	2	Cork	Son
	Annie Sweeny	R.C.	11mth	Cork	Daughter
7.	Arthur McCloskey	R.C.	30	Donegal	Assistant Keeper
	Kathleen McCloskey	R.C.	28	Donegal	Wife
	John McCloskey	R.C.	8	Wicklow	Son
	James McCloskey	R.C.	7	Wicklow	Son
	Annie McCloskey	R.C.	5	Wicklow	Daughter
	Mary McCloskey	R.C.	4	Wicklow	Daughter
	Daniel McCloskey	R.C.	2	Mayo	Son
	Alfred McCloskey	R.C.	10mth	Cork	Daughter
8.	Isabel Blakely	C.I.	29	Down	Wife
	Terence Blakely	C.I.	5	Kingstown	Son
	Reginald Blakely	C.I.	1	Down	Son
	Robert Blakely	C.I.	3mth	Cork	Son
9	Edward Smith	C.I.	35	Wicklow	Assistant Keeper
	Henry Bent	C.I.	28	Dublin	Artificer

Fastnet Bell

In 1912 the Submarine Signal Company, the London subsidiary of an American company, offered a submarine bell buoy to Irish Lights on a one year trial. They were anxious to have it moored off the Fastnet and prove its benefit as an aid to navigation. The submarine bell, which was rung by wave action, was to act as an additional warning to shipping. The Commissioners agreed to place one there and to buy it for £400 should the year trial prove successful.

On the 15th of August 1913 Hubert Cook, the Secretary of Irish Lights, issued the following Notice to Mariners "Bell Buoy moored in 23 fathoms of water about 4 ½ cables, 228° (W.S.W. Magnetic) from the Fastnet Lighthouse. The Buoy also carries a Submarine Bell".

In January 1914 R. Deane, Irish Lights Inspector, checked how audible the bell was. He listened on the *Alexandra* for the bell at four km. from the Fastnet. "I could not detect the double strike referred to in the report of the Submarine Bell Co.'s Engineer". He wanted the buoy to be taken into Schull for repair as "the rock shelves away from the [Rock Island] Pier below the level of low water mark and renders the pier an unsafe place to berth steamers alongside of, that are fitted with bilge keels". Also the crane there was not certified to lift the weight of this buoy[269].

On the 15th of February 1914 at 2 p.m., prior to removing the buoy for repairs, it broke its moorings during a "moderate westerly gale". It drifted off towards Cape Clear. A few days later Captain Brady on the *SS Ierne* found it about five miles south of Baltimore. He brought it into Baltimore where it was put under the charge of the Harbour Master Augustus P. Dennis. Dennis had it moored around 1 km from Baltimore in the track of vessels. As a result it had to be lit which cost the Harbour Master £26/4/2, an amount the Submarine Signal Co. proved very reluctant to pay as they believed the buoy had been left on Schull pier. It was later agreed that the buoy would be re-moored at Fastnet for a further trial period of 12 months and so it was re-laid on the 20th of July. In March 1915 the Submarine Signal Co was charged £4/13/9 for the paint used on repainting the buoy: 49lbs (22kg) Ralityens Composition; 1¾ gallons (8ltr) Corsite Green paint; 1½ gallons (6.8ltrs) Corsite Black paint. Submarine Signal Co. men did the actual painting at Rock Island[270].

The final reference to the buoy was a letter from the Submarine Signal Co. dated the 1st of July 1921 "we shall be glad to know if the work upon the buoy removed from the Fastnet, which you were kind enough to undertake has now been completed, as we anticipate shortly to be able to complete arrangements for establishing this buoy in the approaches to the Clyde".

Mizen Head Station

As a result of a number of shipwrecks at Mizen Head around the close of the nineteenth century, it was decided in the early 20th Century to establish a fog signal station there. R. Deane, Irish Lights

---

[269] Irish Lights Work File 1914/76.
[270] Irish Lights Work File 1914/104.

Rock Island

Inspector, calculated the following costs in October 1907 associated with running the Mizen station[271]:

> Three Assistants @ 3/3 per day with two on duty receiving 1/9 per day rock allowance and £2 per year garden allowance.
> 1,000 detonators @ 9 ½d each   £395/16/8
> 3 ½ tons coal – lighthouse
> 10 ½ tons coal – dwellings
> 63 tons – total coal Crookhaven dwellings
> £50 – medical attendance
> 3,150 gallons of paraffin for three stations @ 5 ¼d per gallon

Doherty, the Acting Secretary of Irish Lights, wrote to the Board of Trade on the 21st of October 1907 requesting approval to spend £7,850 to establish a fog station at Mizen "with dwellings at Crookhaven [Rock Island] under the Principal Keeper of Fastnet". Doherty wrote "I understand it is the intention of the Board, when Mizen Head works are completed, that Fastnet, Crookhaven and Mizen Head are to be treated as a combined station". He anticipated that the new fog signal would be first sounded around the 1st of October 1908[272]. It was not however not operational until the 3rd of May 1909[273].

In January 1908 the G.P.O. notified Irish Lights that it would increase the postal deliveries to Mizen Head from four to six days a week "whilst the Engineering work there is in progress".

A note on file indicates that in 1914, Mizen Head was using two explosives every 7 ½ minutes during fog. During the day they used Cotton Powder Charges @£35 per thousand; at night they used Flash Sound Signals @£45 per thousand[274].

In 1924 the keepers requested a Principal Keeper for Mizen[275]. However Mizen Head remained under the control of the Fastnet

---

[271] Irish Lights Work File 1907/998.
[272] Irish Lights Work File 1907/998.
[273] Journal No.45, Commissioners of Irish Lights, 3rd May 1909.
[274] Irish Lights Work File 1914/234.
[275] Journal No.50, Commissioners of Irish Lights, 30th May 1924.

Principal Keeper until 1931 when the Assistant Engineer's recommendation that it have its own principal keeper was accepted[276].

On the 4th of November 1933 P. Sheehan, a labourer, was injured and later died whilst dismantling a two ton crane at Mizen Head. His family were later awarded £100 by the Circuit Court Judge[277].

Explosives Magazine & IRA Raids

On the 1st of October 1901 James Twohig PK provided head office with a record of the number of cotton powder charges and detonators used on Fastnet over the previous three months:

July   1,506
August   1,790
September   950

He requested further supplies which were received on the 14th of October from the *SS Cragside*. The 8,580 cotton powder charges and 9,705 detonators were stored in the Rock Island magazines. These charges and detonators had replaced rockets about 12 years previously with each fuse and detonator costing 9d. They were supplied by the Cotton Powder Co. of London[278].

The Fastnet PK T. P. Murphy asked in February 1919 whether the Goleen police should be notified every time explosives were moved form Rock Island to Mizen Head, presumably because of the ambush potential from the local I.R.A.

On the 1st of February 1920, the following charges and detonators were stored in the area:

Fastnet	4,937 2 oz Tonnite Charges	7,869 Detonators
Fastnet Reserve Store (Rock Island)	1,200 2 oz Tonnite Charges	1,000 Detonators
Mizen	3,836 2 oz Tonnite Charges	3,497 Detonators
Mizen Reserve Store (Rock Island)	6,600 2 oz Tonnite Charges	11,000 Detonators

---

[276] Committee Minute Book, Irish Lights, 1930-46.
[277] Irish Lights Work File 1933/771.
[278] Irish Lights Work File 1901/1025.

Rock Island

There was obviously concern among local police over the possibility of a raid at Rock Island as the district sergeant and constable visited J. J. Duggan, AK Mizen Head, at Rock Island on the 5th of March 1920. They enquired about the availability of accommodation for a "protective police or military" force on Rock Island. "The sergeant owing to being locally stationed for several years knew about the unoccupied house here". This was probably house no.2, the old Fastnet PK's house.

In a "Summary of Police Reports" concerning the storage of explosives for fog signalling, dated the 22nd of April 1920, the police stated that Mizen Head and Rock Island Reserve store "are not considered safe, they are each guarded by two unarmed men only. It is impossible to afford Police protection". However Fastnet was "considered safe from raids".

On the 16th of May 1920, at 1.30 am, Mizen Head "was raided by armed and masked men (about 100) who carried off the bulk of the Fog Station Explosives at the Station, together with Firing Battery, Station Telescope, Storm Lantern and Morse Lamp". On the 18th of May, F.J. Duffy AK wrote

> It was the intention of the raiders to visit Rockisland on Sunday morning after they had finished with Mizen Head. They asked me was there much powder in the magazine at Rockisland and I told them it would be hardly worth while going there for what they would get, so seeming Rockisland Magazine stands in danger. I had the Sergeant of Police down this evening and he suggested to me to remove the bulk of the powder to some other store.

As one can see from the quantities stored on Rock Island, the IRA would have secured considerably more explosives from raiding Rock Island. Possibly the difficulty of getting off Rock Island with its one narrow road and the proximity to the armed Coast Guard station discouraged the raiders.

Captain Davis, Irish Lights' Inspector, had a discussion with the Deputy Inspector-General of the R.I.C. (Royal Irish Constabulary) the day after the raid. Davis told the officer "if the raiders wanted more of these explosives they could just as easily collect them from our reserve stock at Rockisland as from Mizen Head". This discussion resulted in all the explosives on Rock Island being removed on the 20th of May 1920. A "military guard of the East Lancashire Regiment" arrived that day in a "motor" with the intention of removing them in the vehicle. However the weight was too great and they placed them on the destroyer *HMS Urchin* which was in Crookhaven Harbour. The destroyer then took them to Bantry. Later shipments for the Fastnet appear to have been stored at the Rock Island Coast Guard Station: on the 31st of January 1921 the Commander-in-Chief at Queenstown wrote to Irish Lights stating that he would "convey explosives from Crookhaven [Coast Guard station] to Fastnet in an armed trawler". Also on the 21st of October 1921, 4,000 charges and 2,000 detonators were taken by the British Navy to the Coast Guard station from where the Irish Lights motor tender *Deirdre* took them to the Fastnet.

The Irish Lights Inspector, in a meeting with Sir Hamar Greenwood, Chief Secretary of Ireland in May 1920, stated that all the lighthouse keepers had taken the oath of allegiance, although some reluctantly. He "felt sure that at least 90% of them were absolutely loyal, although in the existing condition of the country, they were liable to contamination".

Fastnet was raided, much to the surprise and embarrassment of the British authorities, on the 20th of June 1920. Two boats, one the *Máire Cáit* from Cape Clear, with IRA men arrived while Anthony Coughlan AK was on duty. John Crowley AK, who was in charge of the Fastnet at the time, had noticed two fishing boats in the vicinity of the Rock at midnight. The weather inner doors for the lighthouse had been left open that night as the weather was "exceptionally fine". According to the Coast Guard "12 raiders landed…The leader appeared to be a refined and educated man with apparently a Dublin accent. His age was about 30…his height was 5'10" [178cm]"[279].

---

[279] Locally the leader was regarded to be a West Cork man by the name of Cotter –O'Meara, Jim, conversation with, 20th of November 2005. Lannin wrote "the Fastnet raid was first mooted by Rickie Collins. He was Captain of the

Rock Island

HMS Truro commanded by Lieut. Commander Baillie-Grahman had gone to the Fastnet around midnight to check out an unknown green light. It then "proceeded to Crookhaven and anchored". The IRA men arrived at 1.00 a.m. and were gone by 1.50 a.m. They took 3,798 charges and 3,930 detonators but left 400 charges and 1,000 detonators. Apparently they damaged the wireless - "the brake adjustment of induction coil being strained it took a few hours to get a spark". By 6.00 a.m. the transmitter was repaired. However it took the Rock Island Coast Guard until 8.00 a.m. to answer the call and inform the Principal Keeper, J. J. Treeby, who was on Rock Island at the time[280]. The other keeper on the Rock at the time was P. Whelan AK.

According to Craig Treeby, his grandfather John Joseph Treeby, Fastnet PK "was held at gun point by the IRA for explosives but to prove it wasn't personal they offered him a drink the next time he was in the pub!"[281]. It is not known where or when this incident occurred.

A second raid occurred at Mizen Head on the 31st of July 1920 at 1.40 a.m. when Jim O'Connor AK was on duty with the "greater portion of the Fog Signal explosives again carried off". Later head office was informed that "seven cases of Day and four cases of Night Charge, also 2,000 detonators" had been taken. As a result of this raid, Irish Lights informed the Under Secretary, Dublin Castle that Mizen Head Fog Signal Station was closed. Due to its isolated location, the British Army had refused to guard the station. The station was raided again by five men on the 1st of July 1921 who cut the telephone lines and took the telephone. It appears that the telephone was only reconnected in November when the "circuit with R.I.C. Guard and Goleen P.O. was restored". By February 1922 J. J. Duggan, AK Mizen, indicated that the "telephone at Rock Island is

---

Goleen Company and a Lightkeeper at the Fastnet from 1912 – 1918" – Lannin, F. "The Raid on the Fastnet Lighthouse", *Mizen Journal*, no.7, 1999, p. 46.
[280] Raiding & Burning by Sinn Feiners, National Archives, London, ADM116/2084.
[281] Treeby, Craig, email, 8th of Mar 2006

now removed". This would appear to refer to the telephone at the former Coast Guard station.

By this time Irish Lights was working with the new Irish government. The Secretary took up the issue of recent raids on Mizen Station with the Chief Liaison Officer who promised to raise the matter with the Officer-in-Charge, 1st Southern Division. The Secretary indicated that there were a total of five raids on Mizen Head over the previous 18 months[282]. With Irish Independence, the Commissioners issued instructions on the 12th of May 1922 that the Irish Lights' Ensign was no longer to be raised at lighthouses on the occasion of British Royal Birthdays[283].

Fran Hollens: reminiscences of a keeper's daughter

Fran Hollens, nee Crowley, left an audiotape of her reminiscences of growing up on Rock Island. She was born in October 1912 at Belmullet, Co. Mayo and christened Mary Francis. Her father, John Crowley, was stationed on Eagle Island at the time. In 1918 he was transferred from Mine Head to Fastnet. He was stationed there until 1923 due to the upheaval caused by the War of Independence and the Civil War. Crowley and his wife Emily, formerly a milliner, had five other children between the ages of 6 months and 12 years when they transferred to Rock Island dwellings: Maureen, Moira, Dora, Michael Benedict and John Joseph. They lived in one of the valley houses, with Alf Rohu and his sister Lily[284] living in the other one. In house no.1 was Danny Hamilton; T. P. Murphy, his wife Mary (nee Hamilton) and four children lived in no.3, the principal keepers house; Andy Coughlan lived in one of the single men's houses (no.4 or 5); and Mr and Mrs Whelan lived in the other single men's house. Jim O'Connor, his wife and son Jim lived in one of the Mizen keepers' houses (no.6 or 7); in the other was Mr Wall who was single.

---

[282] Raid Files, Commissioners of Irish Lights.
[283] Journal No.50, 12th May 1922.
[284] Alfred & Elizabeth Rohu were the children of Edward Rohu, former Fastnet PK.

Rock Island

In 1919 T. P. Murphy was replaced by J. J. Treeby, his wife and two sons. At a later stage the Whelan's were replaced by Harry Stanifore and his sister Elli. Andy Coughlan was replaced by Anthony Henihan. Mr & Mrs Donovan replaced Mr Wall; and the Duggan family replaced the O'Connors. Alf Rohu was transferred to Northern Ireland where he later married in Bangor, Co. Down. He was replaced by Mr & Mrs Fennell and their three children.

While she lived at Rock Island there were three men on the Fastnet at any one time with one ashore. Those on shore were responsible for keeping the paths clean and always wore their uniform in case of an inspection. Reliefs were every fortnight with men on the Fastnet for six weeks and off for two. However reliefs were often two weeks overdue. She recalled the *Alexandra, Tearaght* and *Ierne* undertaking the reliefs. There was no telephone connection with the Fastnet at the time. Instead they used red and yellow flags for semaphore. Frans' mother would semaphore letters of interest and family news to her husband on the Fastnet at pre-arranged times. She did this in front of the white background of what she described as Mrs Williams', her grandmother's house. It appears her grandmother had lived there before and she was describing house no.2 which had been the principal keepers' house. She said this house was used during their time on Rock Island as a store for the Fastnet fog detonators. In winter, presumably because of poorer visibility, husband and wife signalled to each other by Morse Lamp. There was however a wireless connection between Fastnet and Brow Head at the time as she refers to the use of Morse code to transmit information from Fastnet for the Lloyds Shipping Register.

Her father had previously been a sailor during which time he contracted malaria. At the time, one had either to have a trade or five years experience as a sailor to join Irish Lights. Her father had travelled the world and was very knowledgeable on geography and navigation. He was also a "great sportsman" and his hobbies were fishing, shooting and sailing. While out on the Fastnet he always made something which he would bring back to the family when on shore leave. She recalled that he also wrote articles with one on bird migration published. When on shore leave he would take the children to Cockle Strand at the end of Crookhaven Harbour by bicycle, to pick periwinkles and cockles. He also made lobster pots which he set around the lighthouse.

He was the keeper in charge of the Fastnet during the IRA raid on the 20th of June 1920. She described the IRA as wanting the charges to blow up a bridge. Her father "reproached the raiders to no avail". They demanded the keys to the magazine and cut off communications with Brow Head. They did however leave enough powder should there be fog before re-supply. She believed the powder was taken ashore and hidden under manure. It is likely her father was quite familiar with the raiders, as one was probably Rickie Collins who lived in Shanavally, one mile from Rock Island lighthouse. She recalled, after the raid, a party of ten military staying for a week on Rock Island to guard the "ammunition" needed to re-supply the Fastnet. They stayed in house no.2.

Andy Coughlan on his wedding day

She remembered destroyers coming into the harbour and the crew playing polo or football ashore. On one occasion her father was given a cat named Tom by an officer from a destroyer. Apparently the officer was not allowed to bring the cat into Britain.

Her family was obviously musical as they brought an accordion, duce harp, piano, violin, concertina and mouth organs with them. She recalled Andy Coughlan teaching them Irish dancing. She also would cycle to Schull, 12 miles away, every Saturday to the Sisters of Mercy Convent where they were taught music, singing and occasionally French. Monday evening was spent practising music. In summer school friends would come between 3 and 6 p.m. where they would sing and dance on the smooth flagstones around the lighthouse.

Her mother kept chickens and they grew their own vegetables. In autumn they picked crab apples and blackberries for jam making. Her mother also made yeast bread every week. She had a Yorkshire Terrier which she would take along with their two cats and the pram to meet the children returning by foot from school in Goleen where Mrs Glanville taught them (Mrs Glanville was married to James Glanville, who had been a Fastnet keeper). On the way home with their mother they would often swim at "Hamilton's Strand".

Her family was "great friends" with Mrs O'Donoghue at the Rock Island Post Office and her mother Mrs Hamilton. They would collect milk, eggs and the post from there. The Hamilton's/O'Donoghue's always said the rosary at 6.00 p.m. She said there was always a pot of Indian Meal over the fire which Mrs Hamilton cooked for her hens. She also recalled going to Ballydevlin House, 3 km away for a "celebration". The curate in Goleen taught them languages once a week. He was described as "a professor from Maynooth". Their other teacher was Alf Rohu, who taught them cards! Weekly orders were given to the market man on Friday who took them to Schull and returned with them on Saturday.

The Fastnet Race

As a result of the commencement of the Bermuda Race in 1906, British amateur sailors decided to institute their own ocean race. The first race started on the 15th of August 1925 at Ryde. It would later move to Cowes on the Isle of Wight. The course went out past Lizard Point, south-west England, and across the Irish Sea, then around Fastnet Rock and back to Plymouth. Sherman Hoyt, captained the *Nina* in 1928. He wrote the following about rounding the Fastnet:

> By 0700 a rift in the clouds let a ray of sunshine through, which showed up the white lighthouse on the rock right under our bows. We sent our name by semaphore to the keeper on the rock, and he, stout fellow, flagged back the good news that we were first round.

Keepers over the years regularly attempted to signal to the boats, usually letting them know their position.

Weather conditions varied dramatically throughout the years with some races becalmed for days and other enduring almost constant gale-force conditions. The 1979 race was however the worst race of all. Initially force 4 to 5 winds were forecast for the start on the 11th of August, later increasing to force 6 or 7. However by all accounts they were regularly force 10 and gusted to force 11. Many boats lost masts and rudders. Others were overturned. Conditions were so bad that many decided they were safer on their liferafts than on the yachts. Twenty four yachts were abandoned, five yachts sank. Fifteen men died, many of them when their lifelines broke after being thrown overboard. Three men died when they did not have the strength to climb the pilot ladder from the coaster *Nanna*.

Thirteen lifeboats, a number of British helicopters plus other aircraft, the Dutch naval warship *Overijssel*, and *HMS Angelsey* were involved in the rescue attempt[285].

Two Drownings & the Bale of Rubber

On New Year's Eve 1945 a bale of rubber was spotted near the entrance of Crookhaven Harbour. Six men set out from Crookhaven in Charlie Newman's boat: Charles Meade, John (Jackie) Flanagan, Thomas "Florrie" O'Driscoll, John "Florrie" O'Driscoll, John (Jack) Ellis and Jerry O'Mahony.

The Cork Examiner reported the incident on the 1st of January:

> The men went out in a six-oared boat with the intention of salvaging some wreckage which they had seen in the water. In a strong south-east gale and heavy seas, their boat was about a mile off the harbour when it capsized. The men clung to the upturned craft and their plight was seen by the son of the lighthouse-keeper of Rockisland lighthouse, near Crookhaven, who immediately notified Goleen Gardai.

---

[285] Dear, I., Fastnet: the story of a great ocean race, London, 1981, pp. 132-141.

The keeper's son also cycled around to Hanley's house at Castlemeighan, around three km away. From there, with a megaphone, he shouted the message across the harbour "Boat Capsized, Men Drowning". A rescue boat, Patrick "Sonny" O'Sullivan's motorised yawl, *Finín* set out with a crew. She got into difficulties with her engine cutting out – she was later towed in by the Baltimore lifeboat. Four of the men were successfully rescued on another boat and taken to Schull hospital but two drowned: Charlie Meade and Jackie Flanagan. Their bodies were later buried on one of Carbery's Isles. The remnant of their boat was washed up at nearby Spanish Cove. The bale of rubber was later retrieved from the shoreline at the south side of Crookhaven inlet at Yokane.

Dermot Griffin: Attendant 1953-88

Dermot Griffin of Boulysallagh, Goleen took up the new position of Rock Island Attendant in 1953. He was 26 years old and had previously worked on inshore fishing boats. He would cycle down from his home outside Goleen to work at the lighthouse. One of his main responsibilities was to repaint the buoys from around the coast. Initially buoys were painted with tar but when hot, this caused problems on the boat's deck so the tar was replaced with paint. Buoys were winched from the Irish Lights' ships onto the pier. The winch was hand wound by three local men and Griffin. The buoys were placed on the upper pier where they were hand scraped to remove all rust. Prior to Griffin's appointment this work was done by the keepers - in 1937 the Fastnet PK was awarded a £10 per annum allowance "to take over charge of the Crookhaven Light & Buoy Depot".

Where necessary, an Irish Lights' blacksmith would do repairs needed to the shackles. A portable forge was kept in the pier shed. Later, power was installed on the pier to allow an electric brush to remove the rust. This however was not very successful. Other buoy yards operated at Tarbert, Larne and Dun Laoighaire. It became increasingly difficult for Griffin to get local labourers once tax was deducted from their pay at source and the work was eventually transferred to the Dun Laoighaire base. The winch, previously used for lifting the buoys, was dismantled in the early 1980s.

In Griffin's early years on Rock Island the *Nabro* serviced the southwest coast lighthouses. Griffin described her as "top heavy" and slow. She would often moor north of Crookhaven village on the "Nabro" mooring. There was a large fuel container lashed to the south-end of the pier for refuelling the *Nabro*. Also on the pier was a long wooden jib which was a spare for the Fastnet. It would be used to keep men and provisions out from the rocks when being winched up onto the Fastnet.

In February 1842, a relative of his, Michael Griffin emigrated to Montreal and travelled from there down the St. Laurence into New York. Prior to leaving he wrote about the area and stated that there was a working light on Rock Island. This again casts doubt over the recorded establishment date of the 4th of August 1843.

Griffin described how each row of granite blocks used for the building the Fastnet were checked in the valley. A concrete platform was built, which still exists, and the blocks were fitted together to ensure they were correctly cut. This was the second time the lighthouse was "built"; the last time before they were taken out to the Fastnet.

He recalled how the nearest shed to no.2 was the coal shed, there was also an outside toilet and the last shed was the carbide store. He would have to "charge" the acetylene generator every four days. The sludge (used carbide) was placed in a covered hole alongside the generator house. This was then used annually for whitewashing the property. He described it as a lot brighter and more effective than the paint that replaced it. Houses 3, 4 & 5 were not painted on the seafront side. This was to improve the contrast with the exterior wall which acted as a navigational day mark. In June 1964 he was paid for 124 hours for the "annual painting" and 64 hours of whitewashing at 4/2½ per hour. In 1966 Tim Coughlan was paid for 58 trips over 29 days for conveying painters to and from Goleen and Rock Island. The houses were painted as required by Irish Lights painters while

Griffin, annually, painted the lighthouse and the exterior wall which acted as a day-mark.

Annual inspections were undertaken by the Commissioners in his time (currently only half the lighthouses are checked annually). It was the one chance the keepers and families had to ask for improvements to their houses or more often a transfer to another station. The keepers, he recalled, left "in dribs and drabs" throughout the 1950s. When the decision to sell was made, Griffin was offered house no.1 to rent. However he declined the offer.

Griffin, apart from looking after the light and the buoys, also serviced the local perches and beacons. These included the Long Island Beacon and the Alderman Perch. There used to be a basket at the top of the perch which was intended to shelter anyone shipwrecked on the Alderman Rock's. He recalled hearing of another beacon on the Alderman to the south of the present one which was destroyed in storms (most likely the one erected by Head, Ashby & Co. in 1862). The basket was removed and replaced with the present top which can be picked by radar[286].

Lighthouse Pier

In August 1860 approval was made for the following purchases:
H R Briggs   300 gallons of oil for Crookhaven   £51/5/0
H R Briggs   400 gallons of oil for Crookhaven   £68/6/8[287]
This would seem to have been the oil needed for the two lights (Crookhaven & Fastnet).

In May 1863 Isaac Notter and W. Camier submitted proposals to buy the old empty casks located at Crookhaven which probably had contained oil or water. Notter's offer of £1/4/3 was accepted. Later, in August 1866, Rev Fisher tendered for 18 barrels, presumably empty, stored at Crookhaven lighthouse

---

[286] Griffin, Dermot, conversation with, 30th October 2005.
[287] Journal No.19, Corporation for Preservation & Improving The Port of Dublin & Co., 10th August 1860.

Henry Gardiner asked for permission in July 1869 to sell the empty casks at the station. Gardiner informed the Secretary in May 1870, that 448 old barrels were put on a steamer. In July he sold a number of empty oil casks for between two shillings and two shillings six pence; he sent the Secretary a postal order for £1/2/0. A further postal order for £3/12/6 was sent for oil casks sold in late August.

Isaac Notter offered "9/4 per cut of old lead lying at Rock Island and 6/ for old water cask" in May 1872. He was told that the lead was required for works and was anyhow worth 30/ per cut. Again on the 8th December 1886, Isaac Notter offered to buy for £1 an old Gaff Spar laying for years at Rock Island which was condemned for use at the Fastnet. He also offered to buy "condemned old rope". The letter addressed to the Secretary was sent off by George Dunleavy PK. The Secretary replied that the "spare gaff is to be used to make a flagstaff to replace the one lately broken by storm"[288].

A Trinity House Buoy "Flemings Buoy" was found washed ashore at Spain Point near Baltimore. Kearon of the *SS Moya* brought it to the "New Pier, Rockisland" on the 6th of January 1905. Later it was brought to Kingstown for return to England[289].

Irish Lights received approval from the Board of Trade to purchase and erect a new five ton derrick on Rock Island in June 1907. This was needed to replace the old hand-crane "which is too small for existing requirements and is moreover worn out"[290]. Also a large amount of material was to be landed on Rock Island during the building of the Mizen Head Fog Station and according to the Engineer the new derrick "would be of great use". The crane erected was supplied by Henderson & Co. and was "similar to that ordered for Killybeg Harbour". Its total cost was £125/15/2, some £15/15/2 over the quote due to "the necessity for levelling the buoy platform behind the crane"[291].

---

[288] Irish Lights Work File 1886/1859.
[289] Irish Lights Work File 1904/1504.
[290] Irish Lights Work File 1907/510.
[291] Irish Lights Work File 1910/32.

It would appear that the immediate area was in a state of upheaval in March 1922 when J. J. Treeby, PK Fastnet, wrote that a large piece of pine was removed from the Crookhaven Lighthouse buoy yard; also 52 granite ashlars (18"x12"x6") and a pair of old magazine boots were stolen from the Crookhaven district. He asked that the skipper of the *Deirdre* not bring "the empties of Northern Stations here".

The pier was used extensively for landing material for Fastnet and Mizen Head. Fastnet AK James Hegarty was paid 1½d per mile on the 22nd of November 1937 for cycling to Crookhaven (a total return journey of 10 miles) to employ labourers for work on the pier. Most of the work was done by off-duty keepers until the 1950s. Keepers Kennedy and Byrne on the 20th of August 1938, for instance, worked three hours each "unloading 35 empty barrels, boxes and landing stores for Northern Rocks". K. N. Murphy spent two hours in November 1938 loading the *Nabro* with stores. In April 1940, James Hegarty spent four hours assisting the landing of oil for Mizen Head and Fastnet from the *Nabro*. Two days later he worked for three hours landing "powder" for Mizen Head, Fastnet & the Skelligs. Empty oil casks were stored in the "valley gardens" as two keepers took them from there and helped load them on the *Nabro* in October 1941[292].

Four local labourers were employed in December 1950 to assist the keepers to sling buoys and unload the *Granuaille* cutter. The cargo included 23 oil casks for the Skelligs, Tearaght and Fastnet. Those employed were P.J. O'Sullivan, John Driscoll, Paul Sheehan and John Goggin[293].

With the appointment of Dermot Griffin in January 1953, the off-duty Mizen and Fastnet keepers were no longer responsible for maintaining Crookhaven Light. This ultimately spelled the end of the dwellings as the keepers could now live away from the station.

---

[292] D3 Book Crookhaven 1936-55, Inspectors Dept, Commissioners of Irish Lights.
[293] D3 Book Crookhaven 1936-55, Inspectors Dept, Commissioners of Irish Lights.

On the 18th of September 1956, Griffin and J. F. Stapleton, a keeper, were paid to "hoist and store 25 drums of carbide, tonite and detonators landed by *Ierne*". The carbide was presumably for the Crookhaven lighthouse but the explosives were either for Fastnet or Mizen Head as there was no fog signal at Crookhaven. The following year Griffin worked alone on the 22 August to "sling & launch empty paraffin casks".

Tim Coughlan the "car contractor" did two trips in February 1962 from Goleen to Rock Island with chain link fencing. This was in anticipation of the sale of the houses where the pier area would need to be fenced off to prevent potential liability.

Dermot Griffin was replaced as Attendant by Bryan O'Regan in 1989. O'Regan had previously been a lightkeeper for 36 years including a number of years on Fastnet. He retired in October 1999. Stephen O'Sullivan, a former keeper and manager of Mizen Visitors Centre, was appointed Attendant in November 1999.

Painting of Buoys at Crookhaven

The first recorded mention of painting buoys on Rock Island was a request from W. Williams, the Fastnet PK, in July 1869 for instructions concerning the buoy in Crookhaven harbour[294]. His request to allow the painter at Rock Island an allowance of £1/10/0 to paint the buoy was allowed.

When Henry Stocker asked about payment owed to E. Wilson for painting a buoy, presumably the Fastnet PK's son, he was told "not to trouble office with things that do not concern him".

The Amelia Buoy at the entrance of Schull Harbour broke adrift on the 19th of August 1934. It was recovered by the *SS Isolda* which collected its replacement from Rock Island[295].

---

[294] E.J. Blake, Crookhaven did write on the 8th of July 1863 "will have Buoys painted and ready for laying out as ordered". However he does not specify the location - Lighthouse Register 1863.
[295] Irish Lights Work File 1934/613.

Rock Island

In June 1946 head office wrote to the PK at Crookhaven concerning the buoys on the pier. He was told "the following buoys were painted in January 1945 and should not require more than a wire brushing and one coat of paint: Danger, Willis, Loo, Cush, Kay and Maiden".

Among Dermot Griffin's responsibilities as Attendant was the servicing of buoys which were brought ashore by the *Ierne*. During the summer months it arrived in Crookhaven twice a week with buoys from Castletownbere to Courtmacsherry. Four men operated the manual derrick with it taking half an hour to lift a buoy. Griffin serviced Courtmacsherry, Danger, Cush, Amelia, Chapel, Horse, Gurteenroe, Loo, Willis, Walter Scott and Maidens Rock buoys.

The keepers, while off-duty, and the attendant were paid 1/10 per hour on top of their salaries in the early 1950s (in the 1930s the keepers had been paid 6½d). For instance, on the 25th of February 1957 two labourers, the attendant and a keeper were paid for 8½ hours, the standard day. Their work was described as "slinging buoys etc.". The next month, on the 13th of March, the same number were employed to "sling and launch Maidens Rock buoy". On the 9th of May, three labourers, the attendant and an assistant keeper were required to "launch 4 buoys & hoist & store 3 buoys".

Labourers at this time were paid for a minimum of 8½ hours. If they worked more than that they were paid for the actual hours. Hourly rates for labourers were as follows:

Year	Rate
1930	1/-
1954	2/5
1958	2/9½
1960	3/ ½
1962	3/7½
1963	3/8½
1964	4/2½[296]

---

[296] D3 Book Crookhaven 1956-68, Inspectors Dept, Commissioners of Irish Lights.

Blacksmiths were regularly employed at the Buoy Yard, presumably doing repairs to buoys. In September 1962 Griffin was paid for assisting the blacksmith. In September 1963 J. C. Harrington supplied two cwts (100 kgs) of coal required in the forge "to heat shackles and pins". Mary McCarthy, in June 1968, supplied two gallons of petrol required by the welder at 11/7[297].

Lighthouse Roadway & Neighbours

Mrs Hamilton was given permission by Irish Lights to put in gateways to her land off the lighthouse roadway allowing "for the passage of her cattle" in June 1887. This agreement allowed however for the passageways to be closed at any time. As a result of this clause Mrs Hamilton decided not to sign the document[298].

Repairs to the lighthouse road costing £18 were paid to M. Hanley in 1909. Fifty per cent of the cost was charged to Crookhaven and fifty per cent to the Mizen Head works.

Mr. Donovan who had come into possession of part of Rock Island requested that Irish Lights put a gateway into his land off the lighthouse entrance road "to enable him to take a cart on and off his property" in 1913[299].

In December 1925 Mrs Elizabeth [Lizzie] O'Donoghue of Rock Island wrote requesting permission to pull down a short section of Irish Lights' wall to allow her to build a new house with the gable end on the same line as the wall. She also asked to put a new gateway in the wall[300]. She indicated that the new house would be to the north of the "existing house". The Fastnet PK James Johnson wrote in response to this request "Mrs O'Donoghue's husband being an ex RIC Head Constable in receipt of a substantial pension she can in my

---

[297] D3 Book Crookhaven 1962-69, Inspectors Dept, Commissioners of Irish Lights.
[298] Journal No.35, Commissioners of Irish Lights, p. 59 & 70.
[299] Journal No.46, Commissioners of Irish Lights, 4th April 1913.
[300] Journal No.5, Commissioners of Irish Lights, 11th December 1925.

opinion be relied upon to make good any alteration to Lighthouse property".

The Commissioners agreed to her request provided that the water from the roof was not discharged onto the road. For this agreement Mrs O'Donoghue paid £2/3/0 in legal cost to Irish Lights. It appears that at the same time Mrs O'Donoghue was trying to buy the field on the other side of the road from T. Donovan with the intention of building her house there. As a result she wrote on the 22nd Of April 1926 to Irish Lights asking them "to retain the correspondence for the present". She however later wrote that "negotiations in this matter, of the field, have fallen through".

By October 1926, Johnson PK was writing to head office to say that work was progressing on the new house and that the walls of this house were now up about "10 to 11 feet all around"[301]. The old house and post office were later pulled down.

In 1928 the need to widen the road and repair the roadway's boundary wall was addressed. C. W. Scott wrote in June:

> Fastnet PK reported that a portion of the wall at the side of the road was cracked and leaning inward and dangerous to cars passing it; also the hairpin bend at the top of the hill above the entrance gate into Crookhaven Light House grounds is so sharp and narrow that motor cars cannot get round it with safety…and there is another bad corner, just above the old post office which ought to be widened sufficiently to enable two cars to pass at this point…the owner of the land, Mrs O'Donoghue, is very anxious to have these alterations carried out…she will make no charge for the encroachments on her land.

Her husband, Richard, had in fact written to the Commissioners in April 1928 to say that the land had been "purchased under the Land Act of 1923". He stated that his wife was the owner and she had no objection to transfer of a small portion for road widening. To support the request to have the road widened, the Fastnet PK,

---

[301] Irish Lights Work File 1926/285.

Andrew Kilgallon, wrote that it "would be invaluable to the keepers especially as the butcher and others could then supply them". Also he stated that the doctor was unable to drive his motor car to the station[302]. As a result of this it appears a local contractor J. Coughlan was awarded the contract for £50 to widen the road and repair the wall[303].

Irish Lights paid for the county council to re-surface the road in 1954. This appears to have cost over £288. Eight years later Dermot Griffin wrote to Irish Lights "the road at present is getting into a bad state, there is a lot of potholes".

Two agreements were entered into, in 1949 and 1957, with Elizabeth Donoghue and George Lannin (her son-in-law) respectively to acquire five small portions of land adjoining the roadway. These were needed for road widening[304].

In the early 1960s Dermot Griffin was being paid a week's wages of 44 hours for maintaining the roadway i.e. cleaning the drains, filling the potholes and cutting the weeds. In July 1963 Cork County Council Engineer Buckley wrote that if the entire road was brought up to standard he "would recommend that it be taken over by the county council for maintenance".

The following year George Lannin asked for the sign above his house to be removed. It stated "Stop, Private Road, No Turning Beyond This Point". He said that Dermot Griffin was involved in putting it up while Irish Lights denied authorising it. Again in 1965 he wrote stating "In the past few years I have laid out a considerable amount of money in establishing fruit garden, apiary & vegetable garden and I sell soft fruits to many holiday makers & tourists who encamped nearby. Notice…would ruin my business".

During that summer of 1965, the Depot Manager F. M. Fitzgibbon went to visit Mr. Lannin. However he went to the lighthouse first and met Mrs Craig-White and Mrs Samuelson who followed him back to Lannin's home. Mr Fitzgibbon wrote that "Mr. Lannin was

---

[302] Irish Lights Work File 1928/267.
[303] Journal No.20, Commissioners of Irish Lights, 22nd June 1926.
[304] Irish Lights Work File 1959/146.

not very co-operative". Lannin wrote to Irish Lights about the meeting "I presume it is the dictates of these two ladies (especially the former [Mrs Craig-White]) you are endeavouring to implement, and that you are really concerned with the traffic on the road". It appears that Mrs Craig-White, in particular, was unhappy with traffic using her carpark to turn.

On the 2nd of June 1966 Irish Lights put up a sign on the entrance to the roadway. It stated "Commissioners of Irish Lights, Private Road (Cul-de-sac) leading to Mr Lannin's farm and Rock Island, No Turning Possible on Road". The sign had been taken down by the 6th. In August Irish Lights asked the County Council to erect a "Cul-de-sac" sign. This was done on the 2nd of March 1967 at a cost of £8/10/0 to Irish Lights. By the 3rd of March the sign was gone. In July 1967, Schull Garda station was writing to Irish Lights that "six previous times this [sign] has been removed, the locals are annoyed". Even signs riveted to the wall were taken down[305].

Sale of the majority of the property

The A.T.G.W.U. (the lightkeepers' union) in December 1958 requested that the dwellings at Rock Island be abandoned due to their "comparatively isolated position" and 22 miles distance from the "nearest railhead at Skibbereen". The following year the intended painting of the station was postponed due to its uncertain future. Writing to the Ministry of Transport in London in November 1960, Irish Lights stated that the keepers "dislike living at these Dwellings and in actual fact the majority of them do not do so, preferring to live elsewhere and to pay for their own housing & travelling expenses". The Inspector wrote in September 1960 "the keepers will not bring their families to live at the dwellings, and as long as conditions exist I am sure there will be discontent". It was estimated that it would cost £4,500 to install bathroom and running water and a further £1,125 to install electricity and cookers. "Even if these

---

[305] Irish Lights Work File 1959/146.

improvements were carried out, the Commissioners consider that there would still be requests from the lighthouse keepers for the abandonment of the Dwellings". It was proposed that by abandoning the dwellings and carrying out the Fastnet reliefs from Castletownbere, where the tender was based, they could save £685. This estimate was based on the following:

Vegetable trips from Crookhaven [Rock Island] to Skibbereen	
One each month at 25/	£15/0/0
Meat trip from Crookhaven to Schull	
say two each month at 22/	£26/8/0
Market trip from Crookhaven to Goleen	
one each week at 10/6	£27/6/0
Rental of telephone and official calls	£15/0/0
Medical Attendance	
Dr. O'Mahony – reduction (£100 - £75)	£25/0/0
Also 6 tons of coal per keeper per annum at £15/8/6 – eight keepers	

As a result the decision to abandon the dwellings was approved.

Irish Lights notified T. Coughlan of Goleen on the 30th of March 1961 that his contract for conveying fresh meat from Schull to Rock Island was terminated. This was due to Fastnet and Mizen Head being converted to non-dwelling stations and the keepers no longer residing at Rock Island. He was however told that he would be invited to submit a quotation for "supplying a car from Goleen to Mizen Head on relief days". He was told a week later that his contracts for supplying a horse and cart from Rock Island to Mizen Head on relief days and the monthly cart trip to Skibbereen to allow the keeper's families to shop were terminated as the dwellings were abandoned.

The Board approved the sale of eight of the dwellings on the 23rd of June 1961 by "Public Auction". The Engineer, in consultation with the Law Agents, decided that the most appropriate method of sale was in one lot[306]. On the 11th of May 1962 the Irish Lights Secretary

---

[306] Irish Lights Work File 1959/146.

submitted a draft advertisement indicating that eight houses were for sale on Rock Island[307]. The same month the property was advertised in the Irish Times, Irish Independent, Irish Press, the Cork Examiner and the Southern Star. The houses for sale were described as follows:

> No.2 with store, chemical closet (with drain to cliff), water tank [later removed]; No.3 porch, hall, livingroom, kitchen (with range), scullery with sink, larder, three bedrooms upstairs, outside coal shed, chemical closet, water tank; No.4 porch, kitchen (with range), scullery (with sink), larder, two bedrooms, outside chemical closet (with drain to cliff), coal store, water tank; No.5 same as no.4 but has Truburn cooker; No. 6 three bedrooms and box room, kitchen (with Truburn cooker), scullery, livingroom, chemical closet (with drain to closet), outside coalhouse; No.7 same as no.6 but with outside store & office; No.8 hall, kitchen (with range), large scullery (with sink), outside store, coal store, chemical closet (with drain to cliff), water tank; No.9 hall, kitchen (with Truburn cooker), livingroom, scullery, no outside store.

Approval from the British Ministry of Transport was also required for the sale and was received in July 1962. Eight of the nine dwellings, and the majority of the site, were sold in April 1963 to retired Colonel John Samuelson of Cloghran, Co. Dublin, and Mrs. Rhona Craig-White of Cahir, Co. Tipperary for £4,100. Although the sale was completed in 1963 it appears that they took possession of the property in 1962. Maxwell Weldon, the solicitors for the sale, charged Irish Lights £113/18/0. A further £110 was paid by Col. Samuelson for "goods and chattels" – ranges, furniture, coal etc. The other bidders were Mary Boland of Corrymeela, Skibbereen who bid £4,023; Alan Best of London (who bought the old Crookhaven Coast Guard station in 1963) £3,100; and W. H. Coombs of Norfolk who bid £1,000[308]. Samuelson's bid was "submitted by me on behalf

---

[307] Journal No.61, Commissioners of Irish Lights Board Minute Book 1962-64.
[308] In November 1960, Aqua-Marine Sports Ltd. of Harrogate, England wrote to Irish Lights indicating their wish to buy the property to be used as a "water-

of some relatives and friends, all British subjects resident in Ireland who would like to have the facilities at Rock Island as holiday homes for our families…this is NOT a commercial enterprise". Desmond Martin, Irish Lights' Engineer-in-Chief thought the £4,100 was "very satisfactory" as "none has either running water nor electricity". Also the £512/10/0 per house compared favourably with £300 per house sold at Blackrock in 1956; £250 per house at Eagle Island in 1957; and £550 at Rathlin O'Birne. The ninth house (no.1) was retained by Irish Lights in case they required an attendant to live on site as the "lighthouse might be interfered with by children or adults".

When the new owners took ownership, No.2 had a Rayburn solid fuel stove with a back-boiler, and a hand pump was used to pump water for the house from the rain water tank beside the sheds. Initially the Craig-Whites used No.2 and the Samuelsons No.3. Oil lamps provided lighting until electricity was installed in 1964. All the houses, apart from No.s 6 & 7, had similar water supplies to No.2 at this time – semi-rotary pumps above the sinks pumped the water from water tanks. No.s 6 & 7 had a gravity water feed from water tanks above the entrance ways.

Stores for Mizen Fog station were sent to Rock Island by ship and taken by truck to Mizen Head at the time of the property's sale[309].

The Craig-Whites bought out the Samuelsons in 1968-69 for the full original purchase price. In April 1969 Mrs Craig-White asked if she could buy the old crane cable to make a new "trot" for her boat around the quay. It was sold to her for £1. She also informed the Commissioners that she had "nine men on the go at the moment". They renovated the houses for holiday rental with Barrys of Skibbereen employed as contractors. The garden area to the east of house No.2, on the sea-front, was filled in and made into a patio area. They installed five 1,000 gallon water tanks above the office attached to No.7 in the late 1960s. Also they had drilled a bore hole on George Lannin's land and put in a pump to supply the property.

---

sports centre" for "water-skiing and skin-diving and underwater exploration" - Irish Lights Work File 1959/146.
[309] Craig-White, Richard, conversation with, 24th September 2002.

Rock Island

However it never produced much water. In August 1967, Mr. Lannin was complaining that the wall beside the well had not been rebuilt even though the work had been done in November 1962.

On the 1st of June 1969 Mr's Craig-White advertised in the Sunday Times "Fastnet Rock to let from Aug. 1, 4 lighthouse cottages (one eight beds, three six beds)"[310]. Craig-White used No.3 themselves when not rented out. She added a double garage attached to No.6 in the 1970s.

In May 1969 P.G. Adams, Irish Lights Secretary informed Major Craig-White that Craig-White's 6.5 m boat would be transported from Cork to Rock Island on board either the *S.S.. Ierne* or the *M.V. Atlanta*. The Craig-Whites also rented the old magazine store for £5 per annum from Irish Lights from September 1970 to September 1972.

The lighthouse with houses no. 2, 3, 4 & 5

In the mid-1990s the property was sold to Geoffrey & Elspeth Kirkland of California, USA, formerly of Oxfordshire, England. A local builder, Vincent Coughlan of Ballydehob, undertook some repairs. Alison Ducker (now O'Sullivan), sculptor, rented house No.2 for two years from the Kirklands. In 1999 the author and his wife,

---

[310] Irish Lights Work File 1959/146.

Crookhaven Lighthouse

Angelique Muller, rented house No.2. They also undertook renovations on houses No.6 & 7. These were rented out to holiday makers from August 2000. On the 7th of August 2002 a new underwater water pipe connecting to the Crookhaven mains supply was turned on providing a regular supply to the property for the first time. House No.4 had to be gutted as a result of dry rot and woodworm which partially affected house No.3. A new kitchen was built replacing the old long and narrow kitchen and exterior rain water tank. Oil central heating was also installed into the two houses. This was completed in July 2004. At the time of writing the Kirklands have the property for sale on the market – total price €3.24 million.

The remaining dwelling retained by Irish Lights (No. 1) was sold in 1998 to Feichin & Margaret McDonagh of Dublin and her two brothers, Kieran and Donnach O'Driscoll, residents of London and Manchester respectively. Considerable improvements were undertaken by them between 1998 and 2000. These included a second storey, electricity, telephone and water supply.

Fastnet Rock Lighthouse

Rock Island

Crookhaven Light Specifications

Latitude:	51° 28.6' N
Longitude:	09° 42.2' W
Optic System:	Fixed cylindrical lens 500mm diameter
Electric Light:	Four 12 volt 35 watt tungsten halogen lamps
Character:	Flashing White/Red every 8 seconds
	2.0 + 6.0 = 8.0 sec
Sectors:	White: over Long Island bay to 281°
	Red: 281° - 340° (59°) outside harbour
	Red: 281° - 348° (67°) inside harbour
	White: 348° towards north shore
Intensity:	White: 5800 cd.
	Red: 1500 cd
Range:	White: 21 kilometres
	Red: 16 kilometres
Height above water:	20 metres
Tower:	White, 14 metres high

CROOKHAVEN COAST GUARD

In 1709, there were two revenue officers based in Crookhaven. They were John Lee, the Surveyor and William Cook, the Tidewaiter[1]. The Surveyor was essentially the customs officer in charge. It was his job to collect the taxes due from shipping entering the port, supervise the tidewaiters and ensure there were no goods been smuggled into the port. The Tidewaiter role was to watch out for vessels, board them and inspect for contraband. They were so named because they waited to board ships coming in 'on the tide'. The revenue officers were very unpopular as smuggling was endemic on the West Cork coast. All strata of local society were involved in smuggling in this 18th century lawless place. Pococke commented

> a Custom house officer can hardly live amongst them. The surveyors are soon weary & desire to be remov'd, & in all these parts hereabouts to the west of Kingsale, they have a term of hiding an officer, which is knocking in the head and putting him under a turf. There have been many instances of Officers never heard of[2].

It is not known where in Crookhaven harbour they were stationed. However the 1848 British Admiralty Chart has a boathouse located one km east of Crookhaven village on the south side of the harbour where Pick's holiday house is presently located. Possibly this was the location of the early customs office.

The next mention of revenue officers is in 1750 when Charles Smith stated that the following officers resided in the Skibbereen district:

A Surveyor at Crookhaven	£40
Four boatmen at Baltimore and four at Crookhaven	£15 each

---

[1] Customs men did not receive a salary but a fee based on collections. Until the 19th Century "the appointees, even the boatmen, were overwhelmingly Protestant and almost entirely recruited from within the region" - Dickson, Old World Colony, 107.

[2] McVeagh, J., ed., Richard Pococke's Irish Tours, Dublin, 1995.

Again however it is not apparent where these men were stationed for the Crookhaven area. He referred to the area as follows

> More westerly, in a peninsula [from Ballydevlin], formerly called the Aldern Head[3], stands Crookhaven, once a place of some note, but now a small inconsiderable fishing town, near an excellent harbour, and one of the best outlets in Europe for vessels to sail to any place whatsoever

In 1816, the Admiralty set up a special service, the Coast Blockade to prevent smuggling throughout the British and Irish coasts. The local revenue officer that year was Robert O'Neill. He reported Daniel Coghlan of Crookhaven to "the castle for attempting to murder him because he had prevented him from smuggling"[4].

On the 4th of February 1816 the Coast Guard commenced their lease on Rock Island. They leased five acres and one rood (2.13 hectares) from Richard Notter for 998 years. The annual rent was £59/3/10 paid half-yearly on the 25th of March and the 29th of September[5]. It is not clear who was responsible for building the dwellings but the amount of the rent suggests Notter may have borne the cost. There were nine houses built: an officer's house of seven rooms; one cottage of five rooms for the chief boatman; and seven cottages of four rooms each. Each house had an out house and "privy accommodation". There was also a watch-house which had two rooms above for one man. This station was known as Crookhaven Coast Guard Station.

According to the *Southern Reporter*, the Revenue Department on Rock Island was guarded night and day in 1822 as a result of Whiteboy violence[6]. In that year the Coast Guard service came into operation.

---

[3] Aldern Head is now known as Streak Head. The name Aldern can be presumed to have given us the Alderman Rocks as there is no history of Aldermen in the area.

[4] Hickey, Famine in West Cork, 36.

[5] The annual rent in 1901 had only increased to £64/2/6.

[6] Hickey, Famine in West Cork, 39.

In 1831 the Coast Blockade was abolished with its members absorbed into the Coast Guard. The Admiralty decided that year that the Coast Guard would become a reserve of the Royal Navy. All men nominated would be controlled by the Admiralty with ranks equal to those in the navy. Regulations stated "vacant positions of Boatmen [in the Coast Guard] will be filled up, from time to time by Seamen, as Ships of War are paid off". Such seamen could not be older than 30 when appointed to the Coast Guard and had to be at least 5 foot 6 inches high (168 cm)[7].

Each station was in the charge of a Chief Officer who was normally a Royal Navy Lieutenant. Beneath him there was a Chief Boatman, Commissioned Boatmen and Boatmen. Men were moved away from their home area for fear of collusion with smugglers which resulted in a mainly English force in Ireland and many Irish working on the English coast.

In 1834 there was a Chief Officer and five men in Crookhaven. As a result of the "decrease of the contraband trade in the Western Coast" the number of staff employed in the Coast Guard was decreased in 1842. In some places Chief Officers were replaced by Chief Boatmen. In the same year, there were no rewards paid to the Coast Guard in the Skibbereen District which included Crookhaven, for the detention of smugglers[8]. The distribution of "seizure-rewards" was on the following basis: Chief Officer - 25 shares; Chief Boatman - 10 shares; Riding Officer (District Officer) 10 - shares; Commissioned Boatmen - 6 shares; Boatmen - 6 shares.

The Coast Guard in Crookhaven were dealing with a busy port during the days of sail due to the excellent shelter provided in the harbour. It was also the last port for provisioning before crossing the Atlantic and had a telegraph connection to Cork and onwards from 1863. On the 29th of November 1846, for instance, the following ships put in:

---

[7] Webb, W., The Coast Guard, 1976.
[8] Customs Ireland: Salaries & Incidents At Outposts, 1842, National Archives, London, CUST38/18.

> *John St. Barbe* of London; *Davis* from Limerick to London with oats; *Alfred and James* of Milford; *Evans* from Kilrush to Glasgow, oats; *Portia* of Glasgow; *M'Lea* from Tarbert to Glasgow, do; *Wilfrid* of Workington; *Boyd* from Tralee to Liverpool, oats two days out; *Magnes* of London; *Douglas* from Galway to Troon, ballast, three days out; *Thetis* of Cardigan; *Davis* from Llanelly, bound to Tralee[9].

In September 1848, contradicting the apparent significance of the port, the Commissioners of Customs offered their houses for sale to the Ballast Board. It is not known whether they considered removing the Coast Guard fully from Crookhaven or relocating to a nearby site. The Ballast Board had George Halpin inspect them as a potential base for Fastnet keepers. However they decided that it was "too large". Halpin described the premises as having "twelve houses of two stories each and a store and office" with four of the houses "set to tenants at will"[10].

The end of the Crimean War saw control of the Coast Guard service transferred to the Admiralty in 1856. Crookhaven was thus overseen by the Admiral of Queenstown (Cobh). As a result of this, the Coast Guard flag was replaced by the navy flag at all stations. Smuggling was now under control with the lifesaving and naval reserve aspects taking increased priority. In that year men wishing to join the Coast Guard had to have served in the navy for seven years, rather than the previous ten years.

The station seems to have been subject to tithes in the 19th century. The Rev. William Fisher of Kilmoe parish submitted a bill for £1/3/10 in 1865 for tithes payable on the Coast Guard buildings[11]. The Admiralty was informed by D. Godley of the Irish Church

---

[9] Cork Examiner, 4th of December 1846.
[10] Journal No.12, Corporation for Preservation & Improving The Port of Dublin & Co., p. 71.
[11] Coast Guard Correspondence 1865, National Archives, Dublin, OPW5/8/1.

Commission in 1872 that it would cost £17/6/3 to buy out the "tithe rent charge". In September that amount was paid.

Royal Navy supply ships were used to transport families and possessions to stations. It can be expected that the Rock Island pier north-east of the lobster ponds (see chapter VII) was used for loading and unloading as there was previously a road running from there across the townland's spine to the station. The houses were furnished to a certain extent. They were supplied with "one iron double bed, a half tester [type of bed], two small bedroom tables, one six-foot kitchen table, six Windsor chairs, one dresser built into the wall of the kitchen, and three sets of fenders and fire-irons, and a coal box"[12].

The Coast Guard and the Famine

In 1845 the Inspector-General of the Coast Guard in Ireland was appointed to the temporary famine Relief Commission[13]. The Coast Guard agreed to assist with regard to relief when they "can be done without interfering with the duties of the service". It was obvious that saving lives was not their first responsibility. They even attempted to get paid for the assistance they provided which was however denied[14].

---

[12] www.coastguardsofyesteryear.org.

[13] "The temporary Relief Commission was established in November 1845 in response to the failure of the potato crop, to administer temporary relief...The members of the first commission represented the various government departments in Ireland which were expected to coordinate relief, such as the Irish Constabulary (police), the Coast Guard, Poor Law Commission, the Army, Board of Works and the Chief Secretary's Office in Dublin Castle. The remit of the Relief Commission was to advise the government as to the extent of potato loss and distress within Ireland, to oversee the storage and distribution of Indian corn and meal and to direct, support and coordinate the activities of local relief committees." - www.nationalarchives.ie

[14] Coastguard Minute Book January 1844 – March 1849, National Archives, London, CUST29/42, p.268.

Rock Island

In 1846 Henry Baldwin[15], Rock Island Chief Officer, took government officials around in a Coast Guard boat with Alexander O'Driscoll, a "local middleman" to show the effect of the potato famine in the area. O'Driscoll asked the government to supply meal by steamer and have it distributed by the Coast Guards[16]. The following year in February 1847, according to Captain Thomas, "bread-stuffs" were sent by the British Relief Association on board the *H.M.S. Rhadamanthus* to the Rock Island Coast Guard station but Baldwin was not allowed to distribute them. A few bags of flour were sent to Goleen[17]. Later that same month, some 500 labourers from the local famine relief road works, carrying their shovels, went to Baldwin to demand food. The *H.M.S. Protheroe* had just arrived in the harbour with 109 tons of bread-stuffs donated by the British Relief Association. The captain of the ship was ordered by Captain Harston of the British Relief Association to leave for Schull. The local men attempted to prevent the ship's departure with the port pilot refusing to take the ship out of the harbour for fear of the crowd. Eventually it was towed to Schull by another government steamer where it discharged 364 sacks of food. According to Alexander O'Driscoll at the time 25 people a day were dying[18].

Responsibilities of the Coast Guard

The duties of the Coast Guard included
- Preventing smuggling - in November 1856 Lieut. T. Hungerford, the District Officer, wrote from Castletownsend "as the winter season draws on and it is also appearing that

---

[15] Baldwin, while probably stationed on Long Island, had saved a man from drowning when the Lady Charlotte was wrecked on the 23rd of October 1838 on Dromadda Rocks at the west entrance of Long Island Channel. The Coast Guard also recovered $36,000 of silver plate from the sea bed - Bourke, E.J., Shipwrecks of the Irish Coast 1105-1993, Dublin, 1994, p. 138.
[16] Hickey, Famine in West Cork, 127.
[17] Hickey, Famine in West Cork, 179.
[18] Hickey, Famine in West Cork, 188.

smuggling transactions are taking place upon the coast I have to desire that the utmost vigilance may be observed at the several stations and on board the *Bantry*"[19].

- Where goods are suspected of coming from wrecks there were to be seized by "an Officer of Customs Excise or Constabulary Force or Peace Officer"[20].
- In 1844 the Coast Guard agreed to assist the Revenue Police[21] in "the suppression of illicit practices". This primarily meant destroying poteen stills, an activity which made them very unpopular. They were to police the shore line and to carry Revenue Police to offshore islands where required[22].
- Submit reports on the daily wind direction[23].
- Assist the police, when called upon, in the "arrest of a felon"[24].
- In 1852 they were given instructions to capture any Russian vessels in their area[25].
- All movements of "foreign ships of war" were to be reported to the Admiralty. In 1855 all foreign vessels were to be reported to the Collectors and Comptrollers of Ports.
- Register all fishing vessels. In July 1852, Lieut. Hungerford in Castletownsend wrote "measures are to be taken at the several stations to enforce the marking and numbering all Boats agreeably to the Act of Parliament there being no

---

[19] Irish Coast Guard Order Book 1852-60, National Maritime Museum, London, MS85/106.
[20] Irish Coast Guard Order Book 1852-60.
[21] The Revenue Police were "a purely Irish body under the control of the Board of Excise" – Bowen, F., Her Majesty's Coastguard, London, 1928, p. 65.
[22] Coastguard Minute Book January 1844 – March 1849, National Archives, London, CUST29/42, p.47.
[23] Coast Guard and Customs Register, 1907, National Archives, Dublin, OPW5/8/25.
[24] Coast Guard Records, National Archives, London, ADM120/10.
[25] Irish Coast Guard Order Book 1852-60.

- excuse after the repeated warnings the people have had for not having their Boats properly marked"[26].
- Collection of local fishing statistics, as a result of the establishment of the Congested Districts Board to assist the impoverished western counties, including Cork. The Coast Guard also had some discretion to grant fishing boats to "poor peasants"[27].
- On the 15th day of the last month of each quarter, officers were required to send "an account of all stores on hand together with the expenditure of the qtr and a list of stores required"
- Collect air and sea temperatures for the Met. Office.
- Assist the Royal Navy with recruitment.
- Issue certificates of health to vessels or detain them where they may be suspected of infection.
- Protect all shipping property from plunder. They reported on all wrecks in their locality. They were to protect the foreshore below high water mark from the removal of materials.

Pay & Conditions

James Bransted, the Acting Tidewaiter at Crookhaven was paid £1/2/6 in 1820 for having travelled 60 miles to Castletownsend and back. James Lynch was later paid the same amount. When moving from Knockadoon to Crookhaven in 1827, a distance of 115 miles, William Shea was paid 3d per Irish mile.

---

[26] Irish Coast Guard Order Book 1852-60.
[27] Bowen, Her Majesty's Coastguard, 237.

Pay Rates set in 1831 were slightly lower in Ireland than in England and Scotland. Chief boatmen received a salary of £9/4/8 and 2/9 per day served, while boatmen received £4/12/4 and 2/9 per day[28]. Pay rates had only marginally increased in 1834. A chief officer was paid £13/17/0 per annum and 3/8 per day served; a chief boatman was paid £9/4/8 and 2/9¼ per day; a boatman received £4/12/4 and 2/9¼ per day[29].

Drawing of Coast Guard Station & Look-out Tower, J.H. Brocas, 26th of July 1837

In 1842 it was agreed that Royal Navy Lieutenants employed as Coast Guard Chief Officers were to be paid the same as when they were in commission in the Navy. This increased their pay by £18 per annum[30]. The Crookhaven Chief Officer in 1842, Richard Hungerford, received £6/15/0 pay per quarter. On top of this he

---

[28] Webb, W., The Coast Guard.
[29] Coast Guards (Ireland) Parliamentary Papers 1834, National Archives, London, 37.296.
[30] Coastguard Minute Book August 1838 – December 1843, National Archives, London, CUST29/41.

was paid four shillings per day as a "sitter" (possibly refers to days actually worked). In the June quarter he was paid for 42 days. He also received £1/15/0 fuel allowance per quarter. The Chief Boatman, John Cooper received a quarterly salary of £2/6/2. He also received a further £12/14/10 for 92 days as a "sitter". Boatmen were paid £1/3/1 and the same amount per day as the Chief Boatman.

In 1854 boatmen were allowed seven days annual leave without "loss of pay". Leave was to be taken between the 1st May and the 30th of August. The maximum accumulated leave was 28 days.

An instruction was issued in September 1855 "on no account shall they wear mustache (*sic*) or beard except under the chin"[31].

In 1856 the Admiralty set out the Coast Guard's pay relative to the navy. Boatmen were to receive the pay of an Able Bodied Seaman on "continuous service". Commissioned boatmen were paid the same as Leading Seamen, and Chief Boatmen the same as First Class Petty Officers. They also, at this time, received 1/4 per day "in lieu of provisions".

Housing was provided free of charge. Their annual pay in 1856[32] was:

	Pay	Provisions Allowance	Total
Boatman	£28/17/11	£24/6/8	£53/4/7
Commissioned Boatman	£31/18/9	£24/6/8	£56/5/5
Chief Boatman	£36/10/0	£24/6/8	£60/16/8

In 1906, Chief Officers had to retire at 55 with other ranks required to retire at 50.

Griffith's Valuation

The valuation on Rock Island was conducted between the 28th of April 1852 and the 16th August 1852. These dates can be ascertained due to the presence of certain Coast Guards.

---

[31] Irish Coast Guard Order Book 1852-60.
[32] Coast Guard Letters 1856, National Archives, London, ADM114/11.

Crookhaven Lighthouse

The following Coast Guards and values were recorded for the coastguard:

Occupier	Details	Land	Buildings	Total Annual Valuation
Charles Evans	House & Gardens	0/5/0	2/0/0	2/5/0
Samuel Appeldore	House & Gardens	0/5/0	2/0/0	2/5/0
Robert Duckett	House & Gardens	0/5/0	2/0/0	2/5/0
John Hill	House & Gardens	0/5/0	3/0/0	3/5/0
Stephen Goodfellow	House & Gardens	0/5/0	3/0/0	3/5/0
John Webb	House & Gardens	0/10/0	8/10/0	9/0/0
James Mahony	House & Gardens	0/5/0	2/0/0	2/5/0
Richard Barry	House & Gardens	0/5/0	2/0/0	2/5/0

Webb was Chief Officer and therefore in the most valuable house. He died, while still stationed at Rock Island, on the 7th of February 1857 aged 57. He is buried beside St. Brendan's Church, Crookhaven. Hill and Duckett were Commissioned Boatmen and Goodfellow was the Chief Boatman.

The boat house and watch house were regarded as exempt for valuation purposes.

Catherine Goodfellow's Drowning

The following story appeared in the Cork Constitution in 1858:

> Crookhaven. A lamentable accident took place yesterday (Sunday) afternoon about 7 o'clock at Rock Island. Mrs. Goodfellow, wife of the Chief Boatman of the Coastguard station here, left her home, as is supposed, for a short walk, and when tea was ready, she not having returned as expected, search was made, and she was discovered by her husband drowned near the Government quay. Mrs. Goodfellow had not left her house above half an hour when she was found. No one can tell how the sad accident happened. It is remarkable that three persons were drowned near the spot where

Rock Island

> Mrs. Goodfellow's body was taken up, and each event took place on a Sunday[33].

Catherine Goodfellow, born in Schull in 1822, was the wife of Stephen Goodfellow. The Government quay is presumably the one located at the Lobster Ponds on the north side of Rock Island.
Of the other three drownings referred to, one was Alexander Notter in Sunday the 10th of July 1825 aged six. Another one was probably William Thomas Brock who died on Sunday the 27th of August 1848 aged two years. His father was William Brock, Coast Guard Boatman stationed at Crookhaven from 1845 to 1849[34].

Communications

In November 1910 the Admiralty reported that it had received two tenders for "wireless telegraphy". This may have been the equipment necessary to communicate between Brow Head Signal Station and Fastnet. The telegraph address in 1915 for the Rock Island Station was Brow Head which indicates that it probably did not have its own line at this stage.
Later, in 1920, the Post Office was offering to connect the lighthouse on Rock Island to the telephone exchange through the Coast Guard station. As Irish Lights refused the offer, off-duty Coast Guard men were paid 6d to take messages to the lighthouse.[35] By the time of evacuation the line was destroyed, presumably by the I.R.A.

The District Office

James Dombrain, Comptroller General of the Irish Preventative Water Guard, stated that he had established 160 stations with 1,821

---

[33] www.coastguardsofyesteryear.com.
[34] Brock lost another child while stationed on Rock Island: Anna Lavinia who died on the 2nd of September 1845 aged seven months. Both children are buried in St. Brendan's graveyard, Crookhaven.
[35] Irish Lights Work File 1929/583.

men, plus 200 casual boatmen during the winter, around the coast by 1824.

In 1826, the local Inspecting Officer, McNamara, was receiving a quarterly horse allowance of £15 and also a second horse allowance of £7/10/0. He also received a mooring duty allowance of £35 per quarter and a stationery allowance. He appears to have been replaced by James Lister. Lister was responsible in 1827 for (in brackets are the number of men) Crookhaven (9), Long Island (14), Kilcrohane (7), Dunmanus (7), White Horse (8), Barlough (6), Garnish (12), Blackball Head (7), Kilmichealogue (8), Adrigole (6), Baltimore (6), Milk Cove (7), Glandore (12), Castletownsend (9), Castletownbere (7). The stations in the Skibbereen District in 1834 were Castletownsend, Barlogue, Long Island, Whitehorse, Baltimore, Glandore, Dunmanus, Millcove and Crookhaven. In the Castletownbere District there were three stations: Castletownbere, Collaris and Garnish Island. In 1841 the stations within the Skibbereen division were Castletownsend, Garnish Island, Barlogue, Long Island, Whitehorse, Baltimore, Glandore, Dunmanus, Millcove, Collaris, Castletownbere and Crookhaven. These stations were under Captain Le Hardy.

The Divisional Officer, Castletownsend in 1847 was T. Hungerford. He was 44 years old and had been in the service for 20 years. His annual salary was £100 and he also received an allowance of £44. He demanded that "everything may be kept in the most perfect order and that the crews must meet [in Castletownsend] for General Exercise" on the 12th of April 1852. He requested the "men of the District" to assemble on the 24th of May to celebrate the Queen's birthday as they had failed to assemble on the 13th because the weather "was too inclement". The flags at Coast Guard stations were flown at half mast from the 8th to the 18th of October 1853 due to the death of the Comptroller General Captain Alexander Ellis. The Deputy Comptroller General expressed "great satisfaction" to

Hungerford "at the state of discipline and good order in which he found the district"[36].

In 1859 Hungerford instructed the men to assemble in Castletownsend at 11.00 a.m. on the 19th of May "each man with 12 rounds of ammunition" to celebrate the Queen's birthday.

The Rocket Apparatus & Life-Saving

The *Eliza Libby* of St. Andrews with a registered weight of 1,000 tons and a cargo of timber was dismasted on the 6th of October 1846 and went into Dunmanus Bay for shelter. Here she took in water and the men evacuated onto the barque *Mary Fisher* on the 13th. On the 19th she was boarded by four Crookhaven men, John, Dick and John Driscoll and Charles Meade. Later Henry Baldwin of the Coast Guard and his men took her up to "Four-mile water" and safely moored her there.[37]

Every Coast Guard station was supplied with life saving equipment. One of the most innovative was the Rocket Apparatus which was described as follows:

> The entire apparatus is stowed in a light cart supplied for the purpose, so that it can be run over rough ground where horse traction is unavailable. The main object, in aiming the rocket, which carries a very light line made of coconut fibre, is to ensure it passing just above and slightly to windward the wreck, so that the line may fall across it. The men on board instantly seize the line and haul off the block of an endless whip, which they make fast as high as they conveniently can; and, as soon as this is done, the people on shore, by means of the whip, haul off a hawser [thick rope], the end of which is also made fast on board, just above the whip-block. That done, the people on shore, haul off the "travelling life-buoy", or as it is usually called, the "breeches buoy", into which one of the shipwrecked crew places himself, and is

---

[36] Irish Coast Guard Order Book 1852-60.
[37] This report came from Alexander O'Driscoll of Crookhaven - http://freepages.geanealogy.rootsweb.com/~colin/DriscollofCork/Miscellaneous

immediately hauled ashore, the operation being repeated till all are landed. Amongst the first things sent off to a wreck, by means of the rocket-line, is a set of instructions printed in several languages[38]

It was expected that the station lifeboat would "as far as possible be manned by volunteers". This was to allow the Coast Guard to concentrate on working the Rocket Apparatus.

The Rocket Apparatus was successfully used by the Rock Island Coast Guard to rescue the crew of the barque *Wolverine* on the 17th of March 1867 at Crookhaven Lighthouse.

> We, the Undersigned Masters of Vessels have pleasure in bearing testimony to the admirable manner in which the lives of the Crew of the Barque *Wolverine* were saved on Sunday, March 17th, 1867 during a furious storm from the S.E. by the exertions of Mr. Bridger, Chief Officer of Coastguards, and the men under his command at the Rock Island Station. The Rocket apparatus was managed with great skill and judgment and was the means of saving the lives of the Crew and bringing them all safely ashore at the Crookhaven Lighthouse.
>
> Signed J. Stavers Brig *Durham*, J. Cooper Barque *St. Angelo*, August Rudin Ship *Sverige*, A. A. Braburg Barque *Waino*, S. M. Kulints Ship *Victor Emmanual*, Chas Evans Ship *Her Royal Highness*, Isaac Notter, Ship Agent, Crookhaven, John S. Sloane M.R.I.A. Superintendent of Lighthouse Works.[39]

D.L. Wodehouse wrote to the Admiralty in September 1868 to see if there was any objection to building a "shed for Rocket Apparatus". Later in January 1869, C.D. Astley submitted plans for a "Rocket Cart House"[40]. In December 1870, The Paymaster-General wrote to the Board of Works that "a sum of £60/6/4 will be transferred to

---

[38] The Navy & Army Illustrated, 6th July 1901 as per www.coastguardsofyesteryear.org.
[39] www.coastguardsofyesteryear.org.
[40] Coast Guard and Customs Register, 1869, National Archives, Dublin, OPW5/8/5.

Board's credit for direction of Board of Trade for building a Rocket House"[41]. The Rocket House was located on the eastern end of the dwellings.

The Rocket Apparatus was still in use in the 1950s. Known locally as the "breeches buoy" it was used by a local volunteer crew to get the crew of a French trawler off when its anchor drifted and it was swept onto Granny's Island in Crookhaven harbour[42].

The *Odessa*

The following report appeared in the Cork Reporter and in the Dublin Evening Post on the 26th of November 1850:

> The *Odessa* with Indian corn, from Constantinople to Falmouth, arrived safe at the latter port, where she got orders for Westport, proceeded on her voyage thither and got as North as far as the Blasquets when she encountered the gales of Monday and Tuesday last. Unable to make any port of safety, she was driven back, and the captain having been washed overboard, the crew not well knowing where they were, the mate having got charge of the vessel underwent the most deplorable sufferings. At one time they were so near the land that many of the men were in the rigging ready to leap ashore. And they even passed, driven so furiously by the gale, between the Skelligs and the Lemon Rock, and went close by the "Bull, Cow, and Calf" off the Dursey. One man of the crew broke his arm, another dislocated his wrist, and many others were injured and wounded in various places endeavouring to save their lives. At an early hour this morning they were brought ashore in Crookhaven, by the Pilot Hooker, *Mary Drennan*, Mr. D. Noonan, owner, with every loose article of value aboard, the vessel and cargo having been left in charge of the crew of the *Mary Drennan* and some other men who were doing all in their power to work her up into Crookhaven harbour. The wind, however, having, about 11

---

[41] Coast Guard and Customs Register, 1870, National Archives, Dublin, OPW5/8/6.
[42] Griffin, Dermot, conversation with, Goleen, 30th October 2005.

o'clock am. increased almost to a gale, they were obliged to abandon that idea, and ran up for Long Island Channel, where she now rides safely at anchor - her crew all alive and comparatively well in Crookhaven, excepting only the unfortunate master, who met a water and untimely grave. The vessel is guarded by Coast-guards and Constabulary, and is safe excepting only the damage done to her rigging and canvasses. The crew are all Italian but one man, a Pilot from Falmouth, through whom I got the particulars of their sufferings. They had not slept an hour, nor tasted a morsel for the last four days, but those who are disabled are now under proper medical treatment, and they are well cared for in every respect. I believe no vessel ever oftener, or more narrowly, escaped being completely dashed to pieces.[43]

Look-out Towers

The two towers on Rock Island were constructed between 1817 and 1842 according to British Admiralty Charts and the Ordnance Survey. It appears that the westerly one may have been used as a pilotage tower i.e. allowing ships needing a pilot to be seen from some distance. It is described as follows

> Ornamental tower. Square tower (3.5m E-W; H *c.* 11m) on rock outcrop overlooking Crookhaven. Indicated on OS map (1842) as 'Tower'.

Western Tower, previously used as a pilotage look-out

---

[43] Daly, Tony, email, 17th of June 2004.

Rock Island

Four-storey; 1st-floor door in N wall; hood mouldings over 3rd-floor windows. Embattled parapet walls. Similar tower visible to NE[44].

The most easterly of the two towers on Rock Island was leased by the Coast Guard from Thomas Notter from the 17th of February 1863 for an annual rental of £5. It was described as "a look-out tower, 33 ft high, commanding a view of the coast, and is situate about a quarter of a mile east of station". It is incorrectly dated in the Archaeological Inventory of West Cork:

> Ornamental tower. Late 19th-century square tower (2.6m N-S; 2.6m E-W; wall thickness 0.6m; H c. 9m) on rock outcrop overlooking Crookhaven to S. Three-storey; 1st-floor door in N wall, approached by stone stairs. Hood mountings over 2nd-floor windows in E and S wall. Embattled parapet walls. Similar tower visible in SW.

Notter was responsible for repairs; however the Office of Public Works seems to have paid John Crowley £6/5/0 for repairs in 1867.

As a result of building the new station at a higher point than the old one, the Admiralty decided to surrender the lease of the look-out tower. This was done in 1907[45].

Eastern Tower, formerly used by Coast Guard

Later, during World War II the tower appears to have been used by the Local Defence Forces as a look-out against invasion forces.

---

[44] Power, D. (ed.) Archaeological Inventory of County Cork: Vol. 1, Dublin, 1992, p. 381.
[45] Coast Guard and Customs Register, 1907.

The Slipway & Boat House

John Notter was paid £5 in August 1826 for erecting a crane at the station. It is assumed this was at the slipway at the end of the new public road and used for removing boats from the water[46].

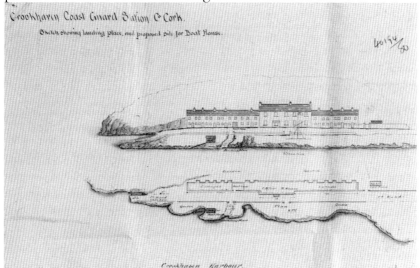

Coast Guard station 1880 with the proposed boat house

In March 1880 the Rock Island Chief Officer Knight (Wright?) asked for sanction from the Inspecting Officer, Castletownsend to have the slipway improved. Knight said he could have O'Sullivan the contractor make a "good job of the slip for £10"[47]. M. Cobb appears to have been the Inspecting Officer at the time as he wrote to District Captain H.B. Phillimore in Kingstown requesting approval to put it "into serviceable condition". As a result of the station's inspection in August 1880 by Prince Alfred, Duke of Edinburgh and Admiral Superintendent of Naval Reserves[48], the Admiralty requested

---

[46] Customs Ireland: Salaries & Incidents at Outposts, 1842, National Archives, London, CUST38/18.
[47] Coast Guard Correspondence 1880, National Archives, Dublin, OPW5/47019/80.
[48] Prince Alfred 1844-1900, son of Queen Victoria.

that the Board of Works (who had responsibility for Coast Guard building projects) have the slipway improved. A.T. Williams, Clerk of Works of the Board of Works for the Cork District, was asked in October 1880 to look at what it would cost to improve the public slipway.

In May 1886, Percy Smith, the Director of Works for the Admiralty in London, wrote to the Office of Public Works requesting that they build a boat house as it was "much required". In August 1886 plans were drawn up by A.T. Williams for a new boat house. It was to be able to accommodate "1 life boat 27 feet in length, 1 gig 24 feet, 1 punt 16 feet and a large crab winch". He wrote at the time "this being a boarding station the crew are constantly afloat and have three boats in use". Boats were painted black on the outside with red inside from 1859. The oars were white and the "gunnel and the bottom boards to be kept cleaned and scrubbed"[49]. They used the slipway at the end of the public road [Griffith's road of 1822] which he described as "roughly cut out of the rock and is in very bad repair". This slip was used "by the Crookhaven Ferry man and parties landing from ships"[50]. "The Life Boat is kept there with a first class double purchase crab winch exposed to all weathers. This very important station stands very much in need of the proposed works, the probable cost of which will be about £300"[51]. At this time, the boat house was within the row of dwelling houses.

Tenders were to be submitted by the 14th of July 1888. There were no plans available for review at the station so the date was put back to the 28th of July. J. McCarthy of Crookhaven had tried to view the drawings there. John Barnett of Goleen won the tender process for the new boat house. The contract was signed on the 14th of August 1888 and the price was £239/4/6. He was required to use limestone

---

[49] Irish Coast Guard Order Book 1852-60.
[50] Coast Guard Correspondence 1880, National Archives, Dublin, OPW5/47019/80.
[51] Coast Guard Correspondence 1889, National Archives, Dublin, OPW5/8954/88.

with red pine lintels. There was a penalty clause for non-completion by the 1st of October 1888 of £2 per week. He however sent a telegram on the 22nd of October 1888 to the Office of Public Works requesting plans as his men were "idle". Isaac Notter of Crookhaven wrote to James Owen, the Office of Public Works Architect, stating that the slipway was being built in the wrong location. He added that his father, Richard Notter was in partnership with Isaac's uncle Sir Thomas Deane who was "an old friend of Mr. Owen who I suppose was your father". In December Barnett was looking for part-payment as he had roofed the boat house. A. T. Williams reported in late March 1889 that the new boat house and slip would be completed "next week"[52].

Isaac Notter wrote again to Owen in March 1889:

> I was looking at the new Boat House Slip at Rock Island Coastguard Station on last Saturday. It is my opinion it is built badly by contractor. He is putting very little cement in the building of the lower course of masonry and if it is not well built with plenty of cement it will not stand as there is a heavy outfall of sea water on the strand in winter months and it would be advisable to send an Inspector to look after the work to secure the foundation of the slip[53].

As a result of the letter Owens requested Williams to make "an early inspection of the work". Williams wrote in October 1889 that he had inspected the slipway and found it satisfactory.

Repairs to the boat house however were required in 1906 as P.J. Lynch sent an estimate of £13/7/4 in July.

---

[52] Office of Public Works, Coast Guard Correspondence, National Archives, Dublin, OPW7/2/2.
[53] Coast Guard Correspondence 1889.

Building Repairs

The station seemed regularly to get a battering from storms. Inspecting Commander Townsend in February 1865 forwarded a letter from John Bridger, Chief Officer, Crookhaven, who reported that "several frames are broken and slates blown off the houses". Townsend gave orders to have the repairs done. John Crowley undertook the glass repairs at a cost of £2/10/0. Townsend was informed in March that part of the "boundary wall has been blown down"[54]. In early January 1866 the Inspecting Commander T.S. Gooch was informed of damage to roofs and windows. Again John Crowley undertook the glazing repairs. This time his charge was £4/13/6. Gooch again informed the Admiralty of storm damage in late March: "14 feet of the boundary wall was blown during the late gale"[55]. John Bridger reported in March 1869 "windows broken, slates and water shoots blown off by recent storms"[56]. John Crowley was paid £4/18/0 for storm damage repairs in January 1870 which were described as "absolutely necessary". In October 1873, John Bridger, Chief Officer, reported "glass broken and slates off roof". Dominic Casey quoted £12/12/0 for these repairs and was accepted. In April 1876 further glass and slating repairs were required as D. Sullivan submitted a quotation[57]. On the 27th of February 1879 the station officer wrote with details of "damage done by recent storm". A.T. Williams prepared specifications of the repair work required which he estimated would cost £58/4/6[58]. A.T. Williams wrote in January 1882 recommending the acceptance of Dominic Casey's

---

[54] Coast Guard Correspondence 1865, National Archives, Dublin, OPW5/8/1.
[55] Coast Guard and Customs Register, 1866, National Archives, Dublin, OPW5/8/2.
[56] Coast Guard and Customs Register, 1869, National Archives, Dublin, OPW5/8/5.
[57] Coast Guard and Customs Register, 1876, National Archives, Dublin, OPW5/8/10.
[58] Coast Guard and Customs Register, 1879, National Archives, Dublin, OPW5/8/13.

tender of £25/12/4 to repair "storm damages"[59]. Further storm damage and drain repairs in October 1883 led to William Casey having his tender for £32/8/4 accepted[60]. The following year, in February, there were storm damage repairs needed with William Casey again getting the work valued at £10/11/2.

In July 1855 J. H. Owens, the Board of Works Architect responsible for Coast Guard buildings, visited the station. His report was paraphrased by the Admiralty[61]:

> The painting inside and out is very much wanted and a drain from the houses to the sea. Nearly all the cottage windows are hung vertically and opening inward which allows the wet to enter freely. He proposes to reverse the frames which will render them nearly water tight. Some new doors and frames are required. Also eave gutters to the back of the cottages, the present wooden ones rotten.
>
> Chief Officers House
>
> Repairs to windows…plastering etc. A new oven and resetting kitchen range. Reslating roofs of sheds and piggery. New doors and hinges to turf house. Repairing, slating and ceiling of Privy – new seat, floor and skirting. Making good middle gutters of roof. Painting woodwork inside £10.
> Repairing ceiling and whitening £3.
> Chimney scraping and preparing walls £2/10.
> Papering sitting and bedrooms £6/16/0.
> Tinting walls of 4 rooms £2.
> Lime whitening out houses £0/15/0.
>
> Boatmans Cottages End House
>
> Repairing slating, new door to shed and hall, making good flue of upper room, lock front door £3/10/0.

---

[59] Coast Guard and Customs Register, 1882, National Archives, Dublin, OPW5/8/16.

[60] Coast Guard and Customs Register, 1883, National Archives, Dublin, OPW5/8/17.

[61] Irish Coast Guard Register, National Archives, London, ADM7/39, p. 156.

Rock Island

House Next Boat House

Repairing plastering hall and ceiling of shed, repair flagging, gathering of flue £2/17/0.

Boat House

Taking asunder and remaking gale doors. Repairing flagging. Plastering and whitewashing £2/0/0.

Mens Houses Generally

Altering front sashes to make them weather tight £5.

Twelve new chimney pots and fixing £2/10/0.

Drain behind houses as specified £20.

Painting cottages inside £6.

Outside £10.

Eave gutters to the back of cottages £6.

Cutting down and levelling the road £5.

Total Cost of the Works Included in Specification £114/0/0.

In March 1856 J.L. Vickery was paid £104/14/6 for repair work, presumably related to the above report[62]. In June, Vickery submitted an estimate of £9/10/0 for supplying a new stove and installing it. This was seen as too expensive and the Board of Works decided to buy a new one from Hodges in Dublin and find someone locally to install it[63]. D. Vickery quoted £3/7/6 which included them paying £1/5 for the old stove, while W. Caglan quoted £4/10/0 with £1 for the old stove.

The Inspecting Commander Gooch sent a list of station defects to the Admiralty in April 1866. This included the Chief Officer's house which had been "left in an unfinished state for more than a year". Among those who tendered for the work was Richard Henry Notter who quoted £84/6/6. The work however was done by John Crowley for £62/4/5.

In May 1868 John Bridger wrote requesting "papering and painting". The following month A.T. Williams estimated the cost of repairs at £215/10/0. He received quotes from J. Crowley, W.H. Jones, J. Wallace, W.A. Lewis and W.H. Jones. John Wallace was awarded the

---

[62] Irish Coast Guard Register, National Archives, London, ADM7/39.

[63] Irish Coast Guard Register, National Archives, London, ADM7/39, p. 268.

contract for £123/6/6. Further estimates for repairs were £91/5/0 in 1870. In 1871 Williams estimated that repairs to the value of £64/10/0 were required. He received two quotes: one from John Crowley and the other from Patrick Desmond of Schull who quoted £20 for "new works" and £47/10/0 for "repairs".

In February 1871 the divisional officer supplied 40 barrels of lime and 6 gallons of tar to Crookhaven, Schull, Baltimore, Barlogue, Castletownsend, Union Hall and Mill Cove. These were to be applied by a contractor. The lime was obviously for painting the buildings exterior[64]. The Divisional Officer reported in March 1878 that Crookhaven "Buildings [were] in a very unsatisfactory state". A.T. Williams prepared specifications of the work required in May. D. Sullivan appears to have got the contract to undertake the necessary repairs for £33/10/0. The station's officer wrote in May 1878 to say that there "was no use in doing [slating] unless lead gutter is taken up"[65].

Leaky roofs in 1871 seem to have led to tenders been received the following year. The following parties tendered: John Moss of Durrus, William Murphy of Bantry and Dominic Casey of Skibbereen. Dominic Casey's tender of £84/18/0 was accepted.

The inspection undertaken by Prince Alfred in August 1880 led to a "complaint as to [the] general condition of premises"[66]. It was agreed to accept John Barnett's quote for £32/15/0 for work on the Chief Officer's House in 1882. The Divisional Officer, Skibbereen was requesting "that immediate steps may be taken to have repairs executed" in August 1883. The Admiralty expected these repairs to cost £121 but a much lower tender from William Casey of £96/4/6 was accepted. Defective "folding doors" also needed repair in August 1894.

---

[64] Coast Guard Letters 18th October – 29th March 1871, National Archives, Dublin, OPW1/2/1/6.
[65] Coast Guard and Customs Register, 1878, National Archives, Dublin, OPW5/8/12.
[66] Coast Guard and Customs Register, 1880, National Archives, Dublin, OPW5/8/13.

Rock Island

1901 & 1911 Census Records

The 1901 Census, taken on the 31st of March, recorded the following

House	Name	Religion	Age	Born	Occupation
1	Patrick Mahony	R.C	49	Co. Cork	Chief Officer
	Ellen Mahony	R C	32	Co. Cork	Housekeeper, sister
2.	John Charles May[67]	C.I.	32	England	Commissioned Boatman
	Sophia May	C.I.	30	England	Wife
	John May	C.I.	3	Co. Dublin	Son
	Florence May	C.I.	2	Co. Dublin	Daughter
	William May	C.I.	1	Co. Cork	Son
	Clarence May	C.I. 2mths		Co. Cork	Son
3.	H. Musselwhite	R.C.	32	England	Boatman
	Sarah Musselwhite	C.I.	33	England	Wife
	Florence Musslewhite	C.I.	3	England	Daughter
4.	Joseph Jupe[68]	C.I.	42	England	Chief Boatman
	Annie Jupe	C.I.	40	England	Wife
	Fanny Jupe	C.I.	20	England	Daughter, Servant
	Jane Jupe	C.I.	18	England	Daughter, Servant
	Daisy Jupe	C.I.	16	England	Daughter
	Ivy Jupe	C.I.	14	England	Daughter
	Joseph Jupe	C.I.	12	England	Daughter
	William Jupe	C.I.	11	England	Son
	Rosina Jupe	C.I.	8	Co. Antrim	Daughter
	Charles Jupe	C.I.	7	Co. Antrim	Son
	George Jupe	C.I.	5	Co. Antrim	Son
	Arthur Jupe	C.I.	3	Co. Antrim	Son
	Dorothy Jupe	C.I.	2	Co. Antrim	Daughter
	Annie Jupe	C.I. 1mth		Co. Cork	Grand-daughter
5.	T. Dwyer	R.C.	33	Co. Cork	Boatman
	Catherine Dwyer	R.C.	35	Co. Cork	Wife
6.	Walter Chamberlain	C.I.	30	England	Boatman
	Mary Chamberlain	C.I.	26	England	Wife
	Alice Chamberlain	C.I.	1	England	Daughter
	Florence Chamberlain	C.I. 2mth		England	Daughter

---

[67] John Charles May, in 1912, was stationed at Cromer, Norfolk, England.
[68] Joseph Jupe, born Carisbrooke, Isle of Wight, 1859, served aboard *HMS Achilles* 1881, stationed at Yarmouth 1891. Wife Annie Kezia, born Cowes, Northwood, Isle of Wight, 1861.

House	Name	Religion	Age	Born	Occupation
7.	W. Flynn	R.C.	36	Co. Waterford	Comm. Boatman
	Margaret Flynn	R.C.	27	Co. Cork	Wife
	Mary Anne Flynn	R.C.	6	England	Daughter
	Isabella Flynn	R.C.	5	England	Daughter
	Margaret Flynn	R.C.	4	England	Daughter
	John Francis Flynn	R.C.	1	England	Son
8	A. Kitcher	C.I.	32	England	Boatman
	Julia Kitcher	C.I.	33	England	Wife
9.	A. Pursey	C.I.	31	England	Boatman
	Elizabeth Pursey	C.I.	22	England	Wife
10.	C. Shaw	R.C.	32	England	Boatman
	Abelia Shaw	R.C.	32	Tralee	Wife
	Violet Shaw	R.C.	8	England	Daughter

The next census in 1911 was taken on the 2nd of May. The following Coast Guard were recorded

House	Name	Religion	Age	Born	Occupation
1.	Charles Hennessy	C.E.	40	Limerick	Chief Officer
	Bessie Hennessy	C.E.	40	England	Wife
	Charles Hennessy	C.E.	12	England	Son
	Kathleen Hennessy	C.E.	9	England	Daughter
	George Hennessy	C.E.	7	England	Son
	Leonard Hennessy	C.E.	5	England	Son
	Herbert Hennessy	C.E.	3	Co. Kerry	Son
2.	Samuel Griffiths	C.E.	40	England	Chief Petty Officer
	Nora Ann Griffiths	C.E.	40	England	Wife
	Nora Marion Griffiths	C.E.	10	Co. Kerry	Daughter
	Rupert Griffiths	C.E.	8	Co. Kerry	Son
3.	James Newton	C.E.	44	England	Petty Officer
	Eva Newton	C.E.	39	England	Wife
	Elizabeth Newton	C.E.	8	England	Daughter
	Jeffrey Newton	C.E.	6	England	Son
4.	Richard Tucker	C.E.	40	England	Coastguard
	Dora Tucker	C.E.	34	England	Wife
	Ernest Tucker	C.E.	8	Co. Kerry	Son
	Victor Tucker	C.E.	7	England	Son
	Arthur Tucker	C.E.	5	England	Son
	Beatrice Tucker	C.E.	3	England	Daughter
5.	Ernest Adams	C.E.	29	England	Coastguard
	Laura Adams	C.E.	31	England	Wife

Rock Island

	House Name	Religion	Age	Born	Occupation
	Vivien Adams	C.E.	3	England	Daughter
6.	William Pocknell	C.E.	36	England	Leading Boatman
	Beatrice Pocknell	C.E.	33	England	Wife
	William Pocknell	C.E.	9	England	Son
	Alice Pocknell	C.E.	5	Co. Cork	Daughter
	Lily Pocknell	C.E.	2	Co. Cork	Daughter

Building of New Station

The need for on-going expensive repairs, often as a result of the old station's proximity to the sea and therefore sea-damage, must have been factors in the decision to build a new station on higher ground above the old station. In June 1904 Patterson & Kempster of Dublin, quantity surveyors, were sent the new stations' plans and specifications. They determined the Bills of Quantities required. Tenders were then sought and were to be received by the 1st of September 1904. By that date four tenders had been received. Robert Kelly successfully tendered for £3,952/6/7[69]. The District Officer, Castletownsend suggested in November 1904 that a look-out tower should be "erected at Western end of Station". There is no evidence of this suggestion being included.

By April 1905 "site is exposed and levelled" as M.J. Burke wrote with regard to paying an instalment of £100 on the new building[70]. Kelly was required to show his insurance policy in January 1906 to demonstrate that he was covered for the contract's value. Later that month he sent proof of cover to the value of £3,952. Kelly wrote in July that he hoped to have the new station finished by the 1st of September. He said he was "hurrying on work as quickly as

---

[69] Once it became known that a new station was to be built, the Admiralty received many brochures from potential suppliers. The Elkay Patent Bath Syndicate submitted details of their baths. G. Worrall & Co. sent details of their railing and gates. C. Kite & Co. sent information on their heating and ventilation equipment - Coast Guard and Customs Register, 1904, National Archives, Dublin, OPW5/8/21.

[70] Coast Guard and Customs Register, 1905, National Archives, Dublin, OPW5/8/23.

possible". He did not however meet the deadline, writing on the 7th of September that he hoped to "have worked finished in five weeks". The work was not to the Admiralty's satisfaction as they wrote "new premises – uninhabitable – ordered men to remove back to old premises". They sent Kelly a list of defects. The Admiral at Queenstown in January 1907 indicated the Admiralty's willingness to take over the new station once "defects specified are completed". They were still waiting for the defects to be "remedied" in late March. The District Officer was finally instructed to take over the new building on the 1st of May 1907.

There was damage inflicted on the station in June 1907 from gales. In August the District Officer submitted details of "storm damages". No record was found to indicate whether this was the old or new station.

The Old & New Stations, probably around 1905-1910

Richard Sanders, Lord Clinton's agent, inquired in September 1905 as to whether the old houses would be let. Sanders had hoped to use the buildings for a "tourist hotel" but the Admiralty saw this as "not desirable". The question of renting the old houses was again raised in June 1907 where the Admiralty "presumed it is not necessary to consult Colonel Notter" (James Lane Notter, the owner). They decided however in November that it was "undesirable to sublet the premises". They appeared to want to demolish the buildings instead, retaining the "watchroom and room over it" for "storage of gear".

The Admiralty replied to a query in October 1905 from the "rural district council" (Cork County Council) on the question of a water supply connection, that the "station has a good supply and admiralty need not subscribe". This is strange as R. Puhreloft & Son submitted an estimate in August 1906 of £22/5/0 for the supply of the wheel gear and pipe needed for a well. The well water supply appears to have been checked for drinking in 1906 as a sample of water was tested by the Government Laboratory, London. In 1911 the well at the station was not considered suitable for human consumption "owing to the presence of copper"[71].

Boathouse, watchhouse and rocket house of old station in foreground, new station at rear (2006)

On the 11th of March 1908, John Barnett wrote to the Admiralty stating that he had omitted to fill up the first page of a tender document and sign his name. As a result he requested a new form. It may have been that the offices and outbuildings were not included in the initial contract. R. Kelly in April requested reconsideration of the decision to disallow his bill for "plastering out offices, painting whole

---

[71] Coast Guard and Customs Register, 1911, National Archives, Dublin, OPW5/8/29.

work inside and out, and also supply of locks". He wrote back the following month accepting the Admiralty's offer which included part payment of his painting claim. Barnett in early August 1908 wrote to say he "expects to complete about 20th" of August". However he was writing the following month to explain why he had not yet completed[72].

Brow Head Signal Station

In July 1903 Lloyds and the Admiralty entered into an agreement relating to Commercial Maritime Signalling. The signalling was taken over by the Coast Guard. They were to be paid by Lloyds seven shillings for day time "telegraphing or telephoning" and 14 shillings for night work. It appears that Coast Guards, who were no longer able to do the occasional arduous work required, were sent to work at the Signal Station which became known as a War Signal Station (W.S.S). For instance, David Laley started serving at Crookhaven in June 1914 at the age of 47. The following June he was transferred to "Brow Head W.S.S." as he was "not suitable for the c.s.". In 1920 he was transferred to Lawrence Cove W.S.S. James Henry Lake, born in 1870 and appointed a Chief Officer in March 1913, was transferred to Brow Head station in August 1919 from Lawrence Cove at the age of 49 from where he was discharged in September 1919[73].

In 1909 Stephen Downey, farmer of Brow Head, wrote that he had been informed "that ye are going to build a fence in front of the Telescope Window". An 1891 lease between the Pelham-Clinton estate and Lloyds included two rights of way to the station by horse and cart. There was a similar agreement entered into between the tenant, John Downey (Stephen's father) of Brow Head and Lloyds. Downey looked for £10 compensation for this portion of land. He added that his landlord was Mr. Sanders (probably Lord Clinton's agent, rather than the landlord). John Downing, Lloyds Sub-Agency,

---

[72] Coast Guard and Customs Register, 1908, National Archives, Dublin, OPW5/8/26.

[73] Coastguard Removals 1886-1905, National Archives, London, ADM175/105.

Malavogue (Brow Head) wrote "I do not remember when the fence was erected, but it was probably many years ago when the use of the old tower as a military station was discontinued".

The Chief Officer, Crookhaven, wrote to his commanding officer, the Divisional Officer, Skibbereen District in January 1912. He indicated that Stephen Downey, who was the tenant at Brow Head, said the Coast Guard had no right to place an iron gate at the entrance to the Signal Station and also had no right to access the station with horses and carts on the route they used. He added "during my time at Station now nearly three years no-one has challenged right of way into Signal Station". He said it was "the only way in which a horse and cart can now get into the Signal Station since the Postmaster General's Wireless Installation is surrounded by a wire enclosure. Page two of lease gives us right to enter with horses and carts". Also he said "this man Stephen Downey has blocked this right of way by erecting a wall of stones across with an opening sufficient only for a person to go thru (*sic*)". At that time "no horse or cart with coal, provisions, men's effects etc. can enter Signal Station". The lease referred to was dated the 19th of June 1907 between Charles S. Pelham Clinton, the landlord, and the Corporation of Lloyds. A supplemental agreement had been entered into between Lloyds and the Admiralty on the 14th of January 1908. The Rear Admiral in Queenstown suggested removing the wall and then see if Downey would take legal action. It appears however that Downey had a case as the Office of Public Works wrote in August 1912 that "when this land was taken from his father, Mess'rs Lloyds Sec. only required a footpath and ordered two stiles to be built at the entrance from the public road". The stile and gateway had been replaced by a double gate in 1909. In a letter to the Admiralty in March 1913, the Office of Public Works stated "his [Stephen Downey's] object is simply to obtain compensation". Local suppliers were unwilling to "use the passage contrary to Downey's wishes". As a result Lloyds suggested paying £5 compensation[74]. Resolution occurred in June 1913 when in return for £3, which Lloyds paid, Downey agreed with the Admiralty to fence the access right of way with posts and wire[75].

The station was described as follows by Bill Boyle who was a wireless operator along with Frank Yelland, Syd Corrin and Richard (Dickie) Knight in 1914:

> The wireless station was housed in an old Martello tower (a watch tower built to withstand Napoleon's cannon). The ground floor was occupied by the batteries, our only source of energy. The first floor was our operating room and also the landline room. The landline room was of the physical dimensions and design of our present day telephone kiosks, but with far less glass and more upholstery. The upholstery was not for our comfort but so that the key clicks and sounder clicks would not interfere with wireless reception! This kiosk stood in a corner of the main room which measured 12' x 10' and about a quarter of this was stoutly wired off for safety. It contained the mushroom spark gap 5kW contained in a sound proof box (which was anything but soundproof), a bank of oil filled condensers, a sliding inductance and a jigger coupling. At the operating bench stood a multiple tuner, a formidable looking combine of teak and ebonite. Also a magnetic detector with its slowly travelling band and its whispered indication that it was functioning. This was our stand-by and a very insensitive one at that. The normal rectifier was a zinzite/bornite combination later to be replaced by a carborundum/steel, and still later by a 4 valve bright emitter. The emergency transmitter was a 10 inch coil that spluttered and zig zagged across the gap to produce a dying duck note. With this we used to communicate to the Fastnet Lighthouse and they would reply by similar means. Above the operating room was the second floor used as the O/C's room, the store room, and

---

[74] Admiralty: Brow Head Signal Station – Question of Right of Way, National Archives, London, ADM1/8365/9.
[75] Abstract of Leases and Lettings, National Archives, Dublin, OPW4/6/12, p.70.

two bunk beds that were available for use of the evening staff if darkness or mist, or wind made it hazardous to go home[76].

It appears that the Brow Head station took on responsibilities for wireless communication from the Crookhaven Post Office in 1920. The following note was recorded by the Admiralty:

> When we decided to close down the G.P.O. W/T Station at Crookhaven, C. in C. [Commander in Chief] Western Approaches represented the necessity of keeping up communication between Brow Hd. W.S.S. (a very important Lloyds station) and the Fastnet. Arrangements were therefore made to maintain a short distance W/T set and we naturally expected that this set would be installed in [Rock Island] C.G. Station. C. in C. decided, however to have it at Brow Hd. W.S.S., which is on top of a hill some 4 miles from Crookhaven [Coast Guard station on Rock Island].

The "military guard" at Brow Head had been withdrawn which the Admiralty writer found unexplainable as Brow Head "is probably the most important War Signal Station in the U.K. at the present". The Marine Guard on Rock Island was supposed to protect Brow Head – an impossible task as it was seven kilometres away by road or four kilometres by sea to Crookhaven and road from there.

The station was attacked four times by the I.R.A. in the month of August 1920: on the 9th, 21st, 27th and 30th. On the 9th at 12.55 a.m. "two pistols, one cutlass, 136 rounds of ammunition, one emergency W/T coil, three pairs of binoculars, one disused spark plug" were taken. Petty Officer William J. Edwards was on watch that night while William Hammond of the Post Office and Jonathon Berry (another statement gave his name as Alfred Parry) were asleep. On the 21st of August 1920 the station was attacked by "about 150 raiders at 12.40 a.m. The crew of the station had been expecting a detachment of Royal Marines under Captain Parsons at the time. They were "taken prisoner and removed to a farmhouse [Stephen

---

[76] www.qsl.net/gm3zdh/coast/ireland/gck.htm

Downey's] while the transmitter was destroyed and two cottages at the station were burned. They were warned not to leave the farmhouse until daybreak. Thomas Hammond when he got back to the station "fired two rockets and reported to Rock Island by flashing lamp". The damage resulted in communications with Fastnet been suspended and Petty Officer Jeremiah Crowley of the station relocating to temporary lodgings in Crookhaven. Later that year Crowley was awarded £500 for the loss of his personal possessions as a result of the cottage fire at Skibbereen Court Sessions. At that time all communications from Crookhaven went through Brow Head.

The I.R.A.'s campaign was effective with the order to vacate the station made on the 28th of August 1920. Notification was issued on the 1st of September that the station had been destroyed "by fire and bomb"[77].

New Coast Guard Station prior to renovation

Closure of Station

The Coast Guard stations were generally treated in a similar manner to Police stations by the I.R.A. during the War of Independence. They were regarded as legitimate targets and representative of the

---

[77] Raids on Irish Coast Guard Stations, National Archives, London, ADM178/108.

British government. All stations were provided with bullet–proof shutters. Bowen refers to the Coast Guard men in Ireland as "intensely proud of this [the King's] uniform and this attitude was a never–ending source of offence" to the nationalist Irish[78]. He added that after World War I they "were hated more than ever as representatives of British power"[79].

According to C.W. Scott of Irish Lights, the Crookhaven "coastguard station was burnt down just afterwards" the offer by the Post Office in 1920 to connect the lighthouse to the telephone system. However this seems unlikely as there was a detachment of 25 Royal Marines stationed at the Coast Guard in December 1920 to protect it and Brow Head. Apparently there were only two Coast Guard men serving there at the time[80].

An Admiralty Fleet Order was drafted in October 1922. It stated "in consequence of the evacuation of Coast Guard Stations in the territory of the Irish Free State…it has been decided that all Divisional Chief Officers are to be placed on the retired list ". Prior to the War of Independence there had been 33 stations in the south of Ireland[81].

Sale & Development

In December 1959 the property was sold to the Commissioners of Public Works by the additional and surviving trustee appointed by Charles James Lane, William Ronayne Crooke Harman. The following year on the 22nd of

The boat house as renovated by Alan Best

---

[78] Bowen, Her Majesty's Coastguard, 235.
[79] Bowen, Her Majesty's Coastguard, 240.
[80] Raids on Irish Coast Guard Stations.
[81] Coast Guard Permanent Records 1922, National Archives, London, ADM120/116.

December 1960, Michael Boland, a solicitor from Skibbereen and his brother Charles Boland, a surgeon from Rathmines, Dublin bought the station buildings and land for £351. They then sold it on to Alan Best on the 31st of August 1963 for £1,800. He gave his address as Rock Street, Crookhaven (where he had bought a house from Mary & Elizabeth Ellis for £100) but his principal residence was in Lambeth, London where he worked as an interior designer. He restored one of the old Coast Guard houses (the Watchhouse) and the Boathouse. Since the departure of the Coast Guard all the houses were in a very poor state as local people had taken slates, stone and wood for their own houses[82].

The property was sold to Peter Shortt and Brian McPhilips in 1990. Peter Shortt bought the Boathouse and the Coast Guard building while Brian McPhilips bought the Watchhouse. The "new" station building and the old Rocket Cart House were restored with the old flat roof replaced with an A-frame roof. The design was by Paul Leech, Architect, and the contractor was Muscrai Construction of Ballyvourney, Co. Cork. They were rented out as holiday accommodation. In 2002 the eight apartments at the main Coast Guard building and the Rocket Cart House were sold to individual buyers.

New Coast Guard Station, renovated

---

[82] O'Driscoll, Denis (Sonny), conversation with, Crookhaven, 2nd December 2001.

NOTTERS & OTHER RESIDENT FAMILIES

From the establishment of the Coast Guard Station in the early 19th century until the late 1950s, the majority of the population was made up of coast guard and lighthouse families who lived on Rock Island for a few years and then moved on to a new station. There were however a number of families who resided here permanently; most owned the land or farmed it.

Notters

The Notters were of German origin and may have settled in the area in 1631[1]. Hickey adds to this by stating "They may have been refugees from the 30 years war"[2]. Pete Notter pretty much substantiates this, saying "Richard Notter left Herrenberg, Germany around 1635 and emigrated to Cork in Ireland. He married Betty Beecher"[3] of Aughadown near Skibbereen. The names vary somewhat in the book From Ilen to Roaring WaterBay:

> Phane Beecher died in 1592/3 and his eldest son Henry, who had married Mary Lyon, daughter of the Protestant Bishop of Cork & Ross, inherited [12,000 acres in Co. Cork]. The eldest son of this marriage was Major Henry Beecher. The latter married Elizabeth Notte (*sic*), eldest daughter of Thomas Notte, who owned an estate at Aughadown and thus by marriage (about 1635-40) the Beechers arrived in Aughadown[4].

---

[1] Murphy, "Rock Island and its Families", 167.
[2] Hickey, Famine in West Cork, 17.
[3] Notter, P., www.rootsweb.com.
[4] O'Brien, B. & Whooley, M., ed., From Ilen to Roaring WaterBay: Reminiscences from the Parish of Aughadown, Skibbereen, p. 34.

Notters & Other Resident Families

With regard to the Notters residing on Rock Island, there is however no mention of them in Smith's list of Noblemen and Gentlemen in the Commission of the Peace in 1773[5].

Within the diocese of Cork and Ross there were a number of Notter marriages in the 18th Century. In 1718 a Thomas Notter married an Elizabeth Hayes. In 1731 a Richard Notter married an Avis Winspear[6]. Later, in 1783 a Henry Notter married Mary Baker. A Thomas Notter had married Dorothy Kingston in 1762; Anne Kingston in 1808; and Mary Screetch in 1802.

The first mention of Notters in the area is in February 1794 when a Richard Notter and his two crew drowned after his boat *Fanny* was wrecked at Ballyrisode. She was a Crookhaven ship "en-route from Dublin to Limerick with iron bedsteads and bedding for soldiers"[7]. This may have been the father of Richard Notter[8] who entered into a lease for "Goleen, Spanish Cove, Snug Harbour, Rock Island and Colleras" with Lord William Riversdale on the 25th of March 1816 for 999 years at a yearly rent of 5 shillings. This lease also mentioned "John Notter of Crookhaven" who was Richard's brother. Notter entered into further leases with Lord Riversdale in 1818 for 1,115 English statute acres (451 hectares) at Lissacaha, near Schull. He bought additional land from Lord Riversdale at Boulysallagh, Goleen and Kilbarry during the 1820s and 1830s. The Tithe Applotment Book of 1828 appears to state incorrectly that it was W. Notter who owned two of the three gneeves[9] of arable land on Rock Island[10]. He also bought land at Enoughter from Andrew Symms for £700 in May 1833[11].

---

[5] Smith, Charles, The Ancient and Present state of the County and City of Cork, Cork, 1893 (reprint), p. 35.
[6] Marriage Licence Bonds: Diocese of Cork and Ross 1623-1750, National Archives, Dublin.
[7] Bourke, Shipwrecks of the Irish Coast, 124.
[8] Richard's parents could have also been Henry Notter and Mary Baker as Richard's son and grandson referred to themselves as Isaac Baker Notter.
[9] A gneeve was approx. 50 acres (20 hectares).
[10] Tithe Applotment Book, 1823-38.
[11] Land Commission, Dublin, EC1332.

Rock Island

Richard Notter appears to have had three wives; his first was Anne Lambert who he married in 1812. She died on the 2nd of September 1817 at "Cove", Cork. They do not appear to have had any children. The following year, on the 8th of August 1818, Richard married Mary Deane at Christchurch in Cork. She was eldest daughter of the deceased architect, Alexander Deane of Cork[12]. She appears to have been the sister of architect Sir Thomas Deane who designed many buildings including much of University College Cork[13]. In 1829 Notter borrowed £1,846 against his land from his wife's relatives, Thomas Deane and Alexander Sharp Deane.

Richard and Mary Notter had four sons: Alexander, Thomas (born 2nd of October 1820), Richard Henry and Isaac. Alexander drowned on Rock Island at the age of six on Sunday the 10th of July 1825. He was buried at St. Brendan's, Crookhaven graveyard. Mary Notter also died in 1825, possibly while giving birth to Isaac.

Notter was residing on Rock Island throughout these years. The 1817 British Admiralty Chart located "Mr. Notter's House" at the location of the factory on Rock Island. The present Rock Island House was not built at this stage. It first appears on the drawings for the initial Ordnance Survey of Ireland conducted in the area on the 11th of February 1842.

Shed near Notter's house with gothic effects, later used for electricity generator

---

[12] Ffolliot, R., Index to Biographical Notices Collected from Newspapers, Principally relating to Cork and Kerry 1756-1827, Cork City Library. Alexander Deane's daughter, Anne married William Thomas Jones of Dublin in 1819. Alexander Deane's youngest daughter, Elizabeth married William Hargrave M.D. of Dublin in 1823. Alexander Deane's son, James married Sarah Greaves. of Cork in 1824.

[13] Sir Thomas Deane (1792-1871) and Joseph Baker, probably the Schull parish tithe proctor, loaned Notter money against his land at Lissacaha.

Notters & Other Resident Families

The Gothic style of the waterside buildings to the east of the house would suggest construction in the 1810s or 1820s as this style was "remarkably popular in south Munster" at that period[14]. Sir Thomas Deane assisted in the house's design although it is of little architectural merit. It appears also that the present structure includes a number of additions which were mainly in place by 1842.

Rock Island House

During the House of Commons Poor Inquiry of 1836, the two landlords of Kilmoe, Richard Notter and Lionel Fleming, made submissions stating that sub-divisions had occurred on their estates since the Napoleonic Wars and tenants had been evicted as a result[15]. Lewis in 1837 refers to the "flourishing state" of Rock Island due to the "spirited exertions of its proprietor R. Notter"[16]. Lewis had astutely listed all the prominent individuals throughout the country. As a result they all ordered copies of the book, once published. One copy was ordered by Richard Notter at his Cork address of "Carrigduve", Blackrock. The house had been designed and built by Sir Thomas Deane who lived nearby in his house "Dundanion". Another copy was ordered by John Notter whose address was "Rock Island House".

---

[14] Dickson, Old World Colony, 160.
[15] Hickey, A Survey, 116.
[16] Lewis, S. Topographical dictionary of Ireland, London, 1837

John Notter, brother of Richard (1787-1852)

In 1835 John Notter, Richard's brother, married Mary Jane McMullen[17]. John Notter in 1839 transferred the ownership of land "with cornstore kiln and other the premises" at South Lowertown to his brother Richard Notter[18]. Richard Notter married his third wife, Margaret Lane, in 1837. She was the eldest daughter of James Lane. They had four children: James, born on the 1st of February 1843, (who used the name James Lane Notter), Catherine, Mary Jane and Margaret, born on the 8th of June 1845. Catherine and Mary Jane did not survive their childhood.

In 1840, according to Hickey, Captain William Thomas (1808-1890), the mining captain/manager of Coosheen mine married a daughter of Richard Notter[19]. Only one of Richard Notter's daughters, Margaret survived childhood and she was born in 1845[20]. The wedding could have possibly been to one of John Notter's daughters or a sister of Richard Notter. In 1845, Mary Anne Notter, Richard's sister, married Henry Thomas (1812-72), presumably William's brother, who was also a mine manager[21].

---

[17] Marriage Licence Bonds: Diocese of Cork and Ross 1751-1845, National Archives, Dublin. It appears she was known as Jane.
[18] Land Commission, Dublin, EC1332.
[19] Hickey, A Survey, 168.
[20] "Thomas Deane Notter, Richard Henry Notter and Isaac Notter were the only children of the said Richard Notter by the said Mary Notter otherwise Deane" - Land Commission, Dublin, EC6810.
[21] Marriage Licence Bonds.

Notters & Other Resident Families

Richard Notter donated the land for the Church of Ireland church in Goleen. He also contributed towards the building cost. The church was built in 1841[22] ending the practice of Goleen area Protestants having to travel to the end of Rock Island and get a ferry across to St. Brendan's Church, Crookhaven. Crookhaven's Catholics continued to make the journey in the opposite direction to Goleen Church.

Richard Notter replied on the 28th of January 1846 from "Rock Island Cottage" to a query from Captain Kennedy of the Scarcity Commission, Dublin Castle concerning local food supplies:

> My opinion is that for the last twenty years there has not been more provision in the Country at this season than there is at present. The disease in the potatoes is not increasing and as a proof there is no want, I never had less trouble in collecting my Rents than I had this Year[23].

Side entrance to Notter's house, most likely used by tenants for paying rent

He was to change his opinion very quickly concerning the impending famine. In March 1846, Notter offered "free of any charge" a store 17 feet wide by 75 feet long (5m by 23m) "for the storage of Provision to meet the approaching scarcity". This was located "on a quay within 100 yds of the Coast Guard station" and still remains in existence as the easterly part of the defunct Cottage Foods' factory. He made the offer to the Earl of Bandon who was

---

[22] Notter, Crookhaven, 10.
[23] Relief Commission Papers, 28th January 1846, National Archives, Dublin, RLFC3/1/429.

Lieutenant for the County[24]. R.B. Hungerford of Ballyrisode supported Notter's offer in April asking that supplies be landed at Crookhaven rather than Skibbereen "as we can get storage free of expense" there[25].

Richard Notter was the chairman of the Kilmoe famine relief committee. Rev. William Fisher, the secretary[26], wrote to the national Relief Commission in May 1846 indicating that Richard Notter had subscribed £10. The following were members of the Kilmoe Committee at the time: R.H. Beecher, Rev. Fisher, Rev. Lawrence O'Sullivan, R.B. Hungerford, John Coughlan, Dr. James McCormick, Rev. Thomas Barrett, H. Baldwin, Dr. Stephen Sweetnam, John Notter, Richard Notter and others[27]. Notter wrote to the Relief Committee, Dublin Castle from the "Goleen Committee Rooms" in August 1846

> we live in a remote district with very few resident Gentry and have received direct refusals from some of the Landed Proprietors. We have an overflowing population who altogether are depending on the Potato Crop which is a total loss…and therefore we hope for your bountiful liberality[28].

In December Major Hugh Parker of the Board of Works "found that deaths were just as frequent in Kilmoe in spite of the best efforts of Richard Notter"[29]. Notter again wrote to the Relief Commission in January 1847. He stated that there was a lack of merchants in the area and therefore a "food depot" in Crookhaven was a necessity. Enclosed with the letter was a statement from Rev. Thomas Barrett

---

[24] Relief Commission Papers, 27th March 1846, National Archives, Dublin, RLFC3/2/6/61.
[25] Relief Commission Papers, 8th April 1846, National Archives, Dublin, RLFC3/1/1331.
[26] Hickey, A Survey, 145.
[27] Relief Commission Papers, 27th May 1846, National Archives, Dublin, RLFC3/2/6/60.
[28] Notter, R., Letter to William Stanley, Relief Committee, 19th August 1846.
[29] Hickey, A Survey, 165.

withdrawing himself from the committee because of the failure to "procure practical and honest working by the…committee". The timing of Barrett's resignation is strange as he and Fr. O'Sullivan were described by Notter as "indefatigable in their exertions" in January 1847.[30] Notter also forwarded details of the donations made to the "General Relief Fund, Crookhaven" from the 15th of August 1846 to the 23rd of January 1847. Some of those who contributed were:

John Notter	£1/10/0
Captain Carter per Doctor McCormac (*sic*)	£3/0/0
Captain of a ship per Doctor McCormac	£0/10/0
A friend from Doctor McCormac	£1/0/0
Don Leahy Esq., Cork per Mr. Notter	£5/0/0
Sir Thos. Deane per Mr. Notter	£10/0/0
Wm. Deane Esq. per Mr. Notter	£1/0/0

Richard Notter collected a further £3, with a total contribution of £64[31].

In February Notter wrote a letter from Rock Island to the Cork Constitution. He stated that the starving people of the parish were becoming

> prey to fever, dysentery and other diseases and are dropping like the blasted leaves of an October tree…Our Relief Committee have two coffins, with sliding bottoms, in which the corpses are carried to the graveyard, and there, deposited in mother earth…From the very windows of where I write, I see a cabin in which the father of 4 helpless children, lie dead, the victim of want and distress; his eldest son died 10 days ago, and his widow and orphans are now left without any earthly means of support…I entreat of them in this hour of need to come and help us[32].

---

[30] Southern Reporter, 12th of January 1847.
[31] Relief Commission Papers, 23rd January 1847, National Archives, Dublin, RLFC3/2/6/61.
[32] Notter, Crookhaven, 22.

Notter was described as in charge of most famine food distribution in the area in April 1847 by the Cork Examiner[33]. However there was criticism of Notter's efforts in May. Alexander O'Driscoll of Crookhaven claimed "part of the cargo of peas sent by the British Relief Association was rotting and sprouting in the depot on Rock Island". He added that a "cargo of flour [from the *Jamestown*] had just arrived and was been placed in Notter's store on Rock Island" but he did not know when it would be distributed. He claimed that the meal had taken only 15 days to get across the Atlantic but it had taken 26 days to get from Cobh to Rock Island. A dispute arose out of O'Driscoll's criticisms, with Fr. Barrett, Pierre Foley and O'Driscoll on one side and Rev. William Fisher, R.B. Hungerford and Richard Notter on the other[34]. This was very much a division according to religious belief: Barrett wrote, with irony, in the *Tablet* that the reason he had to resign from the committee was that "a "Romanist" idolatrous, damnable population of seven thousand were being placed at the mercy of our relief rector"[35]. The story of the rotting food got passed down through the generations with a child telling the Folklore Commission how the food was stored by the landlord who would sell it but not give it away and so "it rotted in the stores and after the famine they sunk it to the bottom of the sea"[36]. In September 1847 O'Driscoll was again criticising Notter regarding the shipment from Notter's Rock Island stores of 90 bags of bread and 17 bags of peas. He claimed "many distressed people assembled on the quay expecting to obtain some of the food were bitterly disappointed[37]".

His store was extensively used during the famine years as seen by this piece in the Cork Examiner on the 23rd of February 1848:

---

[33] Hickey, A Survey, 422.
[34] Hickey, Famine in West Cork, 202.
[35] Hickey, Famine in West Cork, 236.
[36] Hickey, Famine in West Cork, 202.
[37] Hickey, A Survey, 438.

Notters & Other Resident Families

Crookhaven, February 17 – Wind S.W. – Arrived from Cork – *Richard* of Berehaven, Sullivan [captain/owner]. Landed at Rock Island 1 ton of rye meal and 4 sacks of rice for the Rev. Mr. Miles; *Fame* of Baltimore, D. Donovan, landed 35 casks of Indian corn for S.P. Foley of the Crookhaven Copper Mines with two boxes of clothing for the poor of Crookhaven; *Shamrock* of Berehaven, Shanahan, landed for Dr. McCormick 10 casks of provisions at Rock Island – for the Rev. A. Fisher, two boxes of clothing, and for Richard Notter, Esq., 2 boxes of clothing for the poor of the parish.

A story of Richard Notter's supposed brutality during the famine years remains. In one version, a charitable association sent corn to the local magistrate. He was a breeder of turkeys and had a prize flock of some one hundred birds. He supposedly kept all the corn, solely to feed his turkeys. One day a starving woman "crawled on her hands on knees across the fields to the trough where the turkeys were feeding". Notter "rushed out in a towering rage with his horsewhip and whipped the unfortunate creature to death"[38]. In the second version the woman whipped to death for stealing the grain was a servant girl of Notter's[39]. No documentary evidence of the death has been found. Considering the horrid state of the area during the famine years and Notter's position as the local magistrate it is unlikely any charges would have been brought. The author doubts the veracity of the story due to the obvious humanity Notter displayed during the famine years[40].

In 1849 Richard took out a mortgage of £1,050 against part of his estate at Lissacaha and Boulysallagh. The loan was provided by Edward Lane and William Henry Hall. It may have been required due to his generosity and lack of rental income during the famine years.

---

[38] As told to John Feehan during a Cork Historical & Archaeological Association lecture tour. The author does not name Notter. Feehan, J., The Wind that round the Fastnet sweeps, Dublin, 1978, p.130.
[39] O'Driscoll, Dennis (Sonny), conversation with, 2nd December 2001.
[40] He was recalled locally as a "good landlord" - Lannin, Mary, conversation with, 6th of March 2006.

Rock Island

In June 1849 John Notter was removed as a trustee of Richard's will as "he had gone to reside out of Ireland"[41]. He emigrated to "the township of Thurlow in the Victoria District [Canada]"[42]. However the only Thurlow Township in Canada is in Hastings County, Ontario, which appears to be where he settled. One could speculate that he left as a result of the shortage of construction work in the area. He and his wife, Jane McMullen had five children between 1840 and 1851: Richard, Jane, Eliza, James and John Henry[43].

Richard Notter appears to have retired to Carragaline, Cork. He died there on the 3rd of January 1852[44]. Richard Notter's will of December 1850 (his last will) "did appoint and direct that the house which he then occupied at Rock island being part of the premises comprised…should go and belong to his son the said Thos. Deane". Thomas also inherited the lands at Spanish Cove, Snug Harbour and Rock Island. His brother Isaac was left land at Goleen and "Collesetra" (Callaros Eighter?). His brother Richard Henry got the lands at Lissacaha. Their aunt Mary Thomas nee Notter was, during her lifetime, to get a 1/5th share of the estates mining income. The will also left £5 per annum to "his nephew John Notter during his minority"[45].

Thomas Deane Notter was recorded as the principal land owner of Rock Island in Griffith's Valuation which was conducted on Rock Island between April and August 1852. His step-mother Mary was still living there as she was listed as the occupier of a house, office and garden. Charles Thomas (1815-74) was also living on Rock Island in a house belonging to Thomas Notter. Charles was a brother of William and Henry Thomas and like them, was active in mining in West Cork. Charles had been, during the famine, a member of the

---

[41] Land Commission, Dublin, EC6810.
[42] Land Commission, Dublin, EC1332.
[43] Notter, P. www.rootsweb.com.
[44] Land Commission, Dublin, EC6810.
[45] Land Commission, Dublin, EC6810.

Ballydehob relief committee[46]. Henry Thomas appears to have also lived on Rock Island as he addressed a letter to Sir Robert Kane of Queen's College, Cork (presently University College Cork) from there in November 1850. The letter concerned the finding of ancient stone hammers on Richard Notter's land at Boulysallagh[47].

In March 1852 Richard Henry Notter was the only lay subscriber listed as a Protestant to the fund for the new Catholic Church in Goleen which was finished in 1855. Notter was also the church architect.

It appears that the Notter family were compelled to sell some of their properties, due to the high level of mortgages secured against the property, under the Encumbered Estates Acts of 1848 & 1849. As a result of a court order in December 1857 the following were advertised for sale at the Imperial Hotel, Cork on the 8th of May 1858:

Store and Offices on Merchants Quay/Andersons Quay, Cork.
58 Patrick Street, Cork.
11 & 12 Grand Parade, Cork.
Colleras & Goleen: 228 acres held by Isaac Notter – Rent £31/1/6.
North & South Spanish Cove, Snug Harbour & part of Rock Island: 230 acres held by Thomas Deane Notter – Rent £52/0/0.
The entire of the Lands held by these Tenants, Isaac Notter and Thomas D. Notter, containing 458 acres statute measure are held by them under a lease date 25 March 1816, made by the Right Hon. William Lord Riversdale, to Richard Notter, since deceased for the lives of said Richard Notter, the Lessee, and James Deane, son of Alexander Deane, with Covenant for perpetual Renewal on payment of a Pepper Corn Renewal Fine, on the fall of each Life.
That part of Rock Island, containing 5A1R0P [5 acres, 1 rood, 0 perch] which was demised by a separate Lease of the same date to said Richard Notter, for a term of 999 years, and on which a Light

---

[46] Hickey, Famine in West Cork, 94.
[47] O'Brien, W., "The Bronze Age Copper Mines of the Goleen Area, Co. Cork", *Royal Irish Academy Journal*, 2003, p. 16.

House and the Premises thereto belonging now stand, is excepted and forms no part of the Premises to be sold.
The Estates of Lord Clinton, Lionel J. Fleming, Esq., the Rev. Thomas O'Grady and other adjoin the lot.
Richard Notter leased Mining Rights on 1 April 1851 for 31 years to William Nicholson and Thomas Phipps Thomas.

In 1853, according to the advertisement, the properties were owned by Margaret Notter (Richard's widow), Jane Kearn Munroe (nee Deane), Thomas Deane Notter, Isaac Notter and Richard Henry Notter[48]. Some property was sold but it seems unlikely that any of the West Cork property was sold at this time as they appear on later Land Commission records[49].

"Richard Deane Notter of Rock Island" was incorrectly listed as a Cork County magistrate in 1863 - it should have been Thomas Deane Notter. His brother, Richard Henry Notter of Lissacaha Cottage, Schull was also listed[50]. In 1867 Richard Henry Notter was the only Notter in the area listed as a magistrate[51]. Guy's Directory of 1875 includes R.H. Notter of Lissacaha, Lowertown as an "Ex-Officia Poor Law Guardian and a Justice of the Peace"[52]. Richard Henry Notter was still a magistrate in 1881[53].

Margaret Notter was the only daughter of Richard and Margaret Lane Notter to survive childhood. In 1869 she married Lionel Albert Becher. They had two children. Only one however survived "infancy". Margaret Lane Notter died on the 17th of April 1873, aged 27 years. Their surviving daughter, also Margaret, married Arthur

---

[48] Landed Estate Court April-May 1858, Vol. 51, National Archives, Dublin, 4/241/4.
[49] Index to the Published Rentals for Sales in the Incumbered Estates Court 1850-1866, National Archives, Dublin & Land Commission, Dublin, EC1332 & EC6810.
[50] Laing, R.H., Cork Mercantile Directory, Cork, 1863, p.189.
[51] Munster Directory, Cork, 1867, p.6.
[52] Guy's Cork Directory, 1875 – also listed in 1892 Directory.
[53] Thoms Directory, 1881, p. 1252.

Notters & Other Resident Families

Cosby. Lionel Becher was still alive in 1910 "and residing in America"[54].

Thomas Deane Notter of Rock Island House married Elizabeth Thomasin Coles Webb on the 2nd of August 1852. Her father, John Webb, was the Chief Officer of Crookhaven Coast Guard Station at the time. John Webb had joined the Royal Navy in 1820 and was the Master of the *HMS Eagle* prior to his appointment to Crookhaven. Thomas and Elizabeth (known as Eliza) had no children. He died on the 26th of October 1870. He was 50 years of age and was buried at St. Brendan's, Crookhaven graveyard. There is a tablet in his honour in Goleen Church. It reads

> A resident landlord, kind and benevolent to the poor, respected and esteemed by all who knew him.
> This tablet is erected by his widow to the deep and undying affection of him whose voice is now hushed in the still sleep of death.

He left his estate to his wife and upon her death to his half-brother James Lane Notter. James later sold it to the Wilcox family.

In the summer of 1881, Richard Henry Notter had to procure workers from Ulster to carry out harvesting etc., as his "ordinary workers had deserted him". Ulster workers were generally arranged through the Property Defence Association headed by Major Barry Broadley based in Cork City[55]. The Cork Examiner reported his problems with the Land League:

> An Iron Hut for the West
> I have learned that an iron hut is on the way for erection near the residence of Mr. R.H. Notter J.P. He is constantly guarded by police

---

[54] Land Commission, Dublin, EC6810.
[55] Donnelly, J., The Land and the People of Nineteenth Century Cork, London, 1975.

and all his employees; save an old woman, have left him. She too, though with him for 20 years, has treathened also[56].

Richard died on the 12th of August 1909. His wife Maria (nee Peel) had died in April 1909.

Isaac Notter was described as a "pillar of industry" by his grandson, Isaac Nash Notter of Callaros Eighter and later Enaghouter. His nickname as a result of his significance was "Big Pa"[57]. The following short verse has remained in local memory:

> Oh my fie for shame
> Who took the branch away?
> Who took the branch away?
> Big Pa did it
> Big Pa did it[58]

Isaac married twice, firstly to a "Ms. Lambert, a wealthy ship owner's daughter from Liverpool"[59]. There is no indication that they had any children. His second wife was Alicia Maria Nash. Apparently she was a "cousin of Lord Chichester [who was related to the Crookhaven landlord Lord Clinton] and she and Big Pa spent their honeymoon with them"[60]. Isaac Nash Notter said "he built three dwelling houses and three look-out towers for piloting foreign ships into Crookhaven harbour who were seeking orders for their valuable cargoes". One of the houses was Cape View House, outside Goleen which later became the doctor's residence. There were three towers, two on Rock Island, derelict but still in existence, and one to the east of Crookhaven village which was knocked down by the property's

---

[56] Cork Examiner, 3rd of August 1881.
[57] O'Meara, Jim, conversation with, 20th November 2005.
[58] O'Meara, Denny, conversation with, 9th January 2006. Fie is an interjection used to express disapproval. The branch may have been the ferry from Crookhaven to Rock Island.
[59] Notter, Crookhaven, 12.
[60] Notter, P., Email, 8th December 2005.

owner, Bert Mills in the late 1960s. The most easterly tower was rented by the Coast Guard. It is certainly possible that the other tower was built by him for pilotage purposes as piloting was supposedly a very lucrative business[61]. This tower, the westerly one, was marked on 1848 Ordnance Survey maps as "Coughlan's Tower". Isaac Nash Notter appeared to contradict himself later when he wrote "two of the Look Out Stations or Towers were built by the Coughlan's". MacCarthy regarded the tower knocked down by Mills as Coughan's Tower. He states "Coughlan's Tower (or the White Tower) was in the grounds of 'Sea View' to the east of Crookhaven village; the tower was demolished some years ago". He added that "there were three Coughlan brothers ...[one] a pirate, who built Coughlan's Tower south of Crookhaven"[62]. He quotes An tUasal P. Lannin

> there was only one Coughlan's Tower, the other two towers in the area were of Napoleonic war origin and were later used by the Irish Lights. Coughlan's tower was much larger than the other towers...[and served to] aid navigation into Crookhaven harbour[63].

Isaac Notter probably lived at the Welcome Inn and "carried on a brisk and lucrative business with the ship and coal dealers"[64]. As we know he had the victualling and coal supply contract for Fastnet Rock for many years as well as carrying out the reliefs of the keepers. Isaac Notter was also appointed Consul of Belgium of Crookhaven and Skibbereen on the 26th of November 1855, a position he held until he resigned it on the 17th of April 1873. He was appointed by King Leopold of Belgium and approved by Queen Victoria of Great Britain. Queen Victoria in approving him requested that "the said

---

[61] At Roches Point, where there was also a Coast Guard Station and a Lighthouse, there were three towers: "two for the pilot and one for the Coast guard" - www.coastguardsofyesteryear.org/news/ Vol2No7.htm.
[62] MacCarthy, C.J.F., "A Man of War – Jeremiah Coughlan", *Seanchas*, No.2, December 1983, p. 17.
[63] MacCarthy, A Man of War, 18.
[64] Notter, I., Letter to Angela O'Sullivan, Crookhaven, 1983.

Isaac Notter in the exercise of his Office, giving and allowing unto him all the Privileges, Immunities and Advantages thereunto belonging".

The following article appeared in the Cork Examiner on the 14th of June 1861:

> A fearful and melancholy loss of life occurred on Wednesday evening, near the Blasquet (*sic*) Rocks. Two whale boats belonging to Mr. Notter, of Crookhaven, which had been out on a fishing excursion, were returning after a most successful cruise, when near the Blasquet Rocks a sudden squall of wind caught them, for which they were quite unprepared, and one of the boats turned over and sank in a moment. None of her crew, which numbered five men, were saved. The other boat reached Crookhaven in safety. Two of the lost crew, who were unmarried, were the sole support of their widowed mothers. The other three have left wives and children, in a helpless, destitute condition.

Isaac and Alicia had seven children: Thomas, Isaac Baker, William Nash, Mary, John, Joseph (lost at sea) and Richard. Isaac, born 1861, married Hannah Webb in April 1882. She was the daughter of John Thomas Coles Webb, a Royal Navy Lieutenant. John Webb had married Nannie Thomas of the Thomas mining family. He would have met her while his father, also John Webb, was the Chief Officer of Crookhaven Coastguard Station 1848-57. Isaac and Hannah had three children. Isaac's brother John also married one of John Webb's daughter's, Elizabeth Mary, in October 1895 near Bantry. They had five children.

Isaac and John however both left their wives in Ireland and remarried. Isaac's first wife Hannah died in Belfast around 1936. Isaac died in San Francisco aged 71. John's wife Elizabeth died in Portsmouth in 1922 aged 55 years. John went to London after 1904 where he married Irene Westerman in Hammersmith in 1920. They

had a daughter and emigrated to Rochester, New York where he died in July 1930[65].
Willian John was the father of local historian Isaac. William served on Irish Lights' steamers for eight years. He married Mary Jane Love of Ballydevlin. He later farmed around his home, *Fastnet View*, in Callaros Eighter outside Goleen. He died in October 1931.
Richard, the son of Isaac "Big Pa" Notter, married Mary Spencer of Curraglass, Rossmacowen on the Beara penninsula. They lived in a house built by his father in Colleras Eighter. He died in November 1943 while she died in August 1951. Their son Joseph inherited the property. He married B. O'Reilly of Enoughter. He died in March 1968. Their sons John (Sean) and Joseph stayed in the area farming. Sean died January 2006 and is survived by his two sons John and Joseph.
Isaac Notter died on the 7th of May 1893 aged 67, at Warren's Place, Cork predeceasing his wife Alicia Maria[66]. His son Thomas, born in 1855, took over the business and was recorded as a publican, shopkeeper and grocer in the 1901 Census. He was a Catholic while his father was a Protestant. He may have been the author of a letter written to the education authorities by "Thos Deane" on the 21st of May 1894. The author complained that a teacher at Crookhaven National School, Miss K. O'Neill, was living in a "Public House". This was confirmed by the school's inspector. The school manager accepted that she lived there but that they intended to build a house for her. The school authorities refused to continue paying her salary while she lived there and so she left and found alternative accommodation five miles away on the 11th of June[67].
Thomas Notter's wife was Hannah (nee Driscoll); they had six children: William John, Mary, Richard, Alice, Thomas and James. In 1901 the children were aged between two and eight. Thomas Notter died in 1905. His widow remarried Arthur (Daddy) Nottage a former

---

[65] Notter, P., Email, 8th December 2005.
[66] Wills & Administrations 1893, National Archives, Dublin.
[67] Correspondence/Orders Book 1840-1906, National Schools, National Archives, Dublin.

telegraph operator on Brow Head. She died in December 1941 aged 70. Daughters Alice died July 1961 and Mary Harding (nee Notter) died in March 1964 aged 70. Son Richard died in March 1973 aged 78. Richard's son, Thomas and his wife Joan (nee Desmond) reside at Yokane, Crookhaven. They have five children: Richard, Helen, Thomas, Mary and John.

James Lane Notter was a "medical student" in Dublin in May 1865. His mother, Margaret Notter was living on the South Terrace, Cork. She had been left Carrigduve House in Blackrock, Cork. She died on the 17th of April 1866[68]. James married Francis "Fannie" McIlree in 1869. She was the daughter of J.D. McIlree, Surgeon General in the British Army Medical Service. They lived in Carrigduve, which he had inherited. He worked as a Staff Assistant Surgeon in the British Army. Around this time he appears to have owned land at Enaghouter, Middle and Lower Lissacaha, Boulysallagh and Kilbarry. All, apart from Lissacaha, are within three kilometres of Goleen.
By 1872 he had moved with the army to Malta where he was attached to the 10th Brigade of the Royal Artillery. At this time he owned land between Cork & Passage Railway and Carrigduve. He also owned land at Coolackey, West Carbery[69].
In 1893 he wrote a chapter of a book on disease in warm climates. At this time he was a Surgeon and Lieut. Colonel at the British Army Medical School at Netley, England with the title of Professor of Military Hygiene. He had obviously served in India previously as most of his writing referred to the country, for example "in India, woollen garments are frequently hung up, exposed to the sun, and well beaten"[70]. By present day standards he had some unusual views – "its [alcohol] universal use during long ages seems to indicate some necessity for its continuance". Also "in the tropics, spirits should be avoided while the sun is above the horizon" which he proposes

---

[68] Land Commission, Dublin, EC6810.
[69] Land Commission, Dublin, EC1332.
[70] Notter, J.L., "Hygiene in the Tropics" in Hygiene & Diseases of Warm Climates, edited by Davidson, A., Edinburgh, 1893, p. 28.

without any explanation. He later adds "after prolonged fatigue its [alcohol] value is unquestionable, provided rest can be enjoyed afterwards"[71]. He also offers some views on plants which can only be regarded as having the most tenuous of connections with hygiene "in many hills stations [in India] the rhododendrons form a special feature and add greatly to the appearance of the place"[72].

James Lane Notter died on the 24th of October 1923 at a nursing home in Southampton, England. In his will dated 1st December 1922 he appointed his "dear wife Fanny Notter[73], Sir Robert Hamil Firth K.B.E. …and my cousin Charles James Lane Solicitor of 26 South Mall Cork to be the Executors and Trustees". Apart from some possessions he left his estate to his wife. She died in 1931. Their daughter Edith Alice Maud Garton[74] had two daughters at the date of his will: Sheila and Nancy Garton. Sheila married Derrick Norris-Hill while Nancy (christened Ellen Nancy)[75] married the Hon. Dudley Oliver Trench, later to become a Lieutenant Colonel in the British Army. James Lane Notter had directed his trustees to invest in any securities "other than Irish Government Stock or securities". This was probably an understandable reaction, considering his military career and the recent Irish War of Independence. He also instructed that one guinea would be subscribed to the parish of Schull and one guinea also to the parish of Kilmoe.

In 1892 Dr. Robert Farrar Brideoake of Lancashire was living in Rock Island House[76]. He rented the house, probably from James Lane Notter. He seems to have taken over the position of local doctor from Michael English. Also in 1892, Guys Directory named

---

[71] Notter, "Hygiene in the Tropics", 37-38.
[72] Notter, "Hygiene in the Tropics", 79.
[73] Fanny Notter died 28th of June 1931.
[74] Edith Alice Maud Notter (1872-1925) married to William Garton (1867-1934).
[75] Ellen Nancy Trench, granddaughter of Colonel James Lane Notter, died on the 10th of March 1949 – Lonton, Tony, Email, 10th January 2006.
[76] Guys Cork Directory, 1892.

Charles Harcourt as the "caretaker" of Rock Island House. Charles was born in England in 1832. He had married Ellen Elizabeth Bourne in February 1867 in Union Hall where he was presumably stationed in the Coast Guard. Their son Robert was born on Rock Island in 1880 while Charles was stationed there. In May 1894 Brideoake married Charles Harcourt's daughter Emmaline[77]. Brideoake seems to have retired by 1900. In the 1901 Census he, aged 59, and Emmaline, aged 27, were still living in Rock Island House. Charles Harcourt, in 1901, was living with his other daughter Edith, aged 22, at the lighthouse where he was described as a "navy pensioner", aged 68.

By 1911 Emmaline was a widow but now only 34 years old. She described herself as a farmer. Her sister Edith Harcourt, now 29 and single, was living with her at Rock Island House. They had a servant Mary Collins aged 17, living with them. Mary, born the 4th of May 1894, was from nearby Shanavally. She was the sister of Rickie Collins and later emigrated to New York. Emmaline is last recorded as living in the house in 1914[78].

On the 13th of August 1926, Fanny Notter, James Lane Notter's widow, rented the house on a 60 year lease to Charles A. Rowe, the owner of Rowe brothers who established the quarry at Castlemeihigan in Crookhaven Harbour. The rental agreement was transferred in November 1933 from Charles A., Harold C., and Thomas B. Rowe to the Browhead Granite Company Ltd which had presumably been established to operate the quarry. Mr. Hellier, manager of the Browhead Granite Co., lived there up until the quarry's closure in 1939, due to the outbreak of World War II[79]. As a result the house is sometimes referred to as "Hellier's House". It is not clear when exactly the quarry opened. In November 1920 Rowe Brothers & Co.'s request to use the Rock Island Lighthouse crane

---

[77] Casey, W., Email, 16th June 2004.
[78] Guys 1914 Almanac & Directory for Cork.
[79] The second-in-charge of the quarry, "the timekeeper" boarded with the O'Donoghue's on Rock Island at the same time - Lannin, Mary, conversation with, 6th of March 2006.

was refused based on the Irish Lights Inspector's recommendation. The quarry must been opened around this time although another source refers to it as opening in 1925[80].The quarried stone was exported as granite chips for road making in Wales and possibly further afield to the Netherlands. The quarry used an under road tunnel to take the graded chips to the quay and from there onto ships. One of these ships, the Steamer *Slateland*, foundered on the 18th of April 1932 with a full load off Cape Clear Island. She was leaking badly, forcing Captain Douglas and his nine crew to abandon ship. They landed safely in their two small boats on Cape Clear[81]. In the early days there were around 100 working there but that had fallen to 39 by the time of its closure[82].

It was intended to re-open the quarry but this never occurred. Rock Island House was later unoccupied with a local man from Spanish Cove, Mr. Scully, acting as gardener and caretaker. It was used occasionally by its directors as a holiday home until the early 1970s[83]. The house was sold by Dudley Oliver Trench, who had inherited it from his deceased wife, to the Browhead Granite Co. on the 26th of February 1965 for £250. The Browhead Granite Co. was previously bought by the British company Amey Roadstone. Ownership transferred to Amey Roadstone in August 1975. The house was purchased in September 1979 from Amey Roadstone by David & Tony Lonton as a holiday home[84]. They undertook considerable repairs but the house's interior remains in a semi-habitable condition. The house has been on the market since 2002 for €660,000.

---

[80] McCarthy, P. & Hawkins, R., Northside of the Mizen, Cork, 1999, p. 191.
[81] Bourke, Shipwrecks of the Irish Coast, 132.
[82] McCarthy & Hawkes, Northside of the Mizen, 191. This, however, does not agree with the figure supplied in a Dail question dated 10th of December 1941 where "70 to 80 men" were unemployed as a result of the closure.
[83] Toner, N., "Between a rock and hard place", The Sunday Times, 1st September 2002, p. 33.
[84] Lonton, Tony, Email, 10th January 2006.

Rock Island

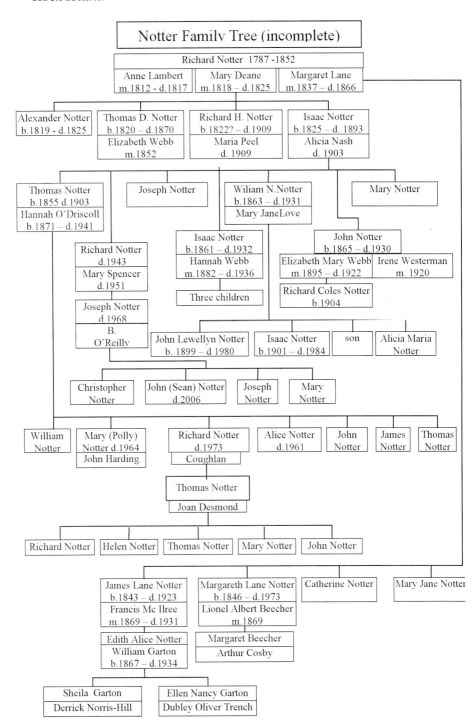

Hamiltons

In February 1834 Richard Hamilton married Mary Sheehan in Goleen. She was a servant to the Notter family. Her father, Jeremiah Sheehane, leased half a gneeve of land on Rock Island in 1828[85]. Rickard Hamilton had apparently come with his brother David to build the Goleen Catholic Church and stayed. They appear to have been the children of Alexander Hamilton of the Coast Guard at Union Hall and his Spanish wife Maria Perrari[86]. Mary Sheehan's sister Ellen married Daniel Coughlan of Spanish Cove in 1835. Her brother, Cornelius, married Anne (Nanny) Donovan, also of Spanish Cove, in 1845. By 1851-53 Rickard Hamilton shared the lease of around 21 acres on Rock Island, including buildings, with his brother-in-law Cornelius Sheehan. The land was leased from Thomas Deane Notter. They also leased an additional 16 acres at nearby Shanavally. The land included the Rock Island quarry from which they supplied the stone for Goleen Catholic Church completed in 1855[87]. By 1859 Cornelius retained the house and garden on Rock Island which was probably located to the north of Lannin's house on the side of the laneway, but his only land holding was at Shanavally.

Rickard and Mary Hamilton had six children: William, born 1835 who had a drapery shop in Schull and died of smallpox in 1872; David, born 1836 who worked for the Liverpool Customs Service; Eliza born 1840 who married lightkeeper Manus Ward[88]; Rickard, born 1845, a lightkeeper; Alexander (Sandy) born 1851; and James who emigrated to San Francisco[89].

---

[85] Tithe Applotment Book, 1823-38.
[86] Roberts, D., Rickard Hamilton, email, 29th June 2004.
[87] Lannin, Mary, conversation with, 6th of March 2006.
[88] A Manus Ward, "Monitor" at Goleen National School had his salary withdrawn on the 30th of November 1886 "owing to failures at results exam" (probably a son of Eliza & Manus Ward) - Correspondence/Orders Book 1840-1906, National Schools, National Archives, Dublin.
[89] Murphy, "Rock Island and its Families", 170.

Rock Island

Rickard Hamilton, the lightkeeper, married Hanora Sullivan. In March 1870, their son David was baptised. His godparents were James Hamilton, and Julia Downey. A daughter, Mary was baptised in April 1871. Her godparents were Jerry Donovan and May/Mary Hamilton, possibly the child's grandmother. They also had a son, William, baptised in June 1874. His godparents were his uncle Alexander Hamilton and presumably his aunt Fanny Sullivan. In September 1876, another son, Richard, was baptised. His godparents were James Stephens and his aunt Eliza Ward (nee Hamilton). They also had a daughter Mary Francis who was baptised in Goleen Catholic Church in September 1878.

Alexander Hamilton married Johanna Donovan of Boulysallagh outside Goleen. They had a son, Rickard, baptised in January 1873. Rickard's godparents were his uncle Rickard Hamilton and presumably his aunt Kate Donovan. Another son, Alexander, was baptised in August 1874[90]. They had a daughter Helena baptised in Goleen Catholic Church in May 1883. Another daughter, Eliza, was baptised in December 1885[91].

Rickard and Alexander's father died in 1886 at the age of 78. The Letters of Administrations of his personal estate were granted to his widow Mary in 1891[92]. The following notice appeared in 1893 "Rickard Hamilton, Effects unadministered £72/10. Letters of Administration of the personal estate of Rickard Hamilton, late of Rockisland, County Cork, Farmer who died 18 September 1886 at same place …were granted at Cork to Rickard Hamilton of Cranfield Point, Kilkeel, Co. Down, Light Keeper the son"[93]. Mary Hamilton may have died between 1891 and 1893.

Eliza Ward appears to have lived at the family home and acted as the Rock Island postmistress during the 1890s[94]. Some lightkeepers

---

[90] Alexander's grandson is Veterinary Surgeon Alexander Hamilton of Bantry who also owns property at Boulysallagh.
[91] Goleen Catholic Church Baptismal Records, Goleen, Co. Cork.
[92] Wills & Administrations 1892, National Archives, Dublin.
[93] Wills & Administrations 1893, National Archives, Dublin.
[94] Guys Cork Directory, 1892.

families did not follow the keepers around the country particularly when they were working on rock stations. In the 1901 census, Eliza's sister-in-law Hanoria Hamilton, 48 years old, was recorded as the head of the family and the postmistress. She was the wife of Rickard Hamilton who was PK at Rathlin O'Birne Lighthouse at the time. She lived with her sons Daniel Joseph aged 17 (who would later become a light keeper and was based on Fastnet in 1913) and Michael aged 16. They also had a widow; Margaret Daly aged 70, described as a domestic servant, living with them. A lighthouse keeper, Cornelius Brennan, aged 29, boarded with the family.

Hanoria and her family were replaced by Alexander Hamilton's family (her brother-in-law) when Rickard sold the farm to him. Alexander was dead by the next census in 1911. His wife, Johanna, aged 61, occupied the family home and worked as a "farmer and postmistress". Her daughters Helena, a National School teacher aged 26, and "Lizzie" (Elizabeth) aged 24 lived with her.

Elizabeth married Rickard Donoghue from Co. Kerry on the 1st of December 1917. Rickard was a member of the R.I.C.. He joined on the 1st of August 1901 at the age of 22 (born 1878-79). Previously he had been a draper's assistant. Initially he served in Kings County (Offaly). He was then transferred to Cork West Riding from May 1903 until November 1912. It may be assumed that he met Elizabeth during this time. Later he was transferred to Waterford, Cork East Riding (during which time they married) and Limerick. He was appointed an Acting Sergeant in October 1912, a Sergeant in November 1914 and a Head Constable in January 1921. He appeared to receive an annual pension of £236/13/4 upon being discharged in July 1922 when the force was disbanded. Their daughter Mary O'Donoghue, born 1928, remained at the family home and married George Lannin[95] who came from the townland of Gubbeen west of Schull. He was a first cousin of Richard (Rickie) Collins[96], resident of Shanavally, I.R.A. member during the War of Independence and

---

[95] George Lannin 22.2.1921-16.1.1993.
[96] Richard Collins, 8.12.1893-7.1.1968.

manager of the "Lobster Fisheries" on Rock Island. George was the head teacher at Lissagriffin National School near Barley Cove until his retirement. They had four children: Maire, born 1952 (married to Teddy O'Brien, Bantry); Eilís (Betty), born 1953 (a teacher who died of cancer in January 1998); Seán (John), born 1958 (lives nearby at Carrigacat and Milleen with his partner Lynn) and Risteard (Richard) born 1960 (head teacher at Lissagriffin, married to Margaret McCarthy, head teacher in Goleen, lives in Durrus).

The Dispensary & Dr. James McCormick

The first dispensary in the parish of Kilmoe was established on Rock Island in 1829. Lionel Fleming, Rev. O'Grady and the Coast Guard Officer "subscribed for a Dr. Orphen, who came and ministered to the poor people". This was a result of the famines of 1817 and 1822, and the threat of the cholera epidemic of 1831-32[97]. It appears that the dispensary was located from 1829 in one of the surplus Coast Guard houses.

Dr. James McCormick was the dispensary doctor throughout the famine. He worked hard as a doctor and within the local famine relief committee. As a result of his efforts he became "ill with fever" in 1847 and was forced to leave the area for a while, being replaced by a Dr. Brady who himself later died from fever[98]. McCormick was back fighting on behalf of the starving locals in June 1848 when he wrote "has not famine alone filled the graves, jails and [transportation] hulks…If the commissions do not immediately interfere, between emigration, starvation and transportation, a population will cease to exist in Kilmoe"[99].

In September 1854 Dr. McCormick was five years rent in arrears to the Admiralty, an amount of £50. He wanted to offset the repairs he had done against the arrears and start paying rent from the 1ˢᵗ of November. The Admiralty was not happy with this proposal saying

---

[97] Hickey, Famine in West Cork, 104.
[98] Hickey, Famine in West Cork, 198.
[99] Hickey, Famine in West Cork, 285.

that he was "as an annual tenant...bound only to keep them wind and water tight". They did however agree to allow £18/17/6 of the expenses he incurred. He offered in January 1856 to pay it off in instalments: £5 every May for four years. The District Inspector suggested he pay £5 half yearly over 2½ years – a total of £25/2/6.

He had vacated the house by November 1855. The Board of Works Architect reported that "he left the house in a most filthy & disreputable condition in every respect". He added that "before it can be inhabited it will require to be thoroughly cleansed, painted and repaired at an expense of probably £50"[100]. At this time, two people offered £10 per annum to rent the house: James Hutchinson Swanton, Lloyds Agent and Robert Matthew, Ship Builder. In December Isaac Notter, the "Belgium Consul", offered to pay £11/10/0 per annum for the house. J.H. Swanton increased his offer to £12 per annum which was accepted in February 1856 as "Mr. Swanton's known respectability gives him the preference"[101]. Swanton surrendered the rental in 1860.

Dr. McCormick was still the local doctor in the Goleen area in 1881[102]. He died in 1884 and according to Hickey was buried "beside Goleen Protestant Church" where his coffin was dug up and his body thrown out on the road as a result of "a dispute with the Land Leaguers"[103]. Another account states he was buried at Kilmoe graveyard and his body was thrown on Barley Cove[104]. It appears more likely that the latter is correct as his wife Eliza was buried at Kilmoe graveyard[105], although it is questionable whether his body was removed.

His descendants lived in Goleen where they owned a hotel which was sold in the 1940s and is now The Lobster Pot bar.

---

[100] Irish Coast Guard Register, National Archives, London, ADM7/39, p. 162.
[101] Irish Coast Guard Register, National Archives, London, ADM7/39, p. 208.
[102] Thoms Directory, 1881.
[103] Hickey, A Survey, p.624.
[104] O'Meara, Denis, conversation with, 21st of November 2005.
[105] Journal of the Association for the Preservation of the Memorials of the Dead, Ireland, Vol. IX, No. 1, 1913, p.239.

Lambs and Others

The Tithe Applotment Book records Patrick Lam, James Lam and Daniel Sullivan as sharing a half a gneeve of land on Rock Island in 1828. Murphy regards Lam as the Anglicisation of Ó'Luain. To the north-east of the lobster ponds on Rock Island is the small island known as Lamb's Island which is presumably related.

John Foley, most likely the Goleen Catholic curate, wrote with from Rock Island in December 1848 "what an abyss of wretchedness this part of the country has fallen into"[106]. John Foley was later responsible for building Goleen Catholic Church.

---

[106] Education Files, National Archives, Dublin, ED1/15 No.110.

ROCK ISLAND SCHOOL

The schoolhouse on Rock Island was a denominational one. It catered primarily for the Protestant children of the Coast Guard station. It was located on land owned by Richard Notter just off Griffith's Road. The school may however have predated this 1822 road as the previous road also went right by the building. Unfortunately nothing remains of the building. We may assume that it was treated, upon its closure, in a similar manner to the old Lissagriffin school where the building material was more valuable than the building.

School was located on left foreground

It seems likely that it was established by The Society for the Education of the Poor (known as the Kildare Place Society). This privately funded charity was established in December 1811. According to Hickey this was the only Protestant school in the parish around 1825. "In Kilmoe parish there were 13 schools. The parish school was at Rock Island where the master was paid £10 per year to teach 45 Protestants and four Catholics in a good slated house. This cost £50, granted from the Lord Lieutenant's school fund. The Kildare Place Society made a grant of books and school requisites"[1]

---

[1] Hickey, A Survey 126.

Rock Island

For the years 1826-27 Christopher Webb, a Protestant, was the Rock Island teacher[2].
The society was later absorbed, along with the London Hibernian Society, into the Church Education Society which was established in 1839. Their focus was on scriptural teaching as espoused by the established church, the Church of Ireland. From the early years these schools were vehemently opposed by the Catholic clergy. The object of the Society was "affording to the children of the Church, instruction in the Holy Scriptures, and in the catechism and other formularies of the [Protestant] Church". Although there may have been an emphasis on religious teaching, high standards were also expected in reading, writing, mathematics and geography. Elementary schools such as Rock Island were to "give a good secular education...arithmetic – compound rules-reduction and simple proportion. Geography – the maps of the World and the British Isles. English Grammar – the Parts of Speech and Simple Parsing"[3]. The Society, until disestablishment of the Church of Ireland, was very much an integral part of the ruling class. The first President of the Cork, Cloyne and Ross branch was the Earl of Bandon. Amongst the Vice Presidents were Lord Viscount Bernard, Lord Viscount Berehaven and Lord Carbery. In 1842 they had the following schools in the parish: Crookhaven, Altar Male and Female, Ballydevlin Male, Ballydevlin Female, Rocky (*sic*) Island, Three Castle Head[4].
The number of pupils attending the school, as per the Church Education Society[5], was:

---

[2] House of Commons Paper, 1826-27, xii, National Library of Ireland.
[3] Fifty-Seventh Annual report of the Church Education Society for Ireland, Dublin, 1896.
[4] Second Annual report of the Church Education Society for Ireland, Dublin, 1841.
[5] Annual Reports of the Church Education Society, Church Representative Body Library, Dublin.

Rock Island School

Year	No. of Pupils	Average Attendance	Local Contributions
1844	39		
1845	30		
1846	70	66	£5
1847	70	66	
1848	101	85	£5
1849	31	24[6]	£5
1850	28		
1851	23		
1852	17	15	£0
1853	19	12	£8/5/0
1854	18	13	£2
1855	26	16	£3
1856	20	12	£0/11/0
1857	32	12	£2
1858	21	7	£9
1859	35	17	£1
1860	26	15	£8
1861	23	12	£0
1862	24	15	£1
1863	20	19	£0
1864	18	9	£9
1865		Closed	
1866		Closed	
1867		Closed	
1868	Not included		
1869	No list of schools[7]		
1870	27	22	£13/10/0
1871	No list of schools		
1894	14	10	
1895	14	10	
1896	15	12	
1897	8	6	
1898	12	7	

---

[6] In 1849, there were 16 male students and 15 female students; with average attendance of 13 for the males and 11 for the females.

[7] The Church Education Society went into terminal decline as a result of disestablishment.

Rock Island

Year	No. of Pupils	Average Attendance	Local Contributions
1899	10	8	
1900	8	7	
1901	8	6	
1902	6	4	
1903	4	4	
1904	12	11	
1905	10	7	
1906	7	6	

It appears obvious that the additional children attending during the height of the famine was due to the distribution of food and clothes at the school. Some of these children can be assumed to have left to attend Goleen National School which was established in 1849.

	1849	1850	1851	1852
Goleen male	71	59	41	46
Goleen female	82	67	45	58
Total	153	126	86	104[8]

Nationally, as with Rock Island, Catholic attendance peaked at Church Education Society Schools in 1848 at 46,367 pupils.

In 1892, while suffering from reduced donations, they looked for grant aid from the Commissioners of National Education but decided they could not accept the conditions attached to the usage of scriptures. Around this time, there was a real sense of being overwhelmed by the Catholic population in rural areas like West Cork "it is just in these districts, where a few Protestant families are surrounded by an overwhelming number of Roman Catholic neighbours, that there is an especial danger to our Protestant children if they attend a Roman Catholic school". Later they stated their aim was "to keep them [Protestant children] from the injurious influences

---

[8] Hickey, A Survey, 557.

of the Roman Catholic National Schools"[9]. The Goleen National School obviously fitted this criteria.

In May 1895 The Rear Admiral at Queenstown directed that £10 be paid for repairs to the school as it was "attended by children of the Coast Guard". On the 21st of June the Goleen Rector, Rev. J. Stoney sent an acknowledgement to the District Captain of the Coast Guard for their £10 donation. The following donations were later made to the school by the Coast Guard "in view of the fact that only children of the Coast Guard men attend the school":

Date of Payment	For year	Amount
20 February 1904	1903	£5
2 March 1905	1902-03	£4
April 1905	1904	£5
10 March 1907	1905	£5

The District Captain was asked in July 1906 by a higher authority in the Coast Guard about the poor attendance of Coast Guard children at Schull and Crookhaven. He wrote "nine children out of 13 and nine out of 21 respectively only attend school. It would be desirable to ascertain why all children do not attend school". In reply the District Captain stated "at Crookhaven, nine children are attending National Schools and twelve Voluntary Schools". The National School could be either the Goleen school (teachers at the time were Joseph O'Driscoll and Mary Wooll), three km walk away or the Crookhaven school (teachers Catherine O'Driscoll plus another) which was 0.5 km by sea and a one km walk from there. It can be assumed that the Protestant children were attending the Rock Island school while the Catholics were attending the National School[10].

---

[9] Fifty-Eighth Annual report of the Church Education Society for Ireland, Dublin, 1897.
[10] ACR Permanent Records, National Archives, London, ADM120/41.

Rock Island

There is no mention of the school in the Church Education Society reports after 1906 with Three Castle Head the only Kilmoe school still in existence in 1907.

ROCK ISLAND POST OFFICE

The Rock Island Post Office was initially based in one of the unused Coast Guard houses. It was located there on the 1848 British Admiralty Chart. According to Hickey, the building of the Skibbereen – Rock Island road, completed in 1826, led to the establishment of post offices at Ballydehob, Schull and Rock Island[1]. However, according to Frank and Strange, Rock Island Post Office was established in 1852[2]. They also state confusing later that its "first appearance" was in 1857. Its postal number was COR255. Crookhaven Post Office had opened in August 1833[3]. In 1848, John Foley, the local priest, wrote from Rock Island applying for the approval of a female teacher for Goleen. He stated "the nearest post town (Rock Islands) is two miles to the south"[4].

The following request was made to the Postmaster General in June 1851

> I beg to recommend that the post "Crookhaven" may be made six days a week instead of only three days as at present at an increased cost of £10 a year to the present Skibbereen and Crookhaven Mail Cart Contractor. If the Contractor objects to perform the additional duty for the above sum, a foot messenger can easily be appointed.

The request was agreed to the same year[5]. A further request for an improved service was made in 1853. This may have involved doing two delivery runs a day to Rock Island and Crookhaven. However the Secretary would not sanction the improvements. He said "the amount of correspondence will not warrant any further outlay". He

---

[1] Hickey, A Survey, 302.
[2] This agrees with An Post who stated the station opened "approx. 1852/57" and closed 1922-25.
[3] Frank, H. & Strange, K., Irish Post Offices and their postmarks 1600-1990, Germany, 1990, pp.138-39.
[4] National School Correspondence, National Archives, Dublin, ED1/15 No.110.
[5] Royal Mail Indexes, Vol. 32, 1851, Royal Mail Heritage, London, p. 138.

did however recommend the establishment of a Goleen Post Office with the proposed salary of £3 per annum for the sub-postmaster. They could not however get someone at that salary and had to increase it to £4[6]. The Goleen Post Office appears to have opened in 1855. Lord Clinton, the principal landowner and absentee landlord of Crookhaven, requested the removal of the Crookhaven Post Office to Rock Island in 1854. This was however refused.

In May 1857 the Mail Contractor was offering "two cars instead of one only" at "no additional expenses". It is not apparent what this involved but it would "allow full advantage afforded by use of the Cork & Bandon Railway"[7]. In 1862 the Mail Car Contractor was being paid £50 per annum. It appears that it was increased to £70 in April 1862 "which is only about £2/9/0 the double mile". The Postmaster General agreed "as proposed by the Surveyor, the driver of the Skibbereen and Rockisland Mail Car may be supplied with a side pouch for the conveyance of letters, to and from, the several ships' officers which are served by the car". We know from the number of ships regularly anchored in Crookhaven harbour that this would have significantly increased the amount of post.

In Guy's Cork Directory of 1875-76 Rock Island was described as a "sub-post-office" to Skibbereen. The daily mail cart went from Skibbereen to Rock Island and back to Skibbereen. The mail from Crookhaven had to be brought by boat over to the Rock Island slipway at the end of the Grand Jury road. This is substantiated by the local historian Isaac Notter, who wrote

> in the days when the mails were brought by horse and side-car by the late Dan McCarthy to the slipway at Rock Island, from Skibbereen, and the late Mr. Florence O'Driscoll, for nearly sixty years; had the contract of collecting the mails each day; and taking them by boat across Crookhaven Harbour[8].

---

[6] Royal Mail Indexes, Vol. 36, 1853, Royal Mail Heritage, London, p. 301.
[7] Royal Mail Indexes, Vol. 44, 1857, Royal Mail Heritage, London, p. 373.
[8] Notter, I., Letter to Angela O'Sullivan, 21st March 1983.

Florence O'Driscoll would also take passengers on the boat. The traditional of taking Crookhaven's post to the Rock Island slipway continued until the late 1940s. Tom "Florrie" O'Driscoll, Florence O'Driscoll's son and the Crookhaven postman, who lived beside O'Sullivan's Bar would row across each morning around 11.00 am and collect the post from the horse and cart driven from Schull[9].

At some stage in the 19th Century, probably around 1855 according to Rickard Hamilton above, the Post Office moved from the Coast Guard buildings to south of the present Lannin house, alongside the lighthouse road. The Rock Island Post Office was closed on the 5th of September 1923[10]. Mrs Elizabeth O'Donoghue (nee Hamilton) would have been the last postmistress, a role her mother, two aunts and probably her grandparents held. With the closure of the Coast Guard station, post levels must have decreased significantly. Also the new Free State government's insistence on balancing its budget is likely to have impacted on marginally economic offices.

---

[9] O'Driscoll, Denis (Sonny), conversation with, 29th of November 2005.
[10] Dalin, C.I., Ireland's Transition: The Postal History of the Transitional Period 1922-1925, Dublin, 1992, p.332.

LOBSTER PONDS

On the 9th of September 1927, the Secretary of the Department of Industry and Commerce consented to the "construction of the lobster tank" on Rock Island[1]. The lobster pond was developed by Pierre Trehiou of Paimpol in Brittany. According to Levis, Trehiou "a Breton nationalist and a respected sea-dog, down to his proverbial wooden leg, was known locally as Captain Perry Trehiou"[2]. Rickie Collins of Shanavally appears to have been involved from the beginning with the operation. Later he managed the ponds.

Isaac Notter referred to the ponds as "an inlet of the sea walled in and fitted with sluice gates for regulating the flow of water. There is an engine operating a pump to spray the lobsters and crayfish; to keep them fresh after being taken from the pond"[3]. Trehiou collected lobster and crayfish regularly along the coast as far up as Carrigaholt, Co. Clare in an old Brixham sailing trawler, the *Thrift*, which had a storage well. He taught the Irish-speaking Blasket Islanders how to count in French.

> For many years Dingle was the only market for their [Blasket Islanders] lobster. That was until the Frenchman Pierre Trehiou came to the area with his large storage ship in the 1920s. He bought the lobster directly from the Islanders. The French vessel had a huge storage tank midship with an iron-mesh net at the bottom, leaving it open to the sea; hundreds of lobsters swam in the tank snapping at one another and feeding from the strips of hanging bacon. The Frenchman and the Islanders got on very well together, and as their relationship grew the Islanders learned to count in French, as well as learning a few French phrases. They had an agreement to exchange goods and got nets, tobacco, wine,

---

[1] Lobster tank on Rock Island, Board of Works (Black Series), National Archives, Dublin, 10155.
[2] Levis, C., Towelsail Yawls: The Lobsterboats of Heir Island and Roaringwater Bay, Cork, 2002, p.84.
[3] Notter, Crookhaven, 2.

rum, or anything else they needed on credit; those items to be debited to their account against the next haul of lobsters[4].

It appears that he may have travelled further up the coast from the following account written in 1930

> The young man [in Connemara] replied that he would like to sell me a lobster, but he was not at liberty to do so. He worked for a man who sold all the lobsters caught in the neighbourhood so that they did not belong to him but to his master.
> To whom does he sell them?
> He said that French trawlers called for them at regular intervals[5].

Lobsters were sent, packed in boxes with sawdust and ice, by lorry to the railway stations at Schull and Skibbereen. Crayfish went by sea to France in 48 hours when conditions were favourable. They were usually shipped in cutters with small engines which relied mainly on sail. Sailings at the peak of the business were every three weeks with each cutter able to carry five tons.

Trehiou also based three traditional Breton lobsterboats at Crookhaven. These were all sailing boats: the 12m *Eugenie* and the 10m *Edmond*, both carrying a "full cutter rig"; and the 14m ketch *Trimardeur*. To allow them to fish legally within three miles of the Irish coast they were all registered in the name of Rickie Collins. The *Edmond* was renamed the *Star of the Sea* at this time. Levis explains their fishing as follows:

> They fished north along the coast as far as Kerry Head at the mouth of the Shannon, the Blasket Islands and Brandon Head being among their favourite fishing grounds. Each boat fished about sixty French barrel-type pots, rather than the withy pots. Initially they practised the French method of fishing the pots in pairs, the boat acting as a mother-ship to a punt which was used to shoot and haul two pots at a time and bring the catch back to be

---

[4] www.dingle-peninsula.ie/blaskets.html.
[5] Morton, H.V., In Search of Ireland, London, 1930, p. 181.

> stored in the well. The Frenchmen always sculled rather than rowed these punts, even in the strongest wind. When the skippers of Trehiou's boats were replaced by locals, they reverted to the Irish method of fishing the pots in trains, usually with fifteen to twenty pots per train[6].

The *Star of the Sea* was wrecked on Roancarrig while fishing in Bantry Bay in 1932. No lives, fortunately, were lost. In 1937 Trehiou also lost the *Thrift* when she was wrecked on Lamb's Island off Rock Island. She was ready to return to Brittany with a full cargo of crayfish and Trehiou at the end of the season. He usually stayed in Ireland for the whole season.

On the 29th of July 1938, Rickie Collins, then manager of the "Lobster Fisheries, Rock Island Pond"[7], made the following request to the Secretary of the Department of Fisheries

> During past two years we have carried out a number of experiments in the cultivation and storage of mussels with a view to establishing an export trade to France and also to Britain. We have found a place here where we believe we can store large quantities, mussels planted here have kept well. The water is pure and the site is convenient to the road for delivery of the mussels.
> Our plan is – provided we get permission – to collect the mussels from the pickers, bring them here and place them in the storage bed where they would re-root and grow again, and then pick the amount to be shipped fresh from the bed, pass them through a purifier and send away direct. In that way we feel we could put a good live and selected mussel on the market, and we hope build up a trade in this class of shellfish.
> We are writing therefore, to ask you if you would be good enough to have the site inspected by an official from your Department with a view to giving us permission to store the mussels and build a small retaining wall about 3 feet [96cm] at entrance to prevent the mussels being disturbed by "ground swell" in winter. All

---

[6] Levis, Towelsail Yawls, 85.
[7] The address for telegrams on the headed paper was "Trehiou, Goleen".

Lobster Ponds

expenses in connection with the scheme would, of course, be borne by us.

If we get permission we would start the work as soon as possible so as to be able to store mussels next winter.

Mussel Storage Bed

The Department replied that they would consider an application for a mussel bed but any licence they would provide "does not confer any right to erect wall or other structures on the foreshore". For this right they would need consent from the Transport and Marine Branch of the Department of Industry and Commerce[8]. Permission would seem to have been forthcoming as the mussel holding area is still there.

Trehiou carried on in business until the start of World War II when he returned to France. In 1941 the ponds re-opened under the management of Hennessy's of Ballineen who leased it from Trehiou. They continued in business throughout the 1940s. Around 1950 they gave up the business and two Bretons leased the pond from Trehiou. They were Jean Oulhen from Primel and his nephew Alain Oulhen from Roscoff who had a company named La Langouste. Jean retired shortly afterwards and was replaced by his son, also Jean who become known as "White John" locally. This was to distinguish him from his cousin, also Jean Oulhen, who came to Crookhaven in 1952 and became known as "Black John". "Black John" went into business independently and employed Patrick (Sonny) O'Sullivan, Crookhaven publican, to manage three holding tanks which were moored in Crookhaven harbour. Sean Collins, T.D. had raised a parliamentary question in 1951 concerning a rumour that a French operation was setting up this second lobster fishery in Crookhaven harbour. The Parliamentary Secretary gave the following reply:

---

[8] Department of Marine, National Archives, Dublin, A2/76/38.

No foreigners may be permitted to fish within the exclusive fishery limits so that special facilities of that nature are ruled out. The Deputy probably had in mind facilities for marketing lobster. There is a lobster pond at Crookhaven managed by a local man, Mr. R. Collins, and it is understood that a French concern have an arrangement with him for storage of lobsters. Being an important lobster fishing centre a number of concerns from Great Britain and the Continent obtain supplies at Crookhaven and it has recently been rumoured that a second French concern are contemplating the erection of another pond there[9].

Rickie Collins at the Lobster Ponds

"White John" and Alain Oulhen had three lobsterboats fishing out of Crookhaven: the *Notre Dame D'Esperance* and the *Ariel*, both 10m and able to carry half a ton of lobster in their wells; and the *Fleur de France*, 14.5m which could hold one ton in its well. These were all auxiliary-powered ketches. Again they were registered in Rickie Collins name to get around the three mile exclusion. Collins remained in charge of the day-to-day running of the pond. The *Fleur de France* was renamed the *St Ita* and was skippered by Dan O'Leary with initially a French crew who, as with the other two boats, were replaced by local crew. These boats again went as far up the coast as Kerry Head. All the Oulhens had buyers around the coast. They would collect the lobster by lorry. Lobsters were collected for the Rock Island pond as far away as Grange, Co. Sligo by Jerry O'Mahony and Denis (Sonny) O'Driscoll of

---

[9] Parliamentary Question by Sean Collins, National Archives, Dublin, MAR/P341/51.

Lobster Ponds

Crookhaven. A number of French boats were used to transfer the catch to France. These included the *Mayannic*, 26m, the *Louton*, 20m, the *Rosco*, 21m, all able to carry five tons of lobster and crayfish; and the *Plumarch*, 23m which could carry ten tons. All were diesel powered. At the height of the lobster boom one of these boats would be leaving the pond every ten days between May and October/November.

The remains of the St. Ita (in middle) at Rock Island

The almost insatiable French demand for lobster and crayfish led to increased prices for local lobster fishermen. In the late 1940s, fishermen were getting 16 shillings per dozen of lobster and 18 shilling to £1 for a dozen crayfish. In the early 1950s this rose to £2 per dozen lobster and £2/10 for a dozen crayfish. By 1957 lobster were fetching £3 per dozen. The increase in value lead to dramatic overfishing and by 1960 this was reflected in the price being dictated by weight. Some fishermen diversified into shrimp and prawn which were also bought by the Oulhens.

On the 19th of August 1959 Jimmy Goggin of "The Barracks", Crookhaven, while cleaning periwinkles on the pier in front of the factory, fell into the sea and drowned. Apparently the hose he was using was not long enough and he gave it a sharp pull resulting in a join coming apart and he falling off in heavy waders. He was only 23 years old.

Rock Island

"Black John" ceased his own operations in 1963 and joined "White John" and Alain at the pond. That year Albert (Bert) Mills, who lived at "The Turrett", Rock Street, Crookhaven, took over the management from Rickie Collins. It appears that Rickie Collins was pushed out of the position and kept using an office on site for some time. Mills, who was originally from Northern Ireland, had lived previously in France and spoke fluent French. He gave employment to many local men with £5 paid for a week's casual work in the early 1960s[10]. At its peak, there were ten full-time employees with another 20 employed during the peak summer months. To cater for the processing and freezing of all the fish a new factory was built by the Bretons on Rock Island in the mid-1960s to a very obvious French design at a cost of £35,000[11].

Factory with old store in middle and ponds on right

Periwinkles, scallops, clams, prawns and salmon as well as other shellfish were kept here and later exported in consignments although some sales were made directly from the factory. A building, Richard Notter's early house on Rock Island, was demolished to build the factory[12]. The west end of the factory had previously been used as a

---

[10] O'Meara, Denis, conversation with, 29th November 2005.
[11] Notter, Crookhaven, 2.
[12] O'Driscoll, Denis (Sonny), conversation with, 2nd of December 2001.

Lobster Ponds

grain store, most likely that used to store food and provisions during the famine.

The business was in decline by the early 1970s

> I talked to the manager of the company [Bert Mills], who was deeply pessimistic about the future of the Irish lobster. He estimated that within the next decade his plant at Crookhaven would have to close down for lack of supplies. Not only were the lobster and crayfish disappearing; the periwinkles, scallops, clams and prawns which were shipped to omnivorous Frenchmen were rapidly dwindling in numbers and in size[13].

The Oulhens sold the business in 1976 to a partnership which included Pat Doherty of Donegal and Mr Samuelson, the former part owner of the lighthouse property. The lobster pond however only survived in business for another two years shutting finally in 1978. Lobster and crayfish had become increasingly scarce and expensive[14]. Celtic Fisheries was the three Oulhen's vehicle for their Rock Island operations. It was established in 1964 with a receiver appointed in 1971. The last accounts were filed in 1976 and the company was struck off the company register in 2000. Celtic Fisheries lease was transferred to Tony Fitzgibbon in April 1991. Fitzgibbon had established Rock Island Foods Ltd. trading as Cottage Foods in 1985. The business made garlic butter on site from imported garlic and Irish butter, along with other products such as cheese fillers. This enterprise employed approximately six people at its peak. Around 2002 the business was sold and employment ceased at the site. Since then there have been two attempts to develop the property: firstly 25 holiday apartments on site and secondly 12 terraced-type houses on the site with proposals to also develop the lobster pond area for recreation. No decision on the latter has been made by the planning authorities to date.

---

[13] Somerville-Large, P., The Coast of West Cork, Belfast, 1972, p. 138.
[14] Levis, Towelsail Yawls, 100.

Rock Island

On Sunday the 28th of September 1997, Denis O'Sullivan of Ballydevlin, Goleen drowned when he became entangled in ropes alongside the Lobster Pond pier. He was a fisherman and the son of Patrick (Sonny) O'Sullivan of Crookhaven.

Fitzgibbon also built a Georgian-style house for his family on Rock Island in the late 1990s alongside Griffith's road about 0.5km from the factory. "Black John" is still a regular visitor to the area having a holiday home in nearby Ballyrisode. He still enjoys catching the occasional lobster from his inshore fishing boat.

Crookhaven Lighthouse

Miscellaneous Events
Rock Island, Fastnet & Mizen Lighthouses

APPENDIX I

1863
John Francis O'Brien wrote to Irish Lights on the 7th of April requesting "that any works to be done in that locality [Crookhaven] may be done quickly"[1]. Two days later, William O'Brien, the Honorary Secretary of Crookhaven Relief committee wrote to the Board requesting the commencement of work to employ the local poor. They were however informed that there was "no work at present".
1864
On the 17th of January, John McKenna, Fastnet PK, was unable to land on the Rock due to "rough weather". It appears he was successful on the 29th of January. Isaac Notter wrote to the Board in June 1864 to say the "coal store and other repairs" were completed.
In October, the keeper reported that the Fastnet landing mast had been "blownaway".
1865
On the 10th of March, James Healy, Fastnet PK, reported the capsizing of a boat with the loss of one of the crew; "the other three were saved by lightkeepers"[2].
In March a crab winch, mast and a gaff were sent to Fastnet with instructions for their installation. It was reported that an O'Driscoll had erected the derrick in May.
1866
James Doyle reported in August that there were between 25 and 30 ton of coal in the Crookhaven stores.
1867
James Healy reported that the Fastnet mast was carried away on the 5th of January. Again in April, Tocker, the foreman on Fastnet was reporting that the "iron mast [was] carried away". Ten days later, on the 27th of April, he reported that a temporary gaff had been erected.
In March 1867, James Doyle, Crookhaven lightkeeper, reported that he had received his annual supply of wicks.
1870
James Thullier, lamp fitter, was employed on Fastnet in April 1870 to fit new pressure lamps.
On the 16th of May, the Fastnet crab winch was swept away by the sea while there were two keepers stationed on the rock.

---

[1] Journal No.21, Corporation for Preservation & Improving The Port of Dublin & Co., p. 214.
[2] Lighthouse Register 1865, Corporation for Preservation & Improving The Port of Dublin & Co.

Rock Island

1872
George Dunleavy A.K. was reported as ill in August by the Fastnet P.K. Wilson. He was off work for 20 days.
Francis Cooper was unable to return to the Fastnet in December due to illness. He resumed work after six days off. Cooper was transferred to Eagle Island in July 1873 and requested £12 to cover his costs of transfer.
1873
Stocker informed head office in July that he had timed the Fastnet light as instructed and it was keeping the correct time.
In October Stocker requested instructions "as to having Flag staff taken down".
In December Stocker sent details of the station's address and stated that Crookhaven should not be on letters. Presumably letters with Crookhaven on them would be sent to Crookhaven and then have to be returned to Rock Island sub-post office.
Thomas Fortune wrote in November that the Fastnet PK Wilson was "laid up with a sore finger".
1883
Approval was given to refloor the AK's dwelling at Fastnet at a cost of £49/19/0. On the 17th of August I. Donovan, AK Fastnet was "severely reprimanded and fined £2" for drunkenness.
1885
In May W. Notter offered to rent a house to a 2nd class AK Fastnet – the Board however decided not to accept it.
1890
Second Class AK R. H. Foster in February asked for a transfer from Fastnet "as he considers his life in danger owing to intimidation".
1893
A request by James Glanville[3] A.K. that his father (a pensioned Coast Guard), his mother and brother would be allowed to live with him on Rock Island until "they can procure a house of their own" was refused[4].
In August Michael O'Reilly, the son of a Lloyds station signalmaster at Brow Head, failed the lightkeepers' entry test[5].

---

[3] James Glanville was born on Rock Island and christened at Goleen Catholic Church on the 19th of January 1870. His parents were Michael Glanville and Margaret McCarthy. His father was in the Coast Guard and based on Rock Island at the time.
[4] Irish Lights Work File 1893/1461.
[5] Irish Lights Work File 1893/852.

Appendices

1900
On the 9th of February J. Reilly P.K. sent a telegraph from Goleen "Self and family all laid up with bad attack of influenza have handed over charge of station to Fastnet shore keeper"[6].

1904
Rev R.T. Hayes of Kilmoe Rectory, Goleen requested permission to visit Fastnet "I am staying here for a short time with my two daughters". The Commissioners allowed the visit but he had to arrange his own transport[7]. However W. F. O'Connor, M.D. Cape View House, Goleen, who wrote on the 8th of November to Irish Lights requesting permission to visit Fastnet Rock "the next time a steamer was going out", was refused. He was "doing temporary medical duty in this district at present"[8].

1908
T. Neville M.D., Goleen wrote on the 15th of September complaining that he had not been paid an allowance for looking after contractors' workers at the new Mizen dwellings on Rock Island[9].

1909
In March J. J. Sweeny, AK was paid compensation of £1/8/7 for his provisions destroyed while landing on the Fastnet[10].
John Tessings, who was unloading cement from the *SS Alexandra* at Rock Island, injured an eye in April[11].
James Twohig PK asked for the transfer of P. J. O'Donnell AK Mizen "as he was insubordinate and declined to carry out his duties at the shore establishment when senior keeper on duty". As a result O'Donnell was transferred to the Aran Island Station in November and lost two years seniority[12].
E. J. Smith AK Fastnet was paid £3/0/0 towards dental work and W. J. Martin was paid £2/2/6 for similar work in November[13]. Twohig was paid fifty percent of his costs of £4/4/- for "artificial teeth"[14].

---

[6] Irish Lights Work File 1900/171.
[7] Irish Lights Work File 1904/674.
[8] Irish Lights Work File 1904/1292.
[9] Irish Lights Work File 1908/654.
[10] Journal No.45, Corporation for Preservation & Improving The Port of Dublin & Co., 19th March 1909.
[11] Journal No.44, Corporation for Preservation & Improving The Port of Dublin & Co, 11th April 1909.
[12] Journal No.44, 5th November 1909.
[13] Journal No.44, Corporation for Preservation & Improving The Port of Dublin & Co., 19th November 1909.
[14] Journal No.44, Corporation for Preservation & Improving The Port of Dublin & Co, 11th November 1910.

Rock Island

1910
Prior to automation, in April 1910, P. Brennan AK was cautioned as the "burner of the lamp had been burnt beyond repair and lamp-glass broken". He, while on morning watch, had not extinguished the light "but left it to burn out to make wicks even". The burner was replaced with the spare one[15].

1911
In December 1911, Dr T Fahilly, a locum for Dr. Neville, claimed a fee of £3/3/- for attending to T. Barry, a mason who had been working on the Fastnet. Barry injured his hand while using potash "that he had been warned not to use" to clean the stairs. The doctor warned that he would place the matter in the hands of his solicitor if not paid. He later settled for £2/13/-[16].
J. J. Sweeny AK at Mizen Head was off duty for two months as a result of a "poisoned hand" which occurred while on duty[17].

1913
On the 22nd of August, the SS *Tearaght* placed AK D. J. Hamilton on Fastnet and took off the temporary keeper.

1914
D.J. Hamilton, AK Fastnet, requested payment in March towards new artificial teeth "to replace those broken by a fall when landing water on Fastnet. The Board agreed to pay half the cost, £2/2/-, from the Donation Fund[18].

1929
In June the *Alexandra* collected and delivered 30 tons of sand to Mizen and five tons to Rock Island[19]. Where the Mizen delivery was unloaded was not provided.

1930
In September J. Driscoll, a temporary keeper, was paid eight shillings a day for 16 days as John Coughlan AK was ill.

1933
B. O'Malley of the "Civic Guard", Goleen was given permission the visit Fastnet on the next relief boat in May[20].

1936
In March J. Mahony was paid £3 for attempting, unsuccessfully, a Fastnet relief due to the illness of Donlon AK[21].

---

[15] Journal No.44, 13th April 1910.
[16] Journal No.46, Commissioners of Irish Lights, 15th December 1911.
[17] Journal No.46, Corporation for Preservation & Improving The Port of Dublin & Co., 21st April 1911.
[18] Journal No.47, Corporation for Preservation & Improving The Port of Dublin & Co., 20th March 1914.
[19] Journal No.50, Commissioners of Irish Lights, 21st June 1929.
[20] Journal No.53, Corporation for Preservation & Improving The Port of Dublin & Co., 5th May 1933.

Appendices

1938
A request from J. Hegarty, in June, to allow his sister to reside with him as his "housekeeper" was not objected to by J. Kennedy PK and was allowed by the Commissioners[22].

1941
In August 1941, Bowler (presumably Edmond or Sylvester) of Crookhaven was paid £4 for one ton of turf supplied "for use of painter living in valley house"[23].

1945
P. S. O'Sullivan, Crookhaven publican, undertook a "special trip relief" on the 6th of September. He was paid £10 after deducting for ten gallons of oil[24].

1947
Don Scanlon recalled while training on the Bailey lighthouse that the PK there was John King. "He was a nice man with some fingers missing from his hand – the result of an accident on the Fastnet Rock Lighthouse early on in his career"[25]. King was the Fastnet PK from 1943-45; no record was found of him have served there earlier.

Lawlor AK at Mizen Head asked for a transfer to Tory Island or Inisheer.
Liam O'Driscoll, of Goleen, was paid £1/4/- to convey the doctor and the Fastnet PK to Mizen Head "on Inspector's direction to contact sick keepers...and give them medication concerning their complaints"[26].

1955
Tim Coughlan, of Goleen, was paid £10/10/- for taking the doctor to Rock Island and then taking the sick keeper William Shanahan to hospital in Cork in August[27].

1956
In March M. MacCarthy was paid £3/13/6 for reserve provisions as his relief was 27 days late.

1960
There were eight keepers attached to Fastnet and Mizen. Four of these lived in the Goleen area, but no longer at the lighthouse – M. A. Boyle, J. T. O'Brien, P. J. Coughlan and B. P. O'Regan. Two other lived at Castletownbere – J. V. Power and J. R. Sugrue[28].

---

[21] D3 Book Fastnet 1926-36, Inspectors Dept, Commissioners of Irish Lights.
[22] Irish Lights Work File 1938/428.
[23] D3 Book Fastnet 1936-55, Inspectors Dept, Commissioners of Irish Lights.
[24] D3 Book Fastnet 1936-55, Inspectors Dept, Commissioners of Irish Lights.
[25] Scanlon, D., Memoirs of an Islander: A Life on Scattery and Beyond, Ennis, 2003.
[26] D3 Book Fastnet 1936-55, Inspectors Dept, Commissioners of Irish Lights.
[27] D3 Book Mizen 1936-55, Inspectors Dept, Commissioners of Irish Lights.
[28] Irish Lights Work File 1959/146.

Rock Island

Crookhaven Lighthouse
Lightkeepers based at Station (incomplete)

APPENDIX II

Name	Rank	Station	Years
Higginbotham		Crookhaven	1861
Marcus Ward		Fastnet	1862-65
John McKenna	PK	Fastnet	1862-64
W J McGinns	AK	Fastnet	1863
J Maginn	PK	Crookhaven	1863-64
Fenis/Ferris	AK	Fastnet	1863
James Healy	PK	Fastnet	1864-65
James Doyle		Crookhaven	1864-67
Robert Butler	AK	Fastnet	1864-66
Daniel Coughlan	AK	Fastnet	1864-83
Robert Blake	AK	Fastnet	1864
William Doherty	AK	Fastnet	1865
J Ward	AK	Fastnet	1866
Thomas Fortune	AK	Fastnet	1867-73
W Williams	PK	Fastnet	1867-71
Henry Gardiner		Crookhaven	1868-71
James McCormick	AK	Fastnet	1869
J Brownell	AK	Fastnet	1870-71
W Wilson	PK	Fastnet	1871-73
Henry Stocker		Crookhaven	1871-73
George Dunleavy	AK	Fastnet	1872
Francis Cooper	AK	Fastnet	1872-73
W Wilson	PK	Fastnet	1872
Tyrell		Fastnet	1874
J Stapleton	AK	Fastnet	1880-81
I Donovan	AK	Fastnet	1883
George Dunleavy	PK	Fastnet?	1886
R H Foster	AK	Fastnet	1890
R Phelim		Fastnet	1890
R Lyons	AK	Fastnet	1890-91
Edward Donovan	AK	Fastnet	1891-93
Harris	AK	Fastnet	1891
J Coughlan	AK	Fastnet	1891

Name	Rank	Station	Years
Kennedy	AK	Fastnet	1891
Maginn	PK	Fastnet	1891
Francis Ryan	PK	Fastnet	1891-95
Henry Gardiner	PK	Crookhaven	1892
James Glanville	AK	Fastnet	1893
George Brownell	PK	Fastnet	1895-96
Edward Rohu	PK	Fastnet	1896-01
J Reilly	PK	Fastnet	1900
John Wills	AK	Fastnet	1900-01
James Twohig	PK	Fastnet	1901-11
Jonathan Wright	AK	Fastnet	1901-04
Alfred Rohu	AK	Fastnet	1901
Cornelius Brennan	AK	Fastnet	1901
William J Martin	AK	Fastnet	1904-11
T P Murphy	PK	Fastnet	1904
Stephen McMahon	SAK	Fastnet	1908
James J Sweeny	AK	Fastnet	1908-10
R Blakely	AK	Fastnet	1909-11
W Snow	AK	Fastnet	1909-11
E Sullivan	AK	Fastnet	1909
P J O'Donnell	AK	Mizen	1909
E J Smith	AK	Fastnet	1909-13
P Brennan	AK	Fastnet	1910
James J Sweeny	AK	Mizen	1910-15
E Sullivan	AK	Mizen	1910-16
A J McCloskey	AK	Mizen	1910-11
P Brennan	AK	Fastnet	1911-16
T P Murphy	PK	Fastnet	1911-19
Jas Devaney	AK	Fastnet	1911-17
M Kennedy	AK	Fastnet	1911-16
J E Clague	AK	Fastnet	1911-15
C Burke	AK	Mizen	1912-16
D J (Danny) Hamilton	AK	Fastnet	1913-16
F J Ryan	AK	Fastnet	1914-18
M Duffy	AK	Fastnet	1915-17
Joseph McCann	AK	Mizen	1915-16

Rock Island

Name	Rank	Station	Years
Andrew Coughlan	AK	Fastnet	1916-22
C Burke	AK	Fastnet	1916-18
Jim O'Connor	AK	Mizen	1916-19
D J (Danny) Hamilton	AK	Mizen	1916-19
Jas Lance	AK	Mizen	1916-18
A J (Alf) Rohu	AK	Fastnet	1917-19
M McMahon	AK	Fastnet	1917-19
W Higginbotham	AK	Fastnet	1918
J R Higginbotham	SAK	Fastnet	1918
Wall			1919
Patrick Whelan	AK	Fastnet	1918-22
John Crowley	AK	Fastnet	1919-24
John Joseph Treeby	PK	Fastnet	1919-24
J J Duggan	AK	Mizen	1919-21
F J Duffy	AK	Mizen	1920-22
Henry Staniforth	AK	Fastnet	1921-24
Patrick Heneghan	AK	Fastnet	1922-26
John Fennell	AK	Fastnet	1921-23
Donovan			
J J Duggan	AK	Mizen	1921
James Johnson	PK	Fastnet	1924-26
John Harding	AK	Fastnet	1924-30
John Keane	AK	Fastnet	1924-26
Patrick McCann	AK	Fastnet	1926-29
Peter J O'Connor	AK	Fastnet	1926-31
Andrew Kilgallon	PK	Fastnet	1928-31
Richard Roddy	AK	Fastnet	1929-32
Andrew Coughlan	AK	Fastnet	1926-31
J Harding	AK	Fastnet	1930
William Hamilton	AK	Fastnet	1930-31
P Roddy	AK	Mizen	1930-37
John (Jer) Coughlan	AK	Mizen	1930-31
P J Staniforth	AK	Mizen	1930
P J O'Connor	AK	Mizen	1930-31
Benjamin Godkin	PK	Fastnet	1931-33
John (Jer) Coughlan	AK	Fastnet	1931-34

Appendices

Name	Rank	Station	Years
P J O'Connor	AK	Fastnet	1931-32
Andrew Kilgallon	PK	Mizen	1931-32
Andrew Coughlan	AK	Mizen	1931-33
David Donovan	AK	Fastnet	1932-35
William J Cahill	AK	Fastnet	1932-36
J A O'Connor	PK	Mizen	1932-34
Eugene Fortune	PK	Fastnet	1933-36
J A O'Connor	PK	Mizen	1933
Michael J Crowley	AK	Mizen	1933-34
Michael J Crowley	AK	Fastnet	1934-35
A McQuaig	PK	Mizen	1934-36
D J Sullivan	AK	Mizen	1934-37
James J O'Connor	AK	Fastnet	1935-38
James Hegarty	AK	Fastnet	1935-38
M J O'Connor	SAK	Mizen	1935
J J Dillon	SAK	Mizen	1935
A J Kennedy	PK	Fastnet	1936-39
John Joe McCann	AK	Fastnet	1936-39
Jas Hegarty	PK	Mizen	1936-38
D Byrne	AK	Mizen	1937-38
T A Murphy	AK	Mizen	1937-38
J Kennedy	AK	Fastnet	1938
T J Lawlor	AK	Fastnet	1938-44
J Hegarty	AK	Fastnet	1938-43
Daniel Hawkins	PK	Fastnet	1939-41
John CW Coughlan	AK	Fastnet	1939-41
Henry Staniforth	PK	Fastnet	1941-43
William Knox	AK	Fastnet	1941-43
Joseph Stapleton	AK	Fastnet	1942-44
Timothy O'Sullivan	AK	Fastnet	1942-46
Gerard Rohu	AK	Fastnet	1943-46
John King	PK	Fastnet	1943-45
James Lavelle	AK	Fastnet	1944-47
William A Hamilton	PK	Fastnet	1945-46
John Glanville	PK	Fastnet	1946-48
Patrick Whelan	AK	Fastnet	1946-49

Rock Island

Name	Rank	Station	Years
Michael Sweeney	AK	Fastnet	1946-48
Edward Cummins	AK	Fastnet	1947
James Power	AK	Fastnet	1947-49
Lawlor	AK	Mizen	1947
Daniel James Sullivan	PK	Fastnet	1948-49
Daniel Coughlan	AK	Fastnet	1948-52
Richard Roddy	PK	Fastnet	1949-51
Joseph Stapleton	AK	Fastnet	1949-51
Denis Cahill	AK	Fastnet	1949-52
Martin Keane	AK	Fastnet	1950-52
George James	PK	Fastnet	1951-52
Kevin Murphy	PK	Mizen	1951-57
Vincent Linnane	AK	Fastnet	1951-52
Thomas Murphy	PK	Fastnet	1952-54
Andrew Coughlan	AK	Fastnet	1952-53
Martin Kennedy	AK	Fastnet	1952-54
Dominick Gaughan	AK	Fastnet	1952-54
Timothy O'Sullivan	AK	Fastnet	1953-55
Michael Crowley	PK	Fastnet	1954-60
Nicholas Lawler	AK	Fastnet	1954-56
William Shanahan	AK	Fastnet	1954-58
Michael Crowley	PK	Fastnet	1954-60
Patrick J Coughlan	AK	Fastnet	1955-59
Thomas Scanlon	AK	Fastnet	1956-59
Bryan O'Regan	AK	Fastnet	1958-62
Thomas Walsh	AK	Fastnet	1959-64
John Sugrue	AK	Fastnet	1959-66
J Power			1959
J Walshe			1959
J Hegarty			1959
D Gaughan			1959

Notes
1. List is incomplete – no separate personnel records retained until 20th century.
2. Additional years may have been served at the station.
3. PK - Principal Keeper; AK - Assistant Keeper; SAK - Supernumerary Assistant Keeper
4. Joe McCann (Fastnet 1915-16) was the brother of Pat McCann (Fastnet 1928). John Joe McCann (Fastnet 1936-38) was the son of Pat McCann

Appendices

Crookhaven Coast Guard Personnel APPENDIX III
Listed according to Rank (incomplete)

Commence Date	Name	Rank	Departure Date
	Robert Robinson	Chief Officer	8 Mar 1820
10 Jan 1820	*John Mills*	*Chief Officer*	*8 Mar 1820*
8 Mar 1820	Richard Medway	Chief Officer	30 Apr 1829
30 Apr 1829	Richard Hungerford	Chief Officer	22 Sept 1842
9 Mar 1843	William Butler	Chief Officer	30 Nov 1843
8 Dec 1843	Charles Wilson Ross	Lt of Station	30 Oct 1845
4 Nov 1845	Henry Baldwin	Chief Officer	11 Aug 1848
25 Aug 1848	John Webb	Chief Officer	7 Feb 1857
1 Feb 1859	John Mullins	Chief Officer 2nd	31 July 1864
27 Sept 1864	John Bridger	Chief Officer	
	William Wright	Act. Chief Officer	
	Thomas Sliney	Chief Officer	
11 Feb 1897	Patrick Maloney	Chief Officer	1 Jan 1902
23 Mar 1909	Charles Hennessy	Chief Officer	29 May 1914
1 July 1915	James Henry Lake	Chief Officer	17 Sept 1919
10 Jan 1820	Thomas Lloyd	Chief Boatman	
	Chad Stevens	Chief Boatman	31 Jan 1826
31 Jan 1826	David Jenkins	Chief Boatman	31 May 1826
31 May 1826	Henry Wodgen	Chief Boatman	5 Jan 1827
5 Jan 1827	William Wingate	Chief Boatman	5 Jan 1828
5 Jan 1828	Robert Brooks	Chief Boatman	4 May 1831
31 July 1831	John Cooper	Chief Boatman	17 Mar 1843
17 Mar 1843	John Downs	Chief Boatman	4 Nov 1846
13 Nov 1846	Jer. Donovan	Chief Boatman	14 Feb 1852
20 Feb 1852	Stephen Goodfellow	Chief Boatman	29 Sept 1859
29 Sept 1859	Joseph Davie	Chief Boatman	28 Dec 1861
28 Dec 1861	James Cobhann	Chief Boatman	22 Oct 1862
22 Oct 1862	Alfred Lillington	Chief Boatman	4 May 1865
20 May 1864	Micheal (S?)ender	Chief Boatman	18 July 1865
16 Aug 1865	James Duggan	Chief Boatman	18 Jan 1868
	Joseph Jupe	Chief Boatman	

217

Rock Island

Commence Date	Name	Rank	Departure Date
	Samuel Griffiths	Ch. Petty Officer	
	James Newton	Petty Officer	
10 Jan 1820	William Crook	Com.d Boatman	5 Mar 1821
10 Jan 1820	William Franks	Com.d Boatman	5 Oct 1821
6 Oct 1821	James Brown	Com.d Boatman	
5 Mar 1821	Matthias Higgs	Com.d Boatman	5 May 1822
	Henry Rees	Com.d Boatman	31 Jan 1826
	Edm,st. Morgan	Com.d Boatman	31 May 1826
5 Apr 1826	Jeremiah Lynch	Com.d Boatman	31 May 1826
31 May 1826	Elijah Wingrove	Com.d Boatman	5 Sept 1828
31 May 1826	John Church	Com.d Boatman	27 Mar 1828
12 May 1828	William Neill	Com.d Boatman	10 Oct 1833
5 Jan 1829	John Cooper	Com.d Boatman	31 July 1831
31 July 1831	Micheal Sweeney	Com.d Boatman	30 Apr 1833
30 Apr 1833	James Nockles	Com.d Boatman	17 Sept 1838
1 Oct 1833	John Hennessy	Com.d Boatman	30 Nov 1835
16 ? 1835	Henry Topple	Com.d Boatman	28 Feb 1837
28 Feb 1837	Thomas Holden	Com.d Boatman	June 1846
17 Sept 1838	Daniel Mortimer	Com.d Boatman	20 Jun 1840
20 Jun 1840	Jeremiah Donovan	Com.d Boatman	13 Nov 1846
13 July 1846	William Brook	Com.d Boatman	1 Mar 1849
28 Nov 1846	Florence McCarthy	Com.d Boatman	23 Apr 1852
19 Mar 1849	Robert David Duckett	Com.d Boatman	16 Aug 1852
28 Apr 1852	John Hill	Com.d Boatman	16 July 1858
16 Aug 1854	Samuel McIlwanie	Com.d Boatman	27 Dec 1859
24 July 1858	Micheal Coughlan	Com.d Boatman	7 Oct 1862
2 Mar 1859	John Mullins	Com.d Boatman	13 July 1863
27 Dec 1859	Thomas Owen	Com.d Boatman	31 July 1863
10 Jan 1862	Thomas Salter	Com.d Boatman	12 Apr 1864
22 Jan 1862	Richard Pillman	Com.d Boatman	27 Sept 1862
7 Oct 1862	John Bell	Com.d Boatman	9 Nov 1864
31 July 1863	Richard R Tippett	Com.d Boatman	
31 Oct 1864	Cornelius Driscoll	Com.d Boatman	
9 Nov 1864	William Higgins	Com.d Boatman	

Appendices

Commence Date	Name	Rank	Departure Date
	John Charles May	Com.d Boatman	
	W Flynn	Com.d Boatman	
	William Pocknell	Leading Boatman	
6 Feb 1820	Richard Waugh	Boatman	
20 Apr 1820	James Lang	Boatman	23 May 1820
20 Apr 1820	Daniel Richards	Boatman	23 May 1820
20 Apr 1820	John Wagstaff	Boatman	23 May 1820
20 Apr 1820	Matthew Higgs	Boatman	5 Mar 1821
6 Feb 1820	James Brown	Boatman	6 May 1821
14 May 1820	Isaac Waugh	Boatman	
14 May 1820	John Jennings	Boatman	
14 May 1820	Laurence Sullivan	Boatman	
21 June 1821	Morris Sheahy	Boatman	
25 July 1821	John Murphy	Boatman	31 July 1828
22 Oct 1821	Jeremiah Murphy	Boatman	
22 Oct 1821	Micheal Burke	Boatman	
26 Oct 1821	Joseph Wilson	Boatman	10 Oct 1827
26 Oct 1821	Thomas Phillips	Boatman	
11 Jan 1822	Timothy McCarthy	Boatman	
11 Jan 1822	James McCarthy	Boatman	
14 May 1822	Daniel Mullins	Boatman	31 Aug 1826
	Thomas Coveney	Boatman	31 May 1826
	John Collins	Boatman	31 May 1826
	John Murphy	Boatman	31 May 1826
	Jas Brady	Boatman	31 May 1826
	Tim Driscoll	Boatman	31 Jan? 1826
	Jeremiah Harrington	Boatman	31 May 1826
	Cornelius Regan	Boatman	31 May 1826
	James Bayley	Boatman	Aug 1830
	Sexton Allen	Boatman	19 July 1826
	Joseph Wilson	Boatman	10 Oct 1827
	William Shea	Boatman	5 July 1829
	Thomas Craig	Boatman	19 Aug 1830
	Micheal Sweeney	Boatman	31 July 1831
	James Noonan	Boatman	18 Sept 1838

Rock Island

Commence Date	Name	Rank	Departure Date
27 Oct 1838	Ralph Charles	Boatman	11 Aug 1840
12 Aug 1840	David Kennely	Boatman	19 Oct 1843
18 Nov 1844?	Walker Henry	Boatman	2 Apr 1844
	Patrick Darragh	Boatman	14 Jan 1845
8 Apr 1844	John William Curtis	Boatman	5 May 1846
14 Jan 1845	William Brock	Boatman	5 July 1846
5 May 1846	Robert David Duckett	Boatman	19 Mar 1849
13 Aug 1846	Florence McCarthy	Boatman	28 Nov 1846
3 Dec 1846	Charles Evans	Boatman	19 Feb 1859
16 Apr 1849	Samuel Appeldore	Boatman	28 July 1856
19 Dec 1849	Richard Barry	Boatman	27 Dec 1859
19 Dec 1849	John Clark	Boatman	16 May 1857
27 May 1851	James Mahony	Boatman	27 Dec 1859
11 Aug 1856	Micheal Coughlan	Boatman	24 July 1858
24 July 1858	Isaae Colenutt	Boatman	7 Apr 1863
27 Dec 1859	Patrick Murphy	Boatman	30 Oct 1861
27 Dec 1859	John Payne	Boatman	29 Aug 1864
10 Jan 1862	John Morgatroyd	Boatman	31 Oct 1864
10 Feb 1862	James Brady	Boatman	22 Apr 1864
20 Dec 1862	Richard Cotter	Boatman	
7 Apr 1863	John Beamish	Boatman	3 Aug 1867
13 July 1863	James Burke	Boatman	
12 Apr 1864	Mortimer Sullivan	Boatman	20 Apr 1865
13 May 1864	Richard Jeffers	Boatman	
29 Aug 1864	James Marshall	Boatman	7 Jan 1867
3 Dec 1866	John Avcutt	Boatman	
Sept 1866	John Harsin	Boatman	
30 July 1867	Henry Merrett	Boatman	
9 Jan 1870	Micheal Glanville		
	Charles Harcourt	Boatman	
	H Musselwhite	Boatman	
	T. Dwyer	Boatman	
	Walter Chamberlain	Boatman	
	A Kitcher	Boatman	
	C Shaw	Boatman	
	Richard Tucker	Coastguard	

Appendices

Commence Date	Name	Rank	Departure Date
	Ernest Adams	Coastguard	
23 May 1894	Henry William Swyer		14 Jun 1895
28 Dec 1901	Alfred Nevitt		28 June 1903
28 May 1903	William Maloney		29 Aug 1904
1 Aug 1904	Henry James Byres		22 Mar 1909
10 June 1914	David W Laley	Boatman	1 Nov 1920
	William B Mulligan		19 Apr 1910

Notes:
1. List is incomplete due to missing service records – Coast Guard Establishment Ireland, National Archives, London, ADM175/--.
2. William Wright served in Crookhaven in 1880 as per Navy List; Thomas Sliney served in Crookhaven in 1892 as per Guy's Cork Directory.
3. Daniel Mullins, Boatman was originally from Crookhaven.
4. Com.d Boatman = Commissioned Boatman

BIBLIOGRAPHY

Irish Lights Archival Records

Committee Minute Book, Irish Lights, 1930-46.
D3 Book Crookhaven 1936-55, Inspectors Dept., Commissioners of Irish Lights.
D3 Book Crookhaven 1956-68, Inspectors Dept., Commissioners of Irish Lights.
D3 Book Crookhaven 1962-69, Inspectors Dept., Commissioners of Irish Lights.
D3 Book Fastnet 1956-68, Inspectors Dept, Commissioners of Irish Lights.
D3 Book Mizen 1936-55, Inspectors Dept, Commissioners of Irish Lights.
Irish Lights Work Files.
Journals No.8-24, Corporation for Preservation & Improving The Port of Dublin & Co.
Journals No.25-50, Commissioners of Irish Lights.
Journal No.61, Commissioners of Irish Lights Board Minute Book 1962-64.
Lighthouse Registers 1862-73.
Lighthouse Wages & Allowances 1930-31, Commissioners of Irish Lights.
Order Book, Commissioners of Irish Lights, 13th May 1903.
Raid Files, Commissioners of Irish Lights.

National Archives, Dublin

Abstract of Leases and Lettings, OPW4/6/12.
Bursary on Crayfish Study Project at Goleen, Co. Cork, MAR/A2/228/68.
Coast Guard and Customs Register, 1907, OPW5/8/25.
Coast Guard Correspondence 1865, OPW5/8/1.
Coast Guard Letters 18th October – 29th March 1871, OPW1/2/1/6.

Bibliography

Correspondence/Orders Book 1840-1906, National Schools.
Department of Marine, A2/76/38.
Education Files, ED1/15.
Index to the Published Rentals for Sales in the Incumbered Estates Court 1850-1866.
Landed Estate Court April-May 1858, Vol. 51, 4/241/4.
Lobster tank on Rock Island, Board of Works (Black Series), 10155.
Map of Mizen Head to Kinsale with proposed Fastnet Cable, BT/5155.
Marriage Licence Bonds: Diocese of Cork and Ross 1623-1750.
Marriage Licence Bonds: Diocese of Cork and Ross 1751-1845.
National School Correspondence, ED1/15 No.110.
Office of Public Works, Coast Guard Correspondence, OPW7/2/2.
Parliamentary Question by Sean Collins, MAR/P341/51.
Relief Commission Papers, 27th March 1846, RLFC3/2/6/61.
Relief Commission Papers, 27th May 1846, RLFC3/2/6/60.
Relief Commission Papers, 28th January 1846, RLFC3/1/429.
Relief Commission Papers, 8th April 1846, RLFC3/1/1331.
Tithe Applotment Book, 1823-38.
Williams, A.T., Office of Public Works Coast Guard file, OPW5/47019/80.
Wills & Administrations 1892 & 1893.

<u>National Archives, London</u>

ACR Permanent Records, ADM120/41.
Admiralty: Brow Head Signal Station – Question of Right of Way, ADM1/8365/9.
Coast Guard Letters 1856, ADM114/11.
Coast Guard Permanent Records 1922, ADM120/116.
Coast Guard Records, ADM120/10.
Coast Guards (Ireland) Parliamentary Papers 1834, 37.296.

Coastguard Minute Book August 1838 – December 1843, CUST29/41.
Coastguard Minute Book January 1844 – March 1849, CUST29/42.
Customs Ireland: Salaries & Incidents At Outposts, 1842, CUST38/18.
Fastnet Foreshore Cable Licence, MT10/615.
House of Commons Parliamentary Papers 1861, 67.461.
Irish Coast Guard Register, ADM7/39.
Raiding & Burning by Sinn Feiners, ADM116/2084.
Raids on Irish Coast Guard Stations, ADM178/108.

Other Contemporary Records

Annual Reports of the Church Education Society, Church Representative Body Library, Dublin.
Cork Examiner, 1846 +.
Goleen Catholic Church Baptismal Records, Goleen, Co. Cork.
Guy's Cork Directory, 1875, 1892 & 1914.
House of Commons Paper, 1826-27, xii, National Library of Ireland.
Ireland Reports & Minutes, Vol. 42, Royal Mail Heritage, London.
Ireland Reports & Minutes, Vol. 47, Royal Mail Heritage, London.
Ireland Reports & Minutes, Vol. 48, Royal Mail Heritage, London.
Irish Coast Guard Order Book 1852-60, National Maritime Museum, London, MS85/106.
Land Commission, Dublin, EC1332.
Land Commission, Dublin, EC6810.
Royal Mail Indexes, Vol. 32, 1851, Royal Mail Heritage, London.
Royal Mail Indexes, Vol. 36, 1853, Royal Mail Heritage, London.
Royal Mail Indexes, Vol. 44, 1857, Royal Mail Heritage, London.
Southern Reporter, 12th of January 1847.
The Parliamentary Gazetteer of Ireland, Dublin, 1844.
Thom's Almanac and Official Directory, 1861 & 1881.

Bibliography

Washington, State of the Harbours and Lighthouses on the South and South-west coasts of Ireland, Dublin, 1849, National Library of Ireland.
Munster Directory, Cork, 1867.

Books & Dissertations

Bourke, E.J., Shipwrecks of the Irish Coast 1105-1993, Dublin, 1994.
Bowen, F., Her Majesty's Coastguard, London, 1928.
Commissioners of Irish Lights, Instructions to Light Keepers, Dublin, 1905.
Dalin, C.I., Ireland's Transition: The Postal History of the Transitional Period 1922-1925, Dublin, 1992
Dear, I., Fastnet: the story of a great ocean race, London, 1981.
Donnelly, J., The Land and the People of Nineteenth Century Cork, London, 1975.
Dickson, D., Old World Colony: Cork and South Munster, Cork, 2005.
Durell, P., Discover Dursey, Beara, 1996.
Fastnet Lighthouse Centenary 1903-2003, Commissioners of Irish Lights, 2003.
Feehan, J., The Wind that round the Fastnet sweeps, Dublin, 1978
Ffolliot, R., Index to Biographical Notices Collected from Newspapers, Principally relating to Cork and Kerry 1756-1827, Cork City Library.
Frank, H. & Strange, K., Irish Post Offices and their postmarks 1600-1990, Germany, 1990.
Gore-Grimes, J., "A Labour of Love", *Beam: The Journal of the Irish Lighthouse Service*, Vol. 24, 1995.
Harrington, G., "The Harringtons and Calf Rock", *Beam: The Journal of the Irish Lighthouse Service*, Vol. 29, 2000.
Hickey, P., Famine in West Cork: The Mizen Peninsula: Land and People, 1800 – 1852, Cork, 2002

Hickey, P., A Survey of Four Peninsular Parishes in West Cork 1796-1855, MA Thesis, UCC, 1980.
Jermyn, N., My Parish, Schull, 2000.
Journal of the Association for the Preservation of the Memorials of the Dead, Ireland, Vol. IX, No. 1, 1913.
Laing, R.H., Cork Mercantile Directory, Cork, 1863
Lankford, E., Fastnet Rock: An Charraig Aonair, Cape Clear, 2004.
Lankford, E., Cape Clear Island: Its People and Landscape, Dublin, 1999.
Lewis, S., Topographical Dictionary of Ireland, London, 1837.
Levis, C., Towelsail Yawls: The Lobsterboats of Heir Island and Roaringwater Bay, Cork, 2002.
MacCarthy, C.J.F., "A Man of War – Jeremiah Coughlan", *Seanchas*, No.2, December 1983.
McCarthy, P. & Hawkins, R., Northside of the Mizen, Cork, 1999.
McVeagh, J., (ed.), Richard Pococke's Irish Tours, Dublin, 1995.
Morrissey, J., A History of the Fastnet Lighthouse, Dublin, 2004.
Morton, H.V., In Search of Ireland, London, 1930.
Murphy, S., "Kevin Murphy, Principal Keeper", *Beam*, Vol. 32, 2003.
Murphy, S., "Rock Island and Its Families", *Mizen Journal*, no.5, 1997.
Notter, J.L., "Hygiene in the Tropics" in Hygiene & Diseases of Warm Climates, edited by Davidson, A., Edinburgh, 1893.
O'Briain, S., "Epilogue", *Beam*, Vol. 26, 1997.
O'Brien, B. & Whooley, M., ed., From Ilen to Roaring Water Bay: Reminiscences from the Parish of Aughadown, Skibbereen.
O'Brien, W., "The Bronze Age Copper Mines of the Goleen Area, Co. Cork", *Royal Irish Academy Journal*, 2003.
Pelly, F. "William Douglass: Designer of Fastnet Lighthouse", *Beam*, Vol. 33, 2004.
Power, D., (ed.), Archaeological Inventory of County Cork: Vol. 1, Dublin, 1992.
Ruttle, Stuart, "Innovative Technology", *Beam*, Vol. 33, 2004

Bibliography

Scanlon, D., Memoirs of an Islander: A Life on Scattery and Beyond, Ennis, 2003.
Scott, C.W., History of the Fastnet Rock Lighthouses, Schull, 1993(reprint).
Smith, Charles, The Ancient and Present state of the County and City of Cork, Cork, 1893 (reprint).
Somerville-Large, P., The Coast of West Cork, Belfast, 1972.
Toner, N., "Between a rock and hard place", *The Sunday Times*, 1st September 2002.
Webb, W., The Coast Guard, 1976.
Wilson, T.G., The Irish Lighthouse Service, Dublin, 1968.

Websites

www.clarelibrary.ie/eolas/coclare/history/frost/chap10_killaloe_protestant_bishops.htm
www.coastguardsofyesteryear.org.
www.dingle-peninsula.ie/blaskets.html
freepages.geanealogy.rootsweb.com/~colin/DriscollofCork/Miscellaneous
www.nationalarchives.ie
www.paulturner.ca/Ireland/Cork/HOB/HOB-12.htm
www.qsl.net/gm3zdh/coast/ireland/gck.htm
www.rootsweb.com

INDEX

acetylene, 19, 20, 21, 22, 107
Admiralty, 10, 23, 24, 48, 68, 69, 124, 125, 126, 129, 132, 134, 137, 139, 140, 141, 142, 144, 146, 147, 151, 152, 153, 154, 155, 156, 158, 159, 162, 186, 195
Agnes (ship), 55
Alderman Rocks, 1, 12, 16, 17, 23-32, 108, 125
Alert, 53, 55, 87
Alexandra, 20, 55, 91, 94, 102, 209, 210, 211
Allen, William, 57
Amey Roadstone, 181
Argus, 31
Ariel, 202
Armstrong, Owen, 63
Atlanta, 59, 120
Baker, Joseph, 5, 162,
Baldwin, Henry, 23, 128, 136,
Ball, Robert, 91
Ballycotton, 42, 84
Ballydehob, 7, 120, 171, 195
Ballydevlin, 1, 5, 13, 57, 59, 104, 124, 177, 190, 206
Bandon, Lord, 24, 25, 165
Barley Cove, 5, 6, 186, 187
barrels, 22, 108, 109, 147
Barrett, Fr. Thomas, 6, 166, 168
Becher, Lionel, 172
Beecher, C., 79
Beecher, Phane, 160
Beecher, R.H., 166
Belgium, 175, 187
Best, Alan, 118, 158

Black Horse, 24, 30, 31
blacksmith, 86, 88, 107, 112
Blake, E.J., 111
Blake, John & W., 29, 50, 51
Blazer, 48
Board of Trade, 19, 20, 21, 22, 25, 26, 27, 30, 31, 51, 54, 61, 62, 65, 69, 72, 73, 74, 76, 78, 80, 81, 87, 96, 109, 138
boat house (coast guard), 133, 142, 143
Boulysallagh, 106, 161, 169, 171, 178, 184
Brideoake, Dr. R.F., 43, 179-180
Britannia, 59
British Relief Association, 128, 168
Brittany, 198, 200
Brock, William, 134, 218
Brow Head, 60, 62, 64, 65, 67, 68, 102, 103, 134, 153, 154, 155, 156, 157, 158, 177, 208,
Browhead Granite Co., 180, 181
Brownell, J., 42
Brownell, George, 43, 73
Bruiser, 48
buoys, 106, 107, 111, 112
Calf Rock, 34, 42, 50, 72, 85
Callaros Eighter, 170, 174, 177
Camier, J. or S., 69
Camier, W., 84, 108
Carbery, Lord, 190
carbide, 20, 22, 82, 107, 110

Index

Carrigduve, 163, 178
Castlemeighan, 81, 106
Castlemeighan quarry, 81, 180, 181, 183
Castletownbere, 54, 56, 59, 79, 82, 84, 88, 111, 116, 135, 211, 212
Castletownsend, 48, 128, 129, 130, 135, 136, 141, 147, 150
Celtic Fisheries, 205
Census, 88, 92, 147, 148, 177, 180
Church Education Society, 191-195
Church of Ireland, 92, 165, 190
Clinton, Lord, 26, 60, 61, 70, 153, 154, 172, 174, 196
coal, 22, 38, 52, 56, 59, 71, 73, 77, 80, 84, 96, 107, 112, 116, 117, 118, 127, 154, 175, 207
Coast Guard, 1, 4, 8, 11, 12, 23, 25, 43, 48, 52, 53, 68, 69, 83, 88, 99, 100, 101, 118, 123-159, 160, 165, 173, 175, 180, 183, 186, 187, 189, 193, 195, 197, 208
Cobh (Queenstown), 45, 50, 52, 87, 99, 126, 151, 167, 193
Collins, Rickie, 100, 103, 180, 198, 199, 200, 202, 204
Connolly, I.,28, 33, 70, 71
Cork County Council, 114, 151
Cottage Foods, 165, 205
Coughlan, Daniel, 10, 41, 183
Coughan's Tower, 175
Cragside, 97
Craig-White, 115, 118, 119
crayfish, 199

Crookhaven Post Office, 62, 155, 195, 196
Crowley, John, 99, 101, 140, 144, 146, 147
Cunningham, 34
Customs, Commissioners of, 69, 126
D'Esperance, 202
Davis, Captain, 99
day mark, 107
Deane, Alexander, 13, 163, 171
Deane, Mary, 162
Deane, R., 19, 20, 44, 45, 65, 66, 95, 96
Deane, Thomas, 13, 144, 162, 163, 164, 167, 172
Deane, William, 167
Deirdre, 78, 79, 99, 109
Dennis, Augustus P., 95
detonators, 74, 96, 97, 98, 99, 100, 102, 110
dioptric, 17, 30
dispensary, 5, 186
Donovan, D., 87
Donovan, Edward 54, 55
Donovan, I., 209
Donovan, Michael, 59
Donovan, T., 112, 113
Douglass, William, 29, 31, 63, 85, 87, 91
Downey, Stephen 153, 154, 156
Doyle, James, 17, 29, 41, 48, 207
Dun Laoighaire (Kingstown), 36, 54, 87, 88, 89, 94, 106, 108, 141
Dunleavy, George 42, 109, 208
Edmond, 199, 211
Eliza Libby, 136

229

Encumbered Estates, 171
Eugenie, 199
Famine, 4, 6, 7, 11, 14, 16, 124, 127-128, 160, 165-169, 170, 171, 186, 192, 205
Fastnet Race, 104
ferry, 4, 142
Fisher, Rev. William, 109, 126, 136, 166, 168, 169
Fitzgibbon, Tony, 205, 206
Flemings Buoy, 108
Fleming, Delaware P., 87, 88, 89, 91
Fleming, Lionel, 5, 163, 172, 186
Fleur de France, 202
Flying Foam, 54, 55
fog, 23, 24, 31, 33, 46, 47, 49, 50, 74, 77, 81, 90, 96, 98, 102, 103, 110
Foley, Pierre, 168, 169
Foley, Rev. John, 187, 194
Foot, Frederick, 78, 88, 89, 90, 91
Fortune, Thomas, 41, 208
Free State, 158, 197
G.P.O., 48, 61, 62, 64, 67, 74, 96, 156
Galley Cove, 61, 63
Gardiner, Henry, 18, 42, 108, 213
Gilhooly, James, 53
Glanville, James, 47, 93, 104, 209
Goggin, Jimmy, 204
Goleen, 1, 3, 5, 35, 43, 45, 48, 53, 55, 57, 59, 74, 82, 86, 87, 91, 97, 100, 101, 104, 105, 107, 110, 116, 128, 138, 142, 161, 165, 166, 171, 172, 174, 175, 178, 179, 184, 185, 187, 188, 189, 193, 194, 196, 197, 201, 207, 209, 210, 211
Goleen Catholic Church, 171, 183, 184, 188, 208
Goleen Protestant Church, 187
Goodfellow, Stephen & Catherine, 133, 134
Grand Jury, 4, 196
Granny's Island, 138
Griffin, Dermot, 74, 81, 105-106, 107, 110, 111, 112, 114, 115
Griffith, Richard, 3, 4, 16, 132, 142, 170, 189, 206
Guilfoyle, James, 61, 62
Halpin, George, 12, 14, 16, 25, 28, 32, 33, 39, 69, 127
Halycon, 53
Hamiltons, 183-186
Hamilton, Alexander, 76, 183, 184, 185
Hamilton, D.J. (Danny), 102, 210
Hamilton, Eliza, 39, 184
Hamilton, Mary, 47, 102
Hamilton, Hanoria, 44, 183, 185
Hamilton, Johanna, 104, 112, 185
Hamilton, Rickard, 43, 47, 183, 184, 185, 197
Harcourt, Charles, 93, 179
Harcourt, Emmaline, 180
Harrington, Jack, 59, 112
Harrington, T., 51, 52
Head, Ashby & Co., 27, 28, 108
Healy, James, 34, 40, 60, 207

Index

Hellier, 180
Hennessy's of Ballineen, 201
Heroine, 53
Higginbotham, 39
Hollens, Fran, 101-104
House of Commons, 11, 24, 25, 27, 53, 163, 190
Hull, William, 2, 3
Hull, Alexander, 74, 75, 76
Hungerford, Richard B.,11, 131, 166, 168
Hungerford, Lieut. T., 128, 129, 135, 136,
I.R.A., 97, 134, 156, 157, 185
Ierne, 56, 57, 87, 88, 89, 90, 91, 92, 95, 102, 110, 111, 119
Irish Lights, Commissioners of, 10, 13, 19, 20, 31, 32, 36, 37, 52, 75, 80, 85, 87, 91, 94, 101, 108, 113, 114, 115, 116, 119, 192, 209, 211
Irish Lily, 25
Isle of Man, 7
Isolda, 59, 111
Jamestown, 168
Johnston, George, 74, 75, 76
Kate Dawson, 51
Kavanagh, James, 90
Kearon, Captain Edward, 54, 55, 56, 57, 64, 88, 109
Kelly, Robert, 74, 150, 152
Kildare Place Society, 189
Kilgallon, Andrew, 79, 114
Kilmoe, 1, 5, 26, 126, 163, 166, 179, 186, 187, 189, 194, 209
Kirkland, Geoffery & Elspeth, 120
Lamb, 8, 72, 188, 200
Lamb's Island, 8, 189, 200
Lambert, Anne, 162
Land League, 53, 173
Lane, Charles James, 158, 179
Lane, Margaret, 164, 172
Lannins, 2, 183, 197
Lannin, George, 114, 115, 119, 180, 185
Le Grand & Sutcliff Boring Engineers, 63
Leonara, 31
Lewis, Samuel, 4, 163
Limerick, T.H., 70, 71
Lissacaha, 161, 162, 169, 170, 178
Lissagriffin, 186, 189
Lloyds, 10, 46, 60, 61, 64, 65, 66, 67, 68, 69, 103, 153, 154, 156, 187, 208
lobster ponds, 198-206
Lontons, 179, 181
look-out tower, 140, 150
Louton, 203
Lowertown, 164, 172
magazine (explosives), 73, 74, 86, 98, 103, 109, 119
Maginn, J., 40, 51
Maginn, William, 54, 55
Mail Car, 196
Máire Cáit, 99
Marconi, 57, 64, 65
Martin, Desmond, 118
Mary Drennan, 138
Mayannic, 203
McCarthy, Dan, 196
McCarthy, J., 5, 53, 142
McCarthy, Mary, 112
McCarthy, Patrick, 81, 82
McCormick, Dr. James, 39, 42, 43, 166, 167, 169, 186, 187,
McCrombie, Captain 53
McDonagh, Feichin, 120

231

McKenna, John, 40, 207
McMullen, Mary Jane, 164, 170
McPhilips, Brian, 159
Mills, Albert, 175, 205
Mizen Head, 5, 46, 47, 48, 63, 68, 74-76, 77, 78, 79, 80, 81, 96-97, 98, 99, 100, 101, 109, 110, 112, 116, 119, 210, 211
Monarch, 63
Morse, 37, 61, 66, 68, 69, 98, 102
Moya, 56, 57, 58, 92, 108
Murphy & O'Connor, 22, 56
Murphy, Kevin, 82
Murphy, T.P., 47, 65, 68, 82, 97, 102
Nabro, 79, 107, 109
Nash, Alicia Maria, 174
Neville, Dr. Thomas, 45, 57, 77, 91, 209, 210
Notices to Mariners, 15, 17, 21, 64, 65, 94
Notre Dame, 202
Nottage, Arthur (Daddy), 177
Notter, 34, 160-182
Notter, Alexander, 134
Notter, Isaac, 28, 29, 42, 50, 51, 52, 53, 54, 55, 60, 84, 109, 143, 172, 174, 175, 176, 177, 187, 207
Notter, Isaac Nash, 174, 175, 196, 198
Notter, James Lane, 151, 164, 173, 178, 179, 180,
Notter, John, 5, 13, 14, 15, 141, 161, 164, 167, 170
Notter, Margaret Lane, 172
Notter, Richard 4, 7, 12, 13, 124, 161, 162, 163, 164, 165, 166, 167, 168, 169, 170, 171, 172, 189, 204
Notter, Richard Henry, 73, 83, 84, 146, 172, 173
Notter, Thomas, 53, 177
Notter, Thomas Deane, 83, 140, 170, 172, 173, 183
O'Donoghue, Rickard & Elizabeth 104, 113, 114, 185, 197
O'Driscoll, Florence, 196, 197
O'Grady, Rev., 186
O'Grady, Thomas, 172
O'Sullivan, Rev. Laurence, 166, 167
O'Sullivan, Patrick (Sonny), 106, 201, 206, 211
O'Sullivan, Stephen, 110
Odessa, 138
Office of Public Works, 7, 140, 142, 143, 154, 158
Old Head of Kinsale, 23, 55, 68
Ordnance Survey, 139, 162, 175
Orwell, 52
Osprey, 51
Owen, James, 143
Oulhen, 201, 202, 205
Penryn, 90, 93
Periera, Francis, 65
Pintsch's Patent Lighting, 20
Plumarch), 203
Pococke, Richard, 1, 123
population, 4, 7, 160, 166, 168, 186, 192
Prince Alfred, 147
Princess Alexandra, 55, 87, 89
Protheroe, 128
Queen Victoria, 141, 175

Index

R.I.C., 99, 101, 185
Rathlin O'Birne Lighthouse, 43, 185
rats, 8, 81
revenue officer, 10, 124
Rhadamanthu, 129
Riding Officer (Coast Guard), 125
Riversdale, Lord, 2, 3, 161, 171
Rocket Apparatus, 83, 136, 137, 138
Rock Island quarry, 76, 183
Rohu, Edward, 43, 46, 63, 93, 102, 213
Rosco, 203
Rowe Brothers, 180
Royal Marines, 156
Royal Navy (British), 37, 44, 125, 127, 130, 131, 173, 176
Samuelson, 115, 118, 205
Sanders, R., 151, 153
Scarlet Fever, 47
Schull, 7, 23, 33, 50, 54, 67, 69, 75, 82, 85, 95, 104, 106, 111, 115, 116, 128, 134, 147, 161, 162, 172, 179, 183, 185, 193, 195, 197, 199, 212
Scott, Charles W., 19, 20, 21, 74, 75, 76, 77, 87, 88, 89, 92, 113, 158
Scully, 181
Scully, C., 55
Scully, Vincent, 26, 27
Self Reliance, 53
semaphore, 62, 63, 66, 102, 105
Shanavally, 2, 103, 180, 183, 185, 198
Sheamon Point, 8, 10, 12

Sheehan, Mary, 183
Sheehan, P., 97
Sheehan, Patrick, 88
Sheehan, Paul, 110
Sheehane, Jeremiah, 183
Shortt, Peter, 159
Sir Richard, 32
Skelligs, 20, 40, 42, 54, 84, 110, 110, 138
Skibbereen, 1, 3, 4, 18, 27, 75, 81, 85, 116, 117, 118, 119, 123, 125, 135, 147, 153, 156, 158, 160, 166, 175, 195, 196, 199
slipway, 141
Sloane, J.S., 17, 30, 34, 35, 36, 41, 48, 50, 60, 71, 73, 83, 137
Snug Harbour, 8, 161, 170, 171
Spanish Cove, 106, 161, 170, 171, 181, 183
St Ita, 202
St. Brendan's Church, 133, 134, 162, 165, 173
Star of the Sea, 199, 200
Stephen Whitney, 23
Stocker, Henry, 18, 42, 111, 208
Stoney, Rev. J., 193
storms, 19, 29, 42, 50, 63, 108, 137, 144, 151
Streak Head, 1, 30, 31, 32, 124
submarine bell, 94
Submarine Signal Co., 95
surveyor, 123, 196
Swanton, James Hutchinson, 187
Tearaght, 54, 76, 102, 110, 210

233

Rock Island

SUPPORTED BY THE HERITAGE COUNCIL

LE CUIDIÚ AN CHOMHAIRLE OIDHREACHTA

This publication has received support from the Heritage Council under the 2005 Publications Grant Scheme.

€ 15.00

ISBN 0 9552684 0 0
978 0 9552684 0 3

9 780955 268403